The Plays of Josefina Niggli

Raleigh, North Carolina; the *News and Record* of Greensboro, North Carolina; the Commonweal Foundation (www.commonwealmagazine.org); and the *Journal of American Folklore* (www.afsnet.org). The Western Carolina University Foundation generously granted permissions to republish Niggli's plays.

University archivist George Frizzell and librarian Priscilla Proctor welcomed us at Western Carolina University's Hunter Library and provided valuable assistance during our visit and after. Niggli's colleagues and dear friends Barbara and Steve Eberly and the late Bill Paulk generously took time to share their memories of the writer. In addition to giving us a tour that included visits to Niggli's residence on a campus hilltop and to the theater that bears her name, these friends provided us with a vivid picture of an artist who touched those around her with her vivacious wit and unflagging energy. Their deep affection for her compelled us to continue in our research and has been a consistent source of inspiration.

Our work on Niggli has benefited immeasurably from conversations with a number of individuals. Among those who read, challenged, shaped, and supported our research are Lauren Berlant, Bill Brown, Chris Catanzarite, Elaine Hadley, Jean Ma, Curtis Márez, Deborah Nelson, Lisa Outar, and Donald Pease. At the University of Chicago, an audience at the American Cultures Workshop—especially Yvette Piggush and Karin Wimbley-Brodnax—provided useful comments on an early version of the introduction. Silvia Spitta supplied invaluable encouragement at a moment when we thought that this volume would never meet a public. At the University of Wisconsin Press, Raphael Kadushin and two anonymous reviewers made useful final-hour recommendations that helped us focus the volume to better represent our original aims.

Philip Bond and David Harriman lived with this project as much as we did. They are our constant collaborators, and the imprints of their influence are apparent in our best work more than they know.

Editors' Note

The spelling of Niggli's first name often varies. "Josephina" is most common in her publications, although she is listed as "Josephine" in her self-published chapbook *Mexican Silhouettes*. Niggli herself seemed to prefer "Josefina," which she consistently used in later publications. Friends referred to her as "Jo."

Josefina Niggli: A Chronology

1910   Josefina Maria Niggli born to Goldie Morgan Niggli and Frederick Ferdinand Niggli in Hidalgo, Nuevo León, Mexico, on 13 July. Outbreak of the Mexican Revolution.

1913   Assassination of Mexican president Francisco Madero. Niggli sent to San Antonio, Texas, to escape the violence of the Revolution.

1920   After spending seven years as itinerant residents of the southwestern United States, Niggli and her family return to Mexico.

1925   Once again sent to San Antonio, this time to begin her university education at Incarnate Word College. Majors in philosophy and minors in history. Before this, she had received all of her education from her mother, save for a year or so that she spent at San Antonio's Main Avenue High School.

1928   Frederick Niggli finances the publication of his daughter's first book, the poetry collection *Mexican Silhouettes*.

1928–32 Writes radio scripts for KTSA Radio in San Antonio.

1931   Earns her Bachelor of Arts degree in philosophy from Incarnate Word. Revised edition of *Mexican Silhouettes* published in San Antonio. During her years as a college student, she publishes poems and short stories in such magazines as *Mexican Life* and the *Ladies' Home Journal*. She wins second prize in a *Ladies' Home Journal* short story contest, and wins the National Catholic College Poetry Contest.

1931–35 Studies playwriting under Coates Gwynne, the director of the San Antonio Little Theater. The Little Theater produces three of Niggli's one-act plays: *Sorella, Yes, Nellie,* and *Grapes Are Sometimes Sweet.*

1935 Enrolls in the master's program in drama at the University of North Carolina at Chapel Hill. Studies playwriting under Frederick Koch and Samuel Selden and is influenced by classmates Paul Green and Betty Smith.

1935–37 Writes most of her acclaimed folk plays in this period, including *Tooth or Shave, The Red Velvet Goat,* and *Sunday Costs Five Pesos.* Also writes a number of historical plays set in Mexico, including *The Cry of Dolores, Soldadera, Azteca,* and *The Fair God.* The Carolina Playmakers performed all of the plays.

1936 Awarded a Rockefeller Fellowship in playwriting.

1937 Submits the three-act play *The Singing Valley* as her thesis, and graduates from the University of North Carolina with a master's degree in drama.

1938 *Mexican Folk Plays* published by the University of North Carolina Press. Receives a fellowship from the Bureau of New Plays and is awarded a second Rockefeller Fellowship in playwriting. Awarded a fellowship to the Bread Loaf Writers' Conference.

1940–42 Works as a secretary and assistant to Paul Green.

1940–41 *The Red Velvet Goat* is performed somewhere in London (in theaters, neighborhood homes, bomb shelters) every night during the blitz of World War II.

1942–44 Teaches radio script writing and production at the University of North Carolina at Chapel Hill.

1945 *Mexican Village* published by the University of North Carolina Press. Publishes *Pointers on Playwriting.*

1946 *Mexican Village* receives the Mayflower Cup Award for the best book written by a North Carolinian during the previous year. Publishes *Pointers on Radio Writing.*

1947 *Step Down, Elder Brother* published by Rinehart. The novel is chosen as a Book-of-the-Month Club selection.

its Revolution, representing "Pancho Villa and Emiliano Zapata as respectively a 'barbarian' and 'The Atilla of the South,' implying that the struggle in Mexico mirrored the savage war of Huns and Romans, with civilization itself at stake."[25] So prominent were cinematic depictions of Mexicans as cowardly greasers and villains that the Mexican government began to censor such films in protest.[26] Niggli's reference to the banana republic view of Latin America highlights persistent notions about Mexico's lack of fitness for self-government. Proponents of these ideas would usually invoke the mixed-race nature of the Mexican people as their chief argument. Hubert Howe Bancroft, the wealthy book dealer and publisher, declared in 1912 that Porfirio Díaz had no choice but to impose dictatorial rule on Mexico because "a nation of mestizos was not, like the Anglo Americans, predisposed toward democratic institutions."[27] Madison Grant—whose *Passing of the Great Race* was among the most influential expressions of the rising eugenic view of immigration in the 1920s—argued that the true achievement of the "melting pot" was best exemplified by "the racial mixture we call Mexican, and which is now [through the Mexican Revolution] engaged in demonstrating its incapacity for self-government."[28]

Leftists of the period also considered Mexico to be a primitive land but looked to that primitivism as an antidote to the "selfish individualism of capitalist society" and to the relentless "onslaught of industrialization."[29] Adherents to this point of view celebrated the cult of the Indian that arose during the Mexican Revolution and continued to thrive in Mexico and the United States through the efforts of Mexico's great muralists José Clemente Orozco, Diego Rivera, and David Alfaro Siqueiros. They emphasized a spiritually incorruptible and pre-modern Indian essence that found influential expression in such texts as John Reed's *Insurgent Mexico* (1913–14) and the early "Mexican" stories of Katherine Anne Porter (1920s).[30] Their narratives, like many others of the time, focus on Mexico's Indians as remaining untouched by the trappings of modernity and thus revealing the most basic humanity shared by all.

One unifying characteristic of Niggli's extraordinarily wide-ranging work is her engagement with prevalent U.S. stereotypes about Mexico and its people. This seems to be in keeping with her response to Usigli—that the United States "needed the folk drama more than Mexico." Along with her artistic ambitions, then, Niggli viewed her writing as a pedagogical opportunity—as a chance to teach audiences in the United States that there was much more to Mexico than the oversimplified representations to which they were accustomed. Thus, while her writings are finely attuned to and informed by Mexico's political and cultural contexts, they also represent Mexico through the lens of U.S. preconceptions. Niggli responds to the U.S. ideals, projections, and desires that shape its image of Mexico by consistently returning to three broad themes, which are neither exhaustive nor mutually exclusive: revolution, gender, and modernity.

Writing the Revolution

Niggli's plays of the Mexican Revolution are often at odds with representations that used the rebellion either to demonize or romanticize Mexican society. While Niggli's childhood experiences with the Revolution would have influenced her decision to write so intensely about it, the cultural and political contexts of the 1930s and '40s also must have played a part. As Richard Slotkin documents, the United States carefully followed the developments of the fighting; Hollywood especially expressed an initially favorable response to the rebellion in both its documentary and fiction films (as noted above, this would quickly change). In many ways, Mexico's recent history of revolution enabled the United States to conceive of its neighbor to the south as a mythic space onto which it could project and possibly resolve various political and cultural questions. Such major films as *Viva Villa!* (1934) and *Juarez* (1939) established Mexico as a place to play out "thought-experiments in the problems of modern revolution."[31]

Niggli was thus producing her plays at a time when U.S. interest in Mexico was at its highest point in years. Moreover, as her reading and writing document,[32] she had a strong personal interest in the figure of Pancho Villa that intersected with his high profile in the United States. *This Is Villa!* (1938) marks her attempt to explain the famous strong man of Mexico to an audience that she believed had failed to grasp his most defining characteristics and, therefore, had failed to understand the Mexican people themselves. Her title forcefully indicates that hers is to be the truest portrait of the general, and, as such, the play provides a suggestive counterpoint to Metro-Goldwyn-Mayer's *Viva Villa!* This cinematic treatment was highly influential, and though Niggli's version of the Villa legend does not respond to the film directly, it does take its cue from images and narratives of the Revolution that were shaped by the Hollywood production.[33] As Slotkin argues, while the film's Villa represents the "legitimate aspirations of the peasantry," he also expresses their "terrible rage—the passion that drives them to uncompromising extremes and in the end perverts their own revolution through terror and excess."[34] At the same time, Villa shows absolute allegiance to Francisco Madero, the historical figure who led the rebellion in its initial stages and whom Slotkin characterizes as the film's "Christ-fool," "a sacred martyr for 'democracy.'"[35] Despite providing a generally unflattering portrait of Villa, *Viva Villa!* redeems its protagonist by emphasizing his populist spirit, thus seeming to support the struggle of the masses. Yet the film is finally only comfortable championing the grievances of the people if they can be contained or made safe through the guidance of the genteel classes. Madero, with his rational temperament and deeply felt sense of justice, represents the ability these elites have to transform the unbridled passion of the people—here embodied by Villa—into a force that will act for the good of Mexico.

In contrast, Niggli's play complicates the relationship between Villa and its Madero-figure, a character known simply as the Professor. The two characters have a great antipathy for each other, largely because each thinks that the other is manipulating the Revolution for his own ends. Villa continually asserts that he stands for the people as no one else can and that "when I speak it is the voice of the people speaking in my mouth" (215), but the Professor emphasizes Villa's appetite for individual glory, his greed, and blazing ambition. The Professor claims to speak for all who fight to meet the Revolution's ideals, but this "dried-up shell of a man" (194) speaks for the ruling elite, for those who fear the reforms that the rebellion might bring. Thus, like many Mexican novels of the Revolution from this period, *This Is Villa!* dramatizes the betrayal of the Revolution by all sides, deromanticizing the rebellion and engaging issues that were of urgency to the Mexican nation.[36] Moreover, to the extent that the play promotes Villa as a representative of the people, it completely reverses the Hollywood fantasy that one could both support and manage the masses. By focusing on the Professor's complete lack of control over Villa, Niggli's play imagines the untamable nature of the people and forces its audiences to confront the possibility of championing the masses without the security that those masses will then acquiesce to the will of their compassionate superiors. In fact, *This Is Villa!* undermines the very idea of a noble elite through its presentation of the Professor's self-interested motives and his ultimately ineffectual commitment to words over actions.

Soldadera, like *This Is Villa!,* deals with issues of representation and the romanticization of the Revolution, viewed largely through the lens of gender. The play focuses on a group of women whose lives have been dominated by death and violence. The only exception is the character Adelita, a young woman who is "the poetry of the Revolution, and the beauty, and she who has seen almost nothing of death finds life very gay" (158). Niggli's choice of name for this character is a telling one. Adelita is one of the great icons of the Mexican Revolution—a figure who quickly reached mythic proportion through her immortalization in legends and corridos.[37] So widespread was the image, that the name was used to refer to any female soldier, or *soldadera,* who took part in the Revolution.[38] While Adelita was understood initially to embody female courage and honor, Arrizón points out that the icon quickly became "shaped and reshaped as it circulated, with numerous corridos providing conflicting interpretations of the figure."[39] Rather than focus on her courage, for example, many versions tend to "emphasize the stoicism of the male rebel soldier as he confronts the prospect of death."[40] Domesticated and romanticized, Adelita becomes the faithful love interest of the troops, a stock character who, as Tabea Alexa Linhard explains, "never challenges her place." She expresses no political motivations or ambitions, and her life as a soldadera is touched neither by the "daily violence nor the emancipatory possibilities of revolutions."[41]

Rather than re-imagine this iconic figure, Niggli simply plucks her Adelita directly from the male-centered corridos described by Arrizón and Linhard. She is the character from the songs, the "beauty" and "poetry" of the Revolution, the iconic female revolutionary that would come to represent an ideal of Mexican womanhood more generally. Yet, while Adelita is one of the play's primary protagonists, she is also one among a constellation

museum meditation on the "Ghost of Maximilian, ghost of Juárez, enemies in life, together" (148). Juárez, the first Indian to lead the nation, is metonymically linked to Marina through shared Indianness. The love plot in *The Fair God,* then, can be read as one between Juárez and Maximilian, whose execution by the former gives birth to a Mexican nation forever secure from foreign invasion.

Although women initially seem to be passive figures in Niggli's historical drama, they emerge, on closer examination, as the figures who actually or symbolically set events into motion. Doña Josefa and Lolita initiate the communication that will lead to Hidalgo's grito, and Marina symbolically stands in for Juárez. This characterization of female will—in contradistinction to a more passive though still traditional masculinity—is more apparent in *The Ring of General Macías,* a drama set during the Mexican Revolution but not involving real historical figures. The play centers on the confrontation between Raquel, General Macías's genteel wife, and Andrés de la O, a peasant revolutionary who invades her home "hunting for the wife of General Macías" (225).

The encounter between Raquel and Andrés de la O first explodes in an exchange of class-based insults but then develops an erotic charge as the two recognize in each other a shared patriotic fervor. A common love of the nation promises to flatten class differences. Andrés, attracted by Raquel's defiant bravery, confidently seizes and kisses her. Although Raquel rebuffs his impudent advance, Andrés continues to admire her, proclaiming, "I can understand why Macías loves you" (227) and then announcing that he has a "very nice present—from your husband" (228). The present is the general's matrimonial band, and Raquel immediately concludes that Andrés must have "stole it from his dead finger" (229). While Andrés assures Raquel that the general is alive, Raquel recognizes that Andrés has taken control of the general's body and with his kiss has assumed the privileges that this symbolically holds. Andrés informs Raquel that if she does not provide sanctuary for him and for his subordinate, Cleto, her husband will be shot.

Upon learning that the Federals are approaching her home in search of the two peasant rebels, Raquel rushes almost instinctively to preserve their lives and thereby her husband's. Earlier in the play she chides a young woman for lamenting the death of her husband in war; honor is more worthy than romantic love. Now she stages a deception to prolong romantic love. Raquel hides Cleto in the closet and conceals Andrés by disguising him as Felipe, her "cousin," who was rendered dumb through wartime imprisonment. In effect, Raquel stages a play. Such plays-within-a-play are familiar in Niggli's work and thematize her relationship to the dramatic form by underscoring her role as author of the events portrayed. This play-within-a-play collapses class differences (and the racial differences that would accompany them) as Raquel convincingly persuades the Federals that Andrés is her relation.

Once the danger posed by the Federals has passed, Cleto asks Raquel why such a brave woman would love a man like the general. Cleto is perplexed because the "general wanted to save his own life. He said he loved you and he wanted to save his own life" (234). The general is thus guilty of the same kind of romantic feeling to which Raquel has succumbed; he subordinates the love of his country to the love of his wife. Raquel recognizes the irony of Cleto's questions: "I saved you from the Federals because I want to save my husband's life. You call me brave and yet you call him a coward. There is no difference in what we have done" (235). Although Cleto claims that Raquel's duties as wife differ from her husband's as military officer, Raquel only feels her hypocrisy and ultimately redeems herself by poisoning Cleto's and Andrés's wine, thereby winning a small victory for her side of the conflict but ensuring the death of her husband. After asking whether "it [is] possible to love a person too much" (237), Raquel agrees with Andrés's affirmative response and bids him join her in a lethal toast to "bright and shining honor" (237). Their final agreement on love conjoins the romance of women with the romance of the peasants. After understanding that the peasants value love of country more than romantic attachments, Raquel concedes that the revolutionaries will win. Yet, the fate of the nation is far from certain at the play's end. Similar to *Soldadera*, *The Ring of General Macías* provides no easy closure. Instead, Raquel takes possession of the ring and of Andrés's mother's religious medal and sits "listening to an empty house" (238). Raquel may have possession of the rewards of battle, but the home and nation continue to lack definition, leaving those who love them expectant, alienated, and waiting.

Mexico, Modernism, Modernity

The historical dramas that we have thus far explored express disillusionment with the Mexican Revolution because it failed to realize its aims. These plays attempt to explain the past rather than imagine a future; however, Niggli thinks in utopian, projective terms in other works and specifically engages the question of how Mexico can be modern. In *The Singing Valley* (1936), the play that she submitted to meet her master of fine arts requirements at the University of North Carolina, Niggli suggests that Mexican modernity requires the integration of both technology and the "modern girl."[47] The first requires the insertion of the machine into a genealogy in which it is viewed as consistent with the Mexican national character, while the second requires a woman who has been seduced by commodity culture and modernist aesthetics to ratify the nation's modernizing aspirations.

The Singing Valley takes place in Abasolo in the Santa Catarina Valley and chronicles Don Antonio's return to the village in 1935 after an absence of fifteen years. Don Antonio fled Mexico for the United States during the Mexican Revolution but has returned to transform the desert village into a "miniature California" by building a powerhouse to "pump water into a spider's web of irrigation ditches" (70). Don Rufino, the town's mayor, resists Don Antonio's plan for modernization. While Don Antonio belongs to a distinguished family that has lived in Abasolo for generations, Don Rufino is a newly established figure in the community, having risen to prominence during his adversary's exile. Don Rufino's authority in the community is rooted in his success as a goatherd, and he resists Don Antonio's plan because it will destroy the valley's ideal grazing conditions. As this brief sketch indicates, the Antonio–Rufino conflict can be read as an example of one of the common themes of American literature: the intrusion of technology into the pastoral scene.

Niggli employs the pastoral with great sophistication in *The Singing Valley*. In her early poems collected in *Mexican Silhouettes* (1928), Niggli frequently depicts pastoral scenes that are figured as a retreat from modernity. Here, the pastoral is the very terrain upon which a new modernity is negotiated. In his classic account of the encroachment of the machine into the pastoral garden, Leo Marx notes that the machine "brings a world which is more 'real' into juxtaposition with an idyllic vision." The pastoral, in Marx's account, differs from the primitive, which is a simple retreat from urban civilization, by being a liminal space "between, yet in transcendent relation to" civilization and nature.[48] Though *The Singing Valley* begins by establishing the Santa Catarina Valley as the site where urban technology and the goatherd come face-to-face, the play quickly complicates this division and, in the process, imagines an alternative modernity that refuses the metropolitan culture of the United States.[49]

The first complication, then, is the introduction of new technology by a figure who is emphatically associated with tradition in the valley. In response to queries about his exile, Don Antonio explains, "The rebel government has laid a hard exile on all of us who were faithful to the old traditions" (63). In his opposition to the rebel government, Don Antonio is not necessarily an agent of the interests that the Revolution opposed. In conversation with his son, Abel, Don Antonio aligns himself with the indigenous and mestizo members of Mexican society: "For centuries my people have been whipped down to the earth, first by the Spaniards and then by men like this Rufino. Protecting them is your duty" (99). Although originally cast as a goatherd—a figure most aligned with nature and land— Rufino is unmasked in the second act as a capitalist exploiter of the goatherds who work for him. Technology, then, is associated with preservation and tradition, and nature's agents with the perpetuation of oppression. Don Antonio's modernization plan bears such a strong resemblance to the land reforms Cárdenas was initiating at the very time Niggli was writing the play that the struggle for the valley can also be read as a struggle for Mexico's future. In this reading, the valley lies between and transcends two nation forms—the United States in all its capitalist prosperity and the Mexico beyond which reformers want to move. As Don Antonio's remarks indicate, transcending these forms involves extricating the oppressive and exploitive capitalism associated with both.

How can the Santa Catarina Valley—and, hence, Mexico—be modern without reiterating the oppressive relationships in U. S. modernity? Niggli addresses this question through the relationship between Don Antonio's children, Abel and Lupita, who were born in Abasolo but raised in the United States. Abel is an engineer who imagines building bridges in the

Many of the themes and stylistic characteristics in Niggli's early works converge in *Mexican Village.* The novel considers, for example, relationships between race and democracy, art and revolution, and the primitive and the modern. It also continues to examine concerns that Niggli expressed as far back as the poems of *Mexican Silhouettes,* including the use of the pastoral to assert the centrality of Mexico's Indians to the burgeoning Mexican nation. Strikingly, most of the reviews—and there were many, appearing in such venues as the *Saturday Review,* the *New York Times,* and *Commonweal*—ignore the book's political and historical themes. They almost uniformly praise its value as a kind of apolitical ethnography, one that infuses enough sentiment into its pages to capture "the spirit of the Mexican people." As Mildred Adams puts it in her *New York Times* review: "Many things make this volume memorable in the modern spate of tales about Mexico. Not the least is the fact that it has no axe to grind, it demands no ideological bias on the part of the reader."[50]

Mexican Village does chronicle the lives of simple people living in a simple Mexican town; however, the novel's concerns go far beyond a mere cataloguing of Mexican folk customs. The central plot line, for example, involves the declining fortunes of the great Castillo family. The story opens just after the end of the Revolution, which has toppled the old system of rule and thereby in many ways rendered the Castillos irrelevant. Yet the family continues to be of great importance to the novel's symbolic storyline, since through them we bear witness to "a bit of Mexican history being played out in terms of family rather than nation."[51] Thus, in the framework of the novel, we sense the significance to the nation as Don Saturnino, the aging patriarch, desperately searches for someone worthy to take his place as head of the family—someone who he believes will be able to maintain its wealth and stature. He has two sons; unfortunately one, Alejandro, dies as a young man from a throat ailment, and the other, Joaquín, is viewed as a disgrace for having fought in the very Revolution that has left the family in decline. Don Saturnino decides to place his faith in Bob Webster, the town's quarry foreman who is haunted by his legacy as the illegitimate son of a Mexican maid and her Anglo boss.

When Bob's Texan father refuses to believe that an "Indian" could be his son and rejects him, Bob moves to Hidalgo, keenly feeling the need to make a connection with the culture his Mexican grandmother spoke about endlessly when he was a child. The townspeople initially view Bob as a "gringo," but he gradually undergoes a kind of symbolic "darkening" process through which he increasingly is identified as a mestizo (the half-Spanish, half-Indian mixture that is said to constitute the Mexican race). This transformation reaches its culminating moment when Bob leaves behind his Anglo identity and re-christens himself Roberto Ortega de Menéndez y Castillo. His status as a mestizo becomes significant when it turns out that Bob is the rightful heir of the Castillo fortune. The Castillo name carries symbolic resonances in that Bob has inherited not only the wealth and stature that are a part of the family's legacy but also, in a sense, Mexico itself, the control of which now passes from the hands of the pure-blooded Spanish Creoles to the mixed-race mestizo classes.

This cursory plot description highlights the novel's concern with the issues that were most pertinent to Mexico's national interests at the time, including the country's increasing investment in establishing a relationship between race and an emerging national identity. Given the centrality of such ideas to the novel, one wonders at the uniformity of the reviews in not only ignoring its political themes but also implicitly (and sometimes explicitly) praising the text precisely for expressing an apolitical sensibility. Ultimately, the reviews seem to reveal more about the U.S. desire for a safe and exotic Mexico—a place fit for exploration by tourists—than they do about the novel itself. Unlike contemporary reviewers and more recent scholars, we consider *Mexican Village* to be foremost a historically and politically engaged novel, one that not only describes the situation of post-Revolutionary Mexico but also asserts a course for transforming the country from a mere "geographical expression" into a viable nation.[52] Niggli's focus on the relationship between race and nation-building places her work in dialogue with some of the most urgently debated ideas of the day and situates her in an intellectual and political realm that includes such Mexican thinkers as Gregorio Fuentes y López, Manuel Gamio, and José Vasconcelos—all figures who influenced her work.

To consider *Mexican Village* exclusively within Mexican contexts, however, would be to overlook the U.S. influences that so profoundly shaped Niggli's vision for her homeland. The web of binational contexts and influences in her work make Niggli a figure who begs to be considered from a post-nationalist perspective, a mode of inquiry that moves beyond the idea of the nation as the organizing principle of U.S. literary studies. Examining *Mexican Village* from an "Americas" as opposed to a strictly "United States" or "Mexican" vantage point raises numerous questions of relevance both to Chicana/o and American studies. For example, how did U.S. paradigms of race and ethnicity inform Niggli's articulation of Mexican *mestizaje* and its relationship to nation-building? What role might her time with the Carolina Playmakers have had in her cultivation of a Mexican pastoral form? How might the place of the Mexican in the U.S. imaginary have influenced her perspective on the Revolution and its consequences? What role did her position as a privileged Mexican expatriate living in the South play in shaping her ideas? And finally, what does the novel reveal about the role of binational political and cultural movements in constituting emerging Chicana/o subjectivities? *Mexican Village,* so uniquely positioned among Mexican American and more broadly "U.S." writings of the period, offers the rare opportunity to explore the answers to such questions.[53]

Mexican Village represented the apex of Niggli's literary career, but not the end of her remarkable life. She would produce two other works of fiction: *Step Down, Elder Brother* (1947) and *A Miracle for Mexico* (1964). Chosen as a Book-of-the-Month Club selection, *Step Down, Elder Brother* takes place in Monterrey and tells the story of tradition-bound Domingo Vázquez de Anda and of Mateo Chapa, whose ascent into the middle class corresponds with the changing social landscape in Mexico. *A Miracle for Mexico* is a historical novel chronicling life in Mexico immediately following the conquest. Set in 1531, the novel's protagonist, Miguel Aguilar, registers the frustration of being mestizo at a time in which Spaniards and criollos held power.

In the second half of her life, Niggli turned her attention to film and teaching. From 1948 through 1956, she worked as a stable writer for Twentieth Century–Fox and Metro-Goldwyn-Mayer in Hollywood. In 1953, she co-wrote the screenplay for *Sombrero,* a musical adaptation of her novel *Mexican Village.* Norman Foster, who had directed several of the Charlie Chan installments, directed the musical, which boasted a star-studded roster that included Cyd Charisse, Yvonne De Carlo, Vittorio Gassman, and Ricardo Montalban. Despite the talent involved, the film failed at the box office and was generally dismissed by critics. Much of the political content of the novel—especially the references to the Mexican Revolution—was excised for the musical; however, the film does begin with a debate about election results in a beauty contest, emphasizing the life of democratic processes in Mexico. Studio productions of the 1950s—especially big-budget musicals—were usually escapist fare for the masses, but one wonders whether there are other cultural factors that contributed to the radically defanged translation of *Mexican Village* for the big screen.

In an unsigned and undated eulogy for Niggli in her papers at Western Carolina University, the eulogist begins with Niggli's recollection of her testimony before the House Un-American Activities Commission. In response to the question, "Josephina Niggli, have you been or were you ever a Communist?" Niggli reportedly replied, "No, darling, I'm a Catholic." A consummate dramatist, Niggli seems to have embellished stories about her life, a striking feature when one considers how remarkable the verifiable narrative of her life is. Whether or not Niggli made the remark, the fact that it would be in her arsenal of anecdotes reveals her concern for Cold War politics. Niggli's arrival in Hollywood corresponded with HUAC's investigations of Hollywood radicals, and her friend Paul Green, who was a member of the leftist Group Theatre and Federal Theatre Project, fell under the committee's scrutiny. In a political climate in which the mere mention of "revolution" made one vulnerable to charges of being a Communist, it is not surprising that Niggli would remove reference to the Mexican Revolution from her postwar literary output. *Sombrero,* then, offers scholars a further possible insight into how Cold War politics affected the cultural production of Mexicans and Mexican Americans.[54]

Niggli would abandon Hollywood for a teaching job in North Carolina in 1956. She credited the actor Lionel Barrymore with encouraging her to pursue teaching.[55] Before assuming her job at Western Carolina University, Niggli studied at the Abbey Theatre in Dublin, Ireland, and at the Old Vic School in Bristol, England. She taught in the departments of English and theater arts until her retirement in 1975. She died on 17 December 1983 and is buried in San Antonio, Texas.

Notes

1. Steve Eberly, interviewed by William Orchard and Yolanda Padilla, Cullowhee, North Carolina, 20 May 2000.

2. Raymund Paredes, "The Evolution of Chicano Literature," *MELUS* 5 (1978): 90.

3. María Herrera-Sobek, introduction to *Mexican Village* by Josephina Niggli (1945; Albuquerque: University of New Mexico Press, 1994), xxi.

4. Alicia Arrizón, *Latina Performance: Traversing the Stage* (Bloomington: Indiana University Press, 1999), 43. Arrizón begins her consideration of Niggli's writing with this terse description/qualification of Niggli's identity.

5. Ibid.

6. Walter Spearman, *The Carolina Playmakers: The First Fifty Years* (Chapel Hill: University of North Carolina Press, 1970), 17.

7. Quoted in ibid., 17–18.

8. Frederick Koch, "American Folk Drama in the Making," introduction to *American Folk Plays,* ed. Frederick Koch (New York: D. Appleton-Century, 1939), xv–xvi.

9. Spearman, *Carolina Playmakers,* 92.

10. Ibid., 32. The resulting play is called *The Thrice-Promised Bride.*

11. Koch, "American Folk Drama," xiv.

12. Charles Zug, "Folklore and the Drama: The Carolina Playmakers and Their 'Folk Plays,'" *Southern Folklore Quarterly* 32 (1968): 291.

13. Quoted in Spearman, *Carolina Playmakers,* 93.

14. For example, see Frederick Koch's introduction to *Mexican Folk Plays,* ed. Frederick Koch (Chapel Hill: The University of North Carolina Press, 1938), vii.

15. See Helen Delpar, *The Enormous Vogue of Things Mexican: Cultural Relations between the United States and Mexico, 1920–1935* (Tuscaloosa: University of Alabama Press, 1992), chapter 1.

16. Two such examples are *The Faces of Deka,* a science-fiction fantasy, and *Miracle at Blaise,* an antiwar drama set in a French convent. Both works were collected in Betty Smith's *25 Non-Royalty One-Act Plays for All Girl Casts* (New York: Greenberg, 1942). *The Faces of Deka* is unique because Niggli published it pseudonymously, under the name "Michael Morgan" (Morgan was her mother's maiden name). Niggli kept meticulous records of her publications and included this play in the set of index cards she used to keep track of her publications and royalties. Aside from this, the play is unique in that it imagines a future in which women rule the world.

17. William C. Parker, "Door Locked on Josephina Niggli, Forced Her to Write First Story," *Raleigh News and Observer,* 29 February 1948, and Paula W. Shirley, "Josefina Niggli," in *Dictionary of Literary Biography Yearbook, 1980,* eds. Karen L. Rood, Jean W. Ross, and Richard Ziegfield (Detroit: Gale, 1981), 283.

18. See chapter 5 of Robert Hemenway, *Zora Neale Hurston: A Literary Biography* (Urbana: University of Illinois Press, 1977), for more on the patronage system and how it affected Hurston and Langston Hughes in particular. There is a more concrete connection between Niggli and Hurston than the similarities we are outlining here. In 1939 Hurston made contacts with the Carolina Playmakers and became friends with Paul Green. In fact, Hurston and Green seriously discussed writing a play, tentatively titled *John de Conqueror.* The play never materialized, but one can see why the Carolina Playmakers and Hurston would have been drawn together given their single-minded focus on "the folk." Strikingly, while Hurston and Richard Wright famously harbored a deep animosity toward each other, both counted Green as a friend and professional collaborator (or potential collaborator in Hurston's case). Wright and Green co-authored the dramatic version of *Native Son* (see ibid., 254–56).

19. For two essays that recount recent criticisms of Hurston, see William J. Maxwell, "'Is It True What They Say about Dixie?' Richard Wright, Zora Neale Hurston, and Rural / Urban Exchange in Modern African American Literature," in *Knowing Your Place: Rural Identity and Cultural Hierarchy,* ed. Barbara Ching and Gerald W. Creed (New York: Routledge, 1997), and Leigh Ann Duck, "'Go there tuh *know* there': Zora Neale Hurston and the Chronotope of the Folk," *American Literary History* 13 (2001): 272–88.

20. Josefina Niggli Papers, box 1, folder 46, Special Collections, Hunter Library, Western Carolina University.

21. Rodolfo Usigli, foreword to Josefina Niggli's *Mexican Folk Plays,* ed. Frederick Koch (Chapel Hill: University of North Carolina Press, 1938), xx.

22. Shirley, "Josefina Niggli," 286.

23. Steve Eberly, "Josefina Niggli," *The Arts Journal* (May 1982): 37.

24. Delpar, *Enormous Vogue of Things Mexican,* 5.

25. Richard Slotkin, *Gunfighter Nation: The Myth of the Frontier in Twentieth-Century America* (Norman: University of Oklahoma Press, 1998), 412.

26. See Helen Delpar, "Goodbye to the Greaser: Mexico, the MPPDA and Derogatory Films, 1922–26," *Journal of Popular Film and Television* 12 (1984): 34–41.

27. Quoted in Rosaura Sánchez, *Telling Identities: The Californio Testimonios* (Minneapolis: University of Minnesota Press, 1995), 30.

28. Quoted in Matthew Frye Jacobson, *Whiteness of a Different Color: European*

Even a spike from the
Sea-green cactus.

Purple hills like amethysts,
Black against the sunset,
Radiant at dawn.

Higher than a man's breath,
Lower than a man's soul:
Jewel studded, military
Hills of Mexico.

(1931)

The Singing Valley

1936

Author's Foreword

In the village of Sabinas Hidalgo on the highway between Monterrey and Laredo, Texas, the passing tourist sees a powerhouse standing in solitary grandeur on the bank of the Santa Catarina River. To this tourist it is only another powerhouse. To the valley it is a monument to the dreams and ambitions of an old man.

Exiled thirty years ago, Don Antonio made his way to Central America where he discovered a gold mine. Here was money, and slowly the dream grew in him to send it back to his valley and change it into the finest orange-producing region in the north. Everything was there . . . the soil, the climate . . . everything but water. So gold was torn out of the ground to send gold back to the ground. When the government discovered what he was doing, his exile was lifted and today one may see him . . . a grand old patriarch with a long white beard . . . sunning himself in the patio of his house in his own beloved village: the living example of a dream come true.

So much, then, for the truth which has still another brief chapter added to it. When Don Antonio returned, he brought with him his children . . . especially one son who had been educated at Oxford. I have often wondered how this son felt when he first saw the village and the valley. Did he love it then as I know he loves it now? Or did he fight it, longing desperately for the old life as does Lupita in this play?

This process of adjustment to environment is a very great problem for many young Mexicans today. The old and the new fight for possession of them. Which wins? That is the problem of this drama. It is also the problem for all of us who have lived too long in a foreign country. Must we, too, like Don Antonio, live in exile, but an exile far more terrible because we are at home?

Premiere Playbill Credits

Singing Valley, by Josefina Niggli, was originally produced by the Carolina Playmakers, on 15 July 1936, in Memorial Hall, Chapel Hill, North Carolina, under the direction of Samuel Selden, who also designed the setting. Costumes were designed by the author and executed with the assistance of Grace Barlow. Make-up was under the supervision of Hester Barlow.

The Cast

DOÑA BECA, a great lady of the valley	Jessie Langdale
DON RUFINO, mayor of Abasolo	Joseph Feldman
FATHER ZACAYA, the village priest	Don Watters
DON PABLO, the civil judge	Wallace Bourne
DOÑA AMPARO, his wife	Jo Humphries
ESTER, DOÑA BECA's niece	Hester Barlow
CONCHA, DOÑA BECA's daughter	Fowler Spencer
DON ANTONIO LOZANO	Robert Finch
GUADALUPE (LUPITA), DON ANTONIO's daughter	Jane Rondthaler
ABEL, DON ANTONIO's son	Alfred Barrett
CARLOS BALDERAS, a candy vendor	Willard Miller
FERNANDO PEREZ, a news reporter	Bedford Thurman
JULIO ROMERO, DON PABLO's son	John W. Parker
PEOPLE FROM THE VILLAGE	G. W. Tidd
	Betty Barlow
	Eleanor Patrick
	Lois Latham
	Naomi Cunningham
	Bruce Higgins

DON RUFINO. Carlos Balderas indeed! What a welcoming committee. You wouldn't leave it to me to do it properly with a band and fine speeches. Oh, no. You had to roost here like chickens on a roof while Carlos Balderas . . . that candy vendor . . . meets them at the station.

DOÑA AMPARO. But Carlos sings so well.

DON PABLO. He will give them a fine welcoming song . . .

DON RUFINO. One man moaning on the wind . . . when I could have been making an elegant speech!

CARLOS (*singing very faintly, off left*).

> The four cornstalks are left all alone.
> On the ranch that is my own.
> The house that's so tiny,
> So white and so shiny,
> Is left very sad.

DOÑA BECA (*excitedly to* FATHER ZACAYA). Do you see them at all?

FATHER ZACAYA (*shading his eyes and peering down at the train*). Not even the ears of the horse. But that is Carlos singing.

CARLOS (*his singing comes nearer and nearer*).

> There's no deer on the mountainside gray.
> Everything is faded today.
> For no birds are flying,
> The roses are dying.
> Since I've been away. Ay-yah!

DON RUFINO (*disgusted*). Now there is a happy ballad to welcome a man home.

DOÑA BECA (*starting toward the house, calling*). Ester! Devil take that girl! Ester! Come out here! (ESTER *runs in from the house. She is a shy, pretty girl of eighteen in a neat pink skirt, a white blouse, and a shawl over her shoulders. Behind her is* CONCHA, *also about eighteen. She wears lavender instead of pink, and flirts with every man from five to eighty.*)

DOÑA BECA. You, daughter! What are you doing here?

CONCHA (*pouting*). I wanted to see Don Antonio come home, Mamá.

DON RUFINO. She wanted to roll the eye at Carlos Balderas.

DOÑA AMPARO. Concha is engaged to our son, Julio. Concha would not roll the eye at any other man.

DON RUFINO. She rolls the eye when she asks for the salt.

DOÑA BECA. Keep your tongue away from my daughter. And you, Concha, behave yourself. (*To* ESTER.) Did you get all the floor tiles washed?

ESTER (*nervously*). I needed kerosene to make them shine, but I didn't have any. No one told me Don Antonio was arriving until this morning . . .

CONCHA. La! He's only a man. He won't notice floor tiles.

DOÑA BECA. Antonio's daughter is not a man.

DOÑA AMPARO. Antonio with a daughter. How wonderful! (*Holding up her parcel.*) I brought her a little present. It isn't much, because I didn't have time to make anything really elegant, but I think she'll . . .

DOÑA BECA. If you crocheted it . . . it's a masterpiece.

FATHER ZACAYA (*excitedly*). I see them! The carriage is almost here. (*He hurries through the gate and off left.*)

DOÑA BECA. You two girls stand against the wall. Don't get in our way. (*The girls, hand in hand, obey her.*)

DOÑA AMPARO. I do hope she'll like my present.

DON RUFINO. It's more important that Antonio like the goat business.

DOÑA BECA (*snorting*). The Devil is shaped like a goat. And you call yourself a good Christian.

DON RUFINO. I'll be in heaven before you! Saint Peter will say, "We want no woman with a sharp tongue here!"

DOÑA BECA. Let me tell you, Rufino Gonzalez . . . (FATHER ZACAYA *enters from the house in time to interrupt them.*)

FATHER ZACAYA (*sharply*). Will no one greet our old friend?

(*As* DOÑA BECA *swings around in confusion,* FATHER ZACAYA *steps aside and,* DON ANTONIO *enters. His American clothes do not look well on his peasant body. But his children are born of city ways.* LUPITA, *very modish, inclined to be sulky, about twenty-one, follows him. With her is* ABEL, *a pleasant young man who has been dominated all his life by both his father and sister. Everyone is looking at* DON ANTONIO *as he faces* DOÑA BECA, *and no attention at all is paid to the last arrival,* CARLOS BALDERAS, *whose candy tray swings from his shoulders. He, alone, is intent on* LUPITA. *There is dignity in him, and something else . . . a kind of private enjoyment of the world around him.)*

DON RUFINO *(importantly)*. As mayor of Abasolo, it gives me true pleasure to welcome you back to . . .

DOÑA BECA *(pushing* DON RUFINO *aside)*. Get out of my way, you fool.

(She and DON ANTONIO *stare at each other, remembering shared memories. Then they fling their arms about each other in the traditional Mexican embrace.* DON PABLO *and* DOÑA AMPARO *sweep down on them, and they, too, embrace* DON ANTONIO *while* DOÑA AMPARO *weeps noisily.* DON RUFINO, *disgusted, retires to the window seat.* LUPITA *superciliously notes the emotional display.* ABEL *quietly "eye-flirts" with* ESTER *and* CONCHA *who giggle silently together, and* CARLOS *still watches* LUPITA *with an amused smile.)*

DON ANTONIO. My friends. My old friends.

DOÑA BECA. You've not aged a day. Not a day.

DON PABLO *(loudly blowing his nose)*. We've missed you, Antonio.

DOÑA AMPARO. I never thought I'd live to see this day.

FATHER ZACAYA. We must not forget that Antonio brings us a beautiful gift . . . the gift of his children.

DON ANTONIO. Indeed. My little family. My girl is named for Our Blessed Lady of Mexico: Guadalupe. We call her Lupita. And the boy . . . I named him for my old friend Father Zacaya . . . He is Abel.

LUPITA *(impatiently)*. You sound as though we were pet dogs. (DON RUFINO *laughs, but the others frown at her disrespect.* CARLOS *smiles and nods thoughtfully.)*

DON ANTONIO *(trying to smooth an awkward moment)*. Eh, Lupita has the blunt nature of her blessed mother, dead these fifteen years. My children, this is Doña Beca of whom you've heard so much . . .

ABEL *(moving forward eagerly)*. Are you the one who threw water on my father when he serenaded you?

DOÑA BECA. That was my dear father. Antonio sang under the wrong window that evening.

FATHER ZACAYA. You must learn our language, my son. Here one does not serenade . . . one sings the rooster.

LUPITA *(dryly)*. How very quaint. (CARLOS *suddenly laughs aloud. Everyone looks at him. He smilingly shrugs his shoulders, and they all look again at* DON ANTONIO.)

DON ANTONIO. And these are my two good friends Don Pablo and Doña Amparo . . . *(To them.)* I heard you were married after I left.

DOÑA AMPARO *(proudly)*. Pablo's the civil judge now . . . a very important man.

DON RUFINO. Because I made him important! *(Moving forward to face* DON ANTONIO.) I am Rufino Gonzales, mayor of Abasolo, at your service. *(He bows grandly.)*

DOÑA BECA. Mayor he calls himself. The truth is, he owns all the goat flocks in the valley, and we need him for his money . . .

DON RUFINO. Deny, if you can, that I am a practical man. *(To* DON ANTONIO.) I've been a good mayor, and I've kept out of the valley every man who might spoil it . . . or seek to change it.

DON ANTONIO. Then you don't approve of progress?

DON RUFINO. I believe in our simple ways. I hope, señor, that you don't plan to change anything.

DON ANTONIO. I have . . . let us say . . . certain plans.

DON RUFINO *(glancing around at the group)*. Interesting . . . very interesting. My office is always open to suggestions. Whether I approve of the suggestions is another matter. And I think you should know, señor, that nothing happens in this valley without my approval. Nothing.

DOÑA BECA *(sharply)*. Pay no attention to this . . . this foreigner, Antonio.

DON RUFINO *(yelling)*. Foreigner! I've been here fifteen years.

DOÑA BECA. Fifty years, and you'd still be a foreigner.

FATHER ZACAYA *(quietly)*. There shall be no quarrels this day . . .

DOÑA AMPARO *(hastily)*. Oh, no. Please. No quarrels *(Turning quickly to* LUPITA.) Dear child, how pretty you are. See, I've brought you a present. *(She extends the parcel.)*

LUPITA *(taking it with her fingertips)*. How very nice of you.

ABEL. Don't be a stick, Lupita. Open it.

LUPITA *(without interest)*. Oh. Oh, yes, of course. *(While she opens the package, the others watch her expectantly, as, baffled, she holds up a crocheted nightgown top.)*

CARLOS. About five years ago, Don Pablo decided that the village wasn't paying the goatherders enough, so he threatened to take the case to the courts in Monterrey.

CONCHA. The day before Don Pablo was to leave, his son, Julio, disappeared.

CARLOS. Of course, Don Pablo couldn't leave then; and he and Doña Amparo nearly went crazy trying to find Julio.

CONCHA. All the world knew it was Don Rufino's doing, but who could prove it?

ABEL. What happened?

CARLOS. Don Pablo finally went to Don Rufino and told him that he'd drop the case in the courts, and the next day Julio came home.

ABEL. Julio could have done something . . .

CONCHA (hotly). Don't blame my Julio! All his money is tied up in goats, and if Don Rufino killed his goats, eh? Why, Julio and I could never marry . . .

ABEL. But surely there are laws . . .

CARLOS. In this valley only Don Rufino's law counts. Personally, I want no dealings with him. That's why I'm a candy vendor.

CONCHA. Have you candy in that box now, Carlos?

CARLOS. That I have, but it's not for you.

CONCHA (she bursts into a laugh, runs over to the kitchen door, and calls). Ester! Ester! Carlos has brought you a fine present!

CARLOS. (upset). Will you stay out of my affairs, daughter of Doña Beca?

ESTER (entering from the house). Why would you bring me a present, Carlos Balderas?

CARLOS (flustered). I'm sorry, Ester. It's not for you. I mean . . . I . . . well, I brought it for . . . for someone else.

CONCHA (delighted). Carlos is blushing! He means Lupita. He means Lupita!

CARLOS (putting the box on the table). I just bring a little present, and all the world has me rolling the eye at her. I'll leave it here where she can find it, and a good afternoon to you!

ABEL (stopping him). Not so fast, friend. How would Lupita feel to get a present secondhand?

CARLOS. Let go of me, Abel. I have work to do in the village.

ABEL. First, Lupita. Ester, go and get her, but not one word about the candy.

ESTER. I swear by the petticoat of Our Blessed Virgin! *(She runs into the house.)*

CARLOS. You're children, all of you, playing games.

ABEL *(dreamily)*. I can see it now. Lupita will come out. Then Concha will guard the house door and I the mountain pass . . . and you'll be alone with Lupita . . .

CARLOS *(yelling)*. No! *(Then with more self-possession.)* You still don't know our customs. A man and girl can only be alone together after they're engaged. Concha, you explain to him . . .

CONCHA *(with solemn mischief)*. You're the man. You tell him.

CARLOS. Listen to me, Abel. I'm no fool. I'm just a candy vendor. What have I to offer your sister? I can't even afford an orchestra to serenade her . . .

ABEL. I'll serenade her for you . . . If you teach me the words to the great song . . .

CONCHA. He means "Shadow of Our Lord, St. Peter" . . .

CARLOS *(shocked)*. Certainly not! Serenades start with simple songs . . . I mean, that's a very important song . . .

ABEL. The words to that song is my price. If you won't teach it to me . . . well . . . your arm, Concha. We'll join Ester in the kitchen and leave Carlos alone here . . .

CONCHA. I think I hear Lupita coming!

> (ABEL *bows and offers* CONCHA *his arm. They make a great ceremony of strolling toward the door.*)

CARLOS. Wait! *(He draws a deep breath and speaks the lyrics.)* "Shadow of Our Lord, St. Peter, the river lures me, the river lures me. And thus your love would my poor love allure . . . my love allure . . ."

ABEL *(surprised)*. Do you mean that's all there is to it?

CARLOS. And enough it is, when you sing it at night . . .

CONCHA. When even the roosters are quiet and there are no dogs barking . . .

CARLOS. A girl will feel so sorry for you she can't help marrying you. Eh, Concha?

(*Before she can answer,* LUPITA *enters from the house, followed by a giggling* ESTER.)

LUPITA. What is all this mystery? Ester looks as though she had swallowed a pound of butter.

ABEL. Carlos has something for you, Lupita.

LUPITA. Really? Good afternoon, Carlos.

CARLOS. Good afternoon, Lupita. I . . . I brought up a . . . a box of candy.

LUPITA. That was nice of you. It's a long climb up the mountainside. (*Opens the box.*) Why this looks delicious. Did you make it yourself?

CARLOS (*straightening and beaming at the others*). All of it. That's burnt milk, and that's made from pumpkin . . . and that from sweet potatoes. Those little round ones are almond paste.

ESTER. Ooh . . . that's feast-day candy . . . the almonds.

CARLOS. Do you like it, Lupita?

LUPITA. I'll have to eat it to see. How much is it? Ester, fetch me my purse.

(*The girls and* ABEL *are embarrassed into silence.* CARLOS *grows very stiff and dignified.*)

CARLOS. Nothing, señorita. I brought it as a gift. I also brought the mail. Good afternoon. (*He gives her a sweeping bow and leaves by way of the gate.*)

LUPITA (*biting her lip*). You, Ester, what are you doing out here? Don't you realize that it's almost time for supper? Don Antonio will be hungry. Into the house with you.

ESTER (*subdued*). Yes, señorita. (*She runs into the house.*)

LUPITA (*turning to* CONCHA). I know you're fond of your cousin, but after all, she has work to do. You mustn't waste her time.

CONCHA. You needn't worry. I'm not staying. I just came to tell you that Mamá is going to pay you a visit this afternoon. (*She turns before she vanishes.*) Good-bye, Abel.

ABEL. Good-bye, Concha. (*He watches her go into the house and then turns furiously on* LUPITA.) You're a fine one!

LUPITA (*defensively*). How was I to know that he was bringing it as a gift?

ABEL. If you weren't always so wrapped up in yourself you would have realized it.

LUPITA. Certainly nobody else is ever concerned about me. You go off down to the plaza with all your friends, with never a thought as to how lonely I might be.

ABEL. You wouldn't be lonely if you tried to make a few friends for yourself.

LUPITA. With Concha, Ester, Doña Amparo, Doña Beca? You expect me to talk to them?

ABEL. Why not? They try hard enough to talk to you. And don't get the idea you're too good for them, either. "He who was born to be a gourd will never become a painted vase."

LUPITA. You're as bad as Father, quoting your village proverbs.

ABEL. I like them better than the bright speeches of your fine friends, which have to cut and hurt other people before they're considered witty.

LUPITA *(catching his shoulders)*. Abel, you're not growing to *(She lets go of him and steps back.)* . . . love this valley are you?

ABEL. I'm finding something here . . . something that I've wanted all my life.

LUPITA *(almost beyond speech)*. Are you being serious?

ABEL. Certainly. You want art. Look at the stone carvings on the outside of the church. It took a great master to change stone into frozen lace.

LUPITA. That isn't art . . . that's design. Art carries the message of a new freedom.

ABEL. I know. Like the statue that bright little friend of yours made . . . What was his name . . . the Russian?

LUPITA. Boris?

ABEL. That's the one. He made a curved line like that . . . *(Gesturing in the air.)* Called it *Flight of a Bird* and expected the world to stand back and gasp. He's still waiting.

LUPITA. The world doesn't always recognize genius. And it does take genius to carve in stone something that is only a flash of light in the air.

ABEL. What kind of genius does it take to carve a man's belief in God so powerfully that he makes others believe, too? And then there's music. The people here don't have to crowd into concert halls to hear a man sing. They open their throats and let the music pour out of their own hearts.

LUPITA. If you can call it music.

ABEL. Of course it hasn't all of the technical tricks of Nancy Moreno's fine compositions. What was her latest effort? That one where she used the factory whistle to show the boy's love for the girl?

LUPITA. Even Pierre Dumarque considered that a masterpiece. And you're just showing up your own ignorance. It wasn't a boy and a girl. It was two robots. She was showing the pulse of the future in sound. The music around here just . . .

ABEL. Shows the pulse of a human heart, and people aren't as important as robots.

LUPITA. I suppose you'll be telling me that they have a great literature here, too.

ABEL. Last month when I was camping out with the surveyors, we'd sit around the campfire at night and listen to some of the traveling goat-herders telling stories. I'd always get a thrill when one of them recited his little opening verse: "The drunkard drinks wine and the boy eats bread. If this tale's a lie it's not out of my head." We'd sit there all wrapped up in our blankets with the stars bending close down above our heads, and the fire protecting us with its warm red glow, and listen to stories of the strongest man in the world who had a bear for a father; of the woman who must weep every night because she betrayed her people to Cortés.

LUPITA. What you're really trying to say is that you want me to release you from your promise.

ABEL *(turning away, slowly)*. Yes.

LUPITA. That's the valley speaking, Abel, not you yourself. I'm holding you to your promise.

ABEL. Then I'll break it.

LUPITA. Not you. You're too much like Father. You won't break it. You said you'd leave just as soon as the powerhouse was finished.

ABEL. Unless something extraordinary happened.

LUPITA. Nothing extraordinary will happen. And then, Abel, we'll go away. You'll forget this valley.

ABEL. I won't live any place near Pierre Dumarque and Nancy Moreno and that crowd. I might put up with her earrings, but not with red polish on his fingernails.

LUPITA. We don't have to live in New York. We can live in London . . . or Paris. *(She sits on the bench, dreaming.)* Think of dressing for dinner again, sitting down to a perfectly appointed table . . . having deft waiters serve you while an orchestra plays softly, and people chatter and laugh all about you. That's living, Abel. Cultured living. That's what we really want . . . not this barbaric place!

ABEL. But if you'd just give it a chance! It's not barbaric . . .

LUPITA. Abel, you promised. Father has always taught us to hold a promise as sacred . . .

ABEL. When I made that promise I didn't know what this valley would mean to me. But now I do . . .

LUPITA. You're talking like a child! Have I ever guided you wrong, Abel? Have I?

ABEL *(reluctantly)*. No.

LUPITA. Dear Abel, this valley is a new toy to you . . . something to play with for a little while. But in time you'll grow bored with it, and then you'll know that the world out there is the only world for both of us.

ABEL *(weakening)*. I never could fight you . . .

LUPITA. My dear brother, my dear baby brother . . . it isn't what we want in this world that's important . . . it's the things we need, to survive as true individuals.

> *(They stare at each other.* ABEL *despondently turns away to gaze out over the valley.* ESTER *enters from kitchen.)*

ESTER. Your pardon, Lupita, but would the reporter like the bananas fried or served with rice?

LUPITA. What reporter?

ABEL *(sulkily)*. He drove out from Monterrey to get a story about the power-house. Father invited him to dinner.

LUPITA *(excitedly)*. A reporter? A man who can talk about something besides goats coming here? Why didn't you tell me?

ABEL. I forgot.

LUPITA *(piteously)*. You forgot! For the first time in three months somebody comes I can talk to . . . And you forgot!

ABEL *(embarrassed)*. I'm sorry, Lupita.

LUPITA *(brushing his comment aside)*. No matter. He's here. He's really here.

Ester, set the table exactly the way I taught you . . . Oh, I wish I had some decent silver and plates. We'll have candles instead of a lamp and . . . (*Turning to* ABEL.) You can sing for us afterwards. Do you remember anything of Nancy Moreno's?

ABEL. No!

LUPITA. Then you'll have to sing Dumarque's "Song without Melody."

ABEL. I can't remember songs that don't have tunes to them.

LUPITA (*horrified*). That's the most important song that's been written in the last twenty-five years. Dumarque says so himself. How could you have forgotten it? (ABEL *does not answer.*) Oh, very well. Sing anything you like . . . but not one of the village songs! I won't have this evening spoiled by a single reference to this valley. Ester, when will he be here?

ESTER. Carlos Balderas is bringing him from the boardinghouse . . .

LUPITA. The boardinghouse! He can't stay in that . . . that flea dump! He'll stay here. How is that room down the hall from Father's? Is it ready for a visitor . . . a very important visitor?

ABEL. A reporter important? When we left New York you wouldn't even speak to a reporter.

LUPITA. When we left New York I didn't know what it was to be so lonely for companionship I'd even talk to myself. (*To* ESTER.) Do try to remember to set the table correctly.

ESTER. I'll try. Do I wait to set it until after Doña Beca leaves?

LUPITA (*blankly*). Doña Beca? What has she to do with this dinner?

ESTER. She's coming to call this afternoon.

LUPITA. Oh, dear. Why should she . . .

ABEL (*sharply interrupting*). Don't forget, she's a good friend to this family. I'd even say she is more important than this reporter.

LUPITA (*coldly*). That is a matter of opinion. Ester, see that the guest room is prepared, and wait to set the table until Doña Beca leaves. (*She looks down into the valley.*) It seems like a dream. I was terrified loneliness would drive me down there to the village. But now I have someone to talk to . . . someone to understand me . . . Ay, it will be wonderful just to be able to talk again! (*She goes into the house.*)

ESTER (*looking after her*). I don't understand her. She can talk. Why, sometimes the words pour out of her like water in the new powerhouse. Of course, they don't seem to mean anything. *(She shrugs and starts into the house.)*

ABEL. Ester! Don't go in. I want to ask you something.

ESTER *(nervously)*. What is it?

ABEL. Why do you run away every time I try to speak to you?

ESTER. Was I not speaking to you earlier this afternoon?

ABEL. But Concha was here then.

ESTER *(nervously)*. She should be here now.

ABEL. Please, Ester, don't you like me just a little?

ESTER. Faces we see . . . hearts no.

ABEL. I'm wearing my heart right up here on my face for you to look at.

ESTER *(not looking at him)*. Then you should wear your hat on the back of your head to show it more plainly.

ABEL *(bending toward her and singing softly)*.

> Oh, moon, can you hear me sing to you?
> If I should be so bold?
> Will love find me at last, at last,
> Before I grow too old, too old?

ESTER *(retreating toward the house)*. Doña Beca will soon be here. She will hear you.

ABEL *(continues his song, and taking her hand)*.

> The moon would say, "Are you afraid, my pretty maid, are
>   you afraid?
> Love's a snare. Love will welcome you if you dare, pretty
>   maid, if you dare."

ESTER *(pulling her hand away from him in some confusion)*. Big pumpkins grow from little ones, and you are a very large pumpkin.

ABEL. Why? Because I . . . like you?

ESTER. You must not say such things. After all, you are the wealthy young Lozano and I am just a village girl. You should keep your songs for your sweetheart in the States.

ABEL. What sweetheart?

ESTER. The one from whom the letter came today. My hair does not hide my face. I know that you are only rolling the eye at me.

ABEL (*laughing*). Nancy Moreno does not mean as much to me as the mosquito that sang in your ear last night.

ESTER. Those are easy words to tumble out of your mouth. I have heard other boys speak them as easily. But the fruit that has been pecked is the one that knows best about birds.

ABEL. You must believe me. Don't you realize, Ester, that . . . (DOÑA BECA *calls from the house.*)

DOÑA BECA (*off left*). Niece! Niece! Where are you?

ESTER. Doña Beca is here. (*He holds her hand tightly. She pulls free, runs up on the stoop, where she turns and looks back at him.*) When the black sky is dyed red, then perhaps I will believe you. (*She runs in, calling.*) I'm coming Aunt Beca . . . I'm coming.

    (ABEL *stands still a moment, then deliberately kicks the bench just as* DOÑA BECA *appears in the doorway.*)

DOÑA BECA. Eh, the temper grows violent, and on such a hot day. (ABEL *shakes her hand.*) What are you doing? Loafing as usual?

ABEL (*shrugging and flinging out his hand*). Now, Doña Beca, I worked this morning. It's too nice a day to waste in work.

DOÑA BECA (*looking up at the sky*). For you it is always too nice a day or too bad a day. Work and hour never seem to meet. (*Suddenly pointing her arm at him.*) And what were you singing a while ago?

ABEL (*innocently*). I was trying to learn a new song.

DOÑA BECA. I doubt if you need any more lessons on it. (LUPITA *enters from the house. She has obviously put on her company manners.*)

LUPITA. A good afternoon to you, Doña Beca.

DOÑA BECA. Um! Lupita, this brother of yours is more worthless than I thought.

ABEL. I am sorry you think that, Doña Beca. Your servant. (*He makes her a little bow and starts into the house.*)

LUPITA. Abel, you're not going down to the village, are you?

ABEL. No. I am going up to my room to . . .

DOÑA BECA. Study singing?

ABEL. To write a letter to Nancy Moreno.

LUPITA (*very pleased*). Are you, Abel? Really?

ABEL (*looking toward the house*). I want to get her opinion of me in writing. (*He nods his head to both of them and goes inside.*)

LUPITA *(staring after him puzzled)*. I wonder what he meant by that?

DOÑA BECA. This Nancy Moreno. She is a friend of yours?

LUPITA. She is my dearest friend.

DOÑA BECA *(puzzled, in her turn)*. Then why do you object to his writing her?

LUPITA. I don't object . . . I'm glad he is, but . . . I feel he's up to some mischief. We had quite a talk this afternoon. He frightened me. He's beginning to like this valley.

DOÑA BECA. And you still hate it. But if you gave yourself a chance you could come to love it . . .

LUPITA. Never! I hate if for stripping me of everything I ever wanted. And worst of all, for what it's doing to Abel. It's actually turning him into a vegetable, without ambition or any memory of our old friends . . . our important friends . . . *(She pauses and looks wonderingly at the door.)* And yet he said he was going to write to Nancy Moreno. Is he reaching out toward her again . . . Could he be thinking of going back, and taking me with him?

DOÑA BECA. You're more American than Mexican. An American girl would go by herself . . .

LUPITA. Father would never let me go . . . and I have no money . . . Oh, if I only had some money of my own! I'd leave on the first train . . . be free of this prison . . .

DOÑA BECA. And free of Carlos Balderas?

LUPITA. Carlos Balderas? What has he to do with me?

DOÑA BECA. That was why I climbed your hill this afternoon . . . to talk to you about Carlos *(Picking up the candy box)*. I see that he has already been here. *(She tries a piece of candy, and nods.)* Umm . . . Carlos is improving. But don't tell him I said so.

LUPITA. Doña Beca, just what is on your mind?

DOÑA BECA. Many things . . . most of them no concern of yours. But I have watched you, Lupita. You like frankness . . . so do I.

LUPITA. Well?

DOÑA BECA. Carlos is really an extraordinary fellow. He followed Pancho Villa during the Revolution. He's quite a hero. Did you know that? (LUPITA *mutely shakes her head.*) And he has also traveled . . . all the way to Mexico City. Someday he may even become mayor of Abasolo. But that is for the future! I am concerned with the present. Has Carlos sung the rooster to you yet?

LUPITA *(amused at* DOÑA BECA's *naïveté).* Certainly not!

DOÑA BECA. He walks slowly, that young man. I must have a talk with him. It is really time that this affair is settled between you.

LUPITA *(beginning to grow angry).* Just what affair are you talking about, Doña Beca?

DOÑA BECA. Your marriage to Carlos Balderas.

LUPITA. My marriage to . . . to that candy vendor! *(She bursts into laughter.)*

DOÑA BECA *(watching her with a frown).* The future mayor of Abasolo.

LUPITA. If he were the future mayor of Monterrey it would still be preposterous!

DOÑA BECA. Why? Because you have lived in the great world? Well, let me tell you something, my girl. Great world or small village, the best cure for your stupidity is an honest husband and a houseful of children.

LUPITA *(really angry).* And let me tell you something, Doña Beca. This conversation has gone far enough. My life is mine . . . mine! It is none of your affair.

DOÑA BECA *(thoughtfully).* Hmm. I could say you are impertinent . . .

LUPITA *(coldly).* If I have offended my father's old friend, I'm sorry. But I won't have everyone in this valley trying to run my life.

DOÑA BECA *(crossing to the patio gate).* Come here, Lupita.

LUPITA. Don't try it, Doña Beca. My father is always pointing out the beauty of the valley. But it is not beautiful to me. It will never be beautiful.

DOÑA BECA. So . . . you are afraid to look at it.

LUPITA. I am not!

DOÑA BECA. Then come here. *(After a moment,* LUPITA *slowly moves toward her.)*

LUPITA *(on a long breath).* Well, I've looked at it.

DOÑA BECA. Notice especially the village . . . that little village of Abasolo that you despise so much. When the first Spaniards came to the north in 1590, they built the church you see down there, with its square tower and its rock walls. That church has seen so much. It has seen gentlemen in plumed hats and ladies in satin with lace veils hiding their dark eyes. It has seen soldiers in steel armor. It has seen swords flashing in the moonlight, and dead men rotting in the sun. It has seen golden dreams, and broken hearts, and much . . . too much . . . ambition.

LUPITA. That's all very romantic, Doña Beca. But I see more than the church. I see the tumbled-down houses, the narrow streets filled with mud and filth, the scrawny chickens and the bony dogs . . .

DOÑA BECA. But you can't see the hearts of the people!

LUPITA. Can I not! The people are worst of all. They keep their eyes fixed on the ground, their hands always curved as though fastened on the plow. They're worse than the chickens and the dogs! They're weeds growing out of the earth.

DOÑA BECA. From the earth comes all life, Lupita . . . and the souls of men.

LUPITA. From the earth comes everything that I hate most in life: stolid peasants, dirt, labor that twists the bones.

DOÑA BECA. And in New York people are not like that? There is no dirt, no misery? Only a great white city shining in the sun?

LUPITA. In New York there are my friends . . . people who understand me . . .

DOÑA BECA. Abel tells me they are people who can be bought with money . . . who love you for your money . . .

LUPITA. That's not true!

DOÑA BECA. Abel says they were always borrowing money from you . . . or trying to sell you their statues and their songs . . .

LUPITA (almost in tears). Abel doesn't understand! Artists can't be bothered with cheap things like . . . like making money. They are put on the earth to create . . . to be supported by less talented people like me. You can't put a value on beauty!

DOÑA BECA. How much does a song cost?

LUPITA. This is a childish argument!

DOÑA BECA. You mean you can't answer my question. But Carlos Balderas could answer it. He knows a song is one of God's gifts . . . like the wind and the flowers and the line of black mountains against the flame of sunset. Beauty that does not come from the heart is worth nothing, Lupita. But beauty from the heart . . . that is what Abasolo has. And until you understand that, Lupita, there is no place for you in this valley. *(She goes quietly into the house.)*

(LUPITA *remains quiet for a moment, then, abruptly, she reaches out and swings the gate shut as* DON ANTONIO, *followed by* FERNANDO PEREZ, *enters from the house.* PEREZ *is a pompous man filled with the importance of* FERNANDO PEREZ. DON ANTONIO *has a worried expression which brightens as he sees* LUPITA.)

DON ANTONIO. Ay, Lupita, I've brought a guest home with me. He's going to put my picture in the paper. Fernando Perez, my daughter, Lupita.

PEREZ *(shaking hands with* LUPITA). Your servant, señorita.

LUPITA *(still rather subdued, but brightening with pleasure of seeing him)*. Your visit gives me pleasure, señor.

DON ANTONIO. We met Doña Beca in front of the house. What mischief has she been up to now? She looked like a mouse that has stolen the cheese from a trap.

LUPITA. Did she, indeed? Perhaps Doña Beca has overreached herself. But no matter. You look tired, Father. Have you been working hard today?

DON ANTONIO. I've been showing the valley to Señor Perez.

LUPITA *(surprised)*. Are you interested in valleys, Señor Perez?

PEREZ. A little, a little, as I am interested in all things. I am a man with very . . . shall I say . . . very wide interests? For example the work of my good friend . . . I trust that you are my good friend, Don Antonio? *(With his hand spread out on his breast and a brief bow toward the older man.)*

DON ANTONIO *(with a smile)*. All the world is my good friend, señor.

PEREZ. You are a lucky man, a very lucky man. As I was saying, the work you are doing here . . . *(He turns to* LUPITA.) But it is magnificent, señorita . . . without parallel. I felt that together we were making history as I watched your father plant the first orange tree today.

DON ANTONIO *(enthusiastically)*. It is the beginning at last, Lupita. With my own hands I broke the soil and started the wealth of this valley.

LUPITA *(anxiously)*. Father, you shouldn't do things like that. It tires you out too much.

DON ANTONIO. Tired? I? *(He laughs, but sinks rather wearily on the bench.)*

Yes, I am a little tired, but it's a good tired that comes from good work well done. Sit down, sit down, señor.

LUPITA. Perhaps the Señor Perez would care to rest before dinner. *(Looking up at the sky.)* It is nearly time to serve it.

DON ANTONIO *(laughing).* You see, señor, my little Lupita is learning to tell time by the sun. Soon she will be as clever as any girl in the village. (LUPITA *steps back and raises her hand to her face as though she had felt him strike her.*)

PEREZ. Me, I learned to read the sun on a boat in the Mediterranean. You see, I have traveled to every place of importance: Paris, London, Naples . . . even Sydney, Australia.

LUPITA *(sincerely).* Ay, señor, it will be fascinating to hear stories of your travels . . .

DON ANTONIO *(sharply).* Not now, Lupita. The Señor Perez is tired. See if the water is hot enough for his bath.

LUPITA. I have already attended to it. *(To PEREZ.)* If you'll follow me . . . naturally you'll stay here as our guest . . . *(She and PEREZ go into the house. Inside, we can hear her calling.)* Ester! You can set the table now.

ESTER *(inside the house).* Very good, Lupita.

> *(In the meantime, DON ANTONIO nervously paces up and down, then sits with folded arms, his face worried. He glances up as ESTER, a folded tablecloth over her arm, comes out.)*

DON ANTONIO. Ester, has Don Rufino been up here this afternoon?

ESTER *(busy at the patio table, clearing it).* I haven't seen him, Don Antonio.
> *(Finding a letter on the table, she hands it to him. He opens and reads it.)*

DON ANTONIO. Where is Abel?

ESTER. I think he's asleep.

DON ANTONIO. Bah! He's so lazy, a dead moth has more life than he!

> *(He is again immersed in the letter. She holds a knife in her hand and looks down at the table puzzled. She looks at him, then back at the table.)*

ESTER. Don Antonio

DON ANTONIO. Umm.

ESTER. Where does the knife go?

DON ANTONIO. On the table.

ESTER *(persisting)*. But where on the table?

DON ANTONIO. Next to the plate. Don't bother me.

ESTER. Yes, Don Antonio.

> *(She picks up the fork, and holds the two of them together. This doesn't suit her, so she changes the fork to her left hand. Again she doesn't like this, so she reverses them, putting the knife in her right hand. Even this doesn't work. Then she has a bright idea. She puts the knife at the top of the plate, the fork at the bottom, then stands off and admires her handiwork. She is interrupted by DON RUFINO's voice calling from the house.)*

DON RUFINO *(off left)*. Is there no one in this house?

ESTER *(tapping the old man on the shoulder)*. Don Antonio, I hear Don Rufino outside.

DON ANTONIO. So he came, eh? Send him in here. And don't you listen at the door.

ESTER. Why, Don Antonio, I wouldn't . . .

DON ANTONIO. Hurry up! Hurry up with you.

ESTER. Before you can say "Mamá."

> *(She runs into the house, DON ANTONIO takes off his glasses, puts them away in their case in his pocket, and standing, faces the door as DON RUFINO enters. The two men look at each other.)*

DON ANTONIO *(jerking his head)*. You wanted to see me?

DON RUFINO. Just a little talk.

DON ANTONIO. With what face do you look at me?

DON RUFINO. A friendly one.

DON ANTONIO. Sit down. (DON RUFINO *sits on the bench*. DON ANTONIO *stands by the table*.) I received a letter today. Do you know anything about it?

DON RUFINO *(shrugging)*. You receive so many letters, Don Antonio.

DON ANTONIO. Not from lawyers' offices in Monterrey.

DON RUFINO. Perhaps if you told me a little about it . . .

DON ANTONIO. It says that the people who own the land in this valley are not going to allow me to dig irrigation ditches on their property.

DON RUFINO. Ay, that is very sad. Without the ditches you can have no farms. And of what use is the powerhouse? All that good money thrown away. You would have done better had you bought goat flocks.

DON ANTONIO. Every dog to his own kingdom. I prefer to buy land.

DON RUFINO (quickly). Land in this valley is not for sale.

DON ANTONIO. Anything is for sale.

DON RUFINO. Don Antonio, I will speak plainly, with my hat on the back of my head to show I hide nothing.

DON ANTONIO. Remember the blind are not always naked. I will listen to you.

DON RUFINO. The shoe factory in Monterrey is very powerful.

DON ANTONIO. Then I shall buy the shoe factory.

DON RUFINO. Ah, but that factory is not a single company. It is owned by men who have other interests, too . . . such as building materials.

DON ANTONIO. Are you threatening to hold up the construction of the new flour mill?

DON RUFINO. Now, Don Antonio, there is no need for anger. I am merely asking you to be sensible.

DON ANTONIO. You mean you want me to leave you alone to rule this valley to suit yourself.

DON RUFINO. Precisely. We've done without you for thirty years. We don't need you now.

DON ANTONIO. For thirty years I've been making plans . . . that never included you.

DON RUFINO (shrugging). That was where you made your mistake. They should have included me. The fish that sleeps is swept away by the current.

DON ANTONIO. So you are beginning to realize that. I thought you imagined only goatherders lived here.

DON RUFINO. That's all they are . . . all they are fit for. You've dazzled them with this money of yours. They don't know what it's going to do to them, but I do. The young men won't be content to stay here any longer. They'll take the money you pay them and go away to the States . . . to the beet fields and to the factories. The girls will leave for the cities. Soon none will be left here but the old and infirm. The roofs of the houses will tumble in. The church will be empty . . . and all of your fine farms will change back to what has always been here: yuccas, flowering thorn, cactus.

DON ANTONIO (with a wry smile). So you're trying to save the valley from my evil influence?

DON RUFINO. You see, you have all misjudged me, Don Antonio. I am really a very humane man. I think only of my people's good.

DON ANTONIO. And goats, incidentally! How do you pay your goatherders?

DON RUFINO. In goats. Property means more to these people than money.

DON ANTONIO. But they need money to buy food and clothes, eh?

DON RUFINO. When they need those things they come and sell me back the goats.

DON ANTONIO. How much do you pay them for their . . . property?

DON RUFINO (virtuously). I pay according to the demands of the shoe factory in Monterrey.

DON ANTONIO. You mean you pay as little as possible. You were right, Don Rufino. You are a very humane man, and as cunning as an eagle with its shoes off!

DON RUFINO. After all, I must look out for my own interests. I have to live.

DON ANTONIO (standing). I think I've been very patient with you. I've listened to everything you have to say.

DON RUFINO (his voice rising). It isn't a question of . . .

DON ANTONIO. Silence! (With the tone of a strong man who knows his mind.) I will build that powerhouse. I will build those irrigation ditches, and neither you, nor the shoe factory, nor all of Monterrey is going to stop me.

(LUPITA enters in a formal evening gown. She pauses in the door of the house to fasten her bracelet, and looks up startled at the two men.)

DON RUFINO (rising angrily). Do not step on thorns with your eyes open, Don Antonio. This is your last chance.

DON ANTONIO. Little man, don't think that you can hinder me! (He shakes the letter at him.) Tie up building material. I'll go elsewhere for them.

DON RUFINO. The railroads won't bring them in.

DON ANTONIO. Then I'll build that flour mill from the rocks in the river bed. Make no mistake, I'll build it.

DON RUFINO. It will never be finished.

DON ANTONIO. It will be finished, if I have to lay every stone with my own two hands. Take your lawyers and your goats and your shoe factories and keep them where they belong, outside of this valley.

DON RUFINO *(frightened).* You can't frighten me. There's more than one way of whipping you down.

DON ANTONIO *(moving toward him).* You'll never find that way. *(With cold fury.)* Now get out! Get out of my house!

DON RUFINO *(retreating).* You will weep over this moment!

DON ANTONIO. I wear shoes against your thorns.

DON RUFINO *(grunting).* We'll see.

> *(He stalks past* LUPITA *who has stepped out of the doorway to let him pass. She gazes after him, then looks in amazement at her father, who is rubbing his hand across his forehead.)*

LUPITA. Father! What . . . what has happened?

DON ANTONIO *(straightening).* He thinks he can whip me down. Nothing can whip me. I can't fail. I've planned too long. *(He walks to the gate.)* Trees pushing up through the soil, their roots drinking the water, their leaves eating the sunlight. And he thinks he can stop it. *(Patting her on the shoulder.)* Don't let it frighten you, Lupita. Nothing can defeat my valley.

LUPITA *(catching hold of him).* You're trembling, Father.

DON ANTONIO. It is only a little storm. But see . . . *(He points out above the wall.)* The moon is rising. Soon the stars will be out. Stars that are the eyes of young virgins who died in love. Stars never shine before rain. No more tempests here. (ABEL, *dressed in a white linen suit, enters from the house.)* My son, is your sleep ended? Why is it that small things can tire a man, when he can work all day in the fields and be strong at evening? Perhaps it is because he has been working in the rich brown earth. *(After a moment.)* The earth is a strong, kind mother, I can't turn away from her now. She put this valley in my trust, and I shan't fail her, no matter what comes. I shan't fail her! *(He sinks down on the chair.* ABEL *looks curiously at* LUPITA, *who shakes her head and puts her hand on her father's shoulder.)*

LUPITA. You should rest for awhile.

DON ANTONIO (*patting her hand*). No, no, I must speak to Abel first. (*He pulls her hand down and looks at it.*) You have such pretty hands, Lupita. They are so warm and firm and strong. Good hands. Hands made for working. You don't have long thin fingers and soft white palms like that newspaper fellow. (*He pats her hand against his cheek as* ESTER *comes to the door.*)

ESTER (*almost in tears*). Lupita! The most terrible thing has happened. (*She begins to weep.*)

ABEL (*anxiously*). What's the matter, Ester? Did you burn yourself? (*She shakes her head, but does not answer.* LUPITA *goes to her.*)

LUPITA. Nothing is that much of a tragedy. What is it?

ESTER (*trying her best to get it out*). Instead of soaking the celery in salt water . . .

LUPITA. Well?

ESTER. I soaked the bananas.

ABEL (*amused but sympathetic*). Poor Ester.

LUPITA (*angrily*). And what of my poor supper? What shall we serve with the rice, eh? (*Catching* ESTER *by the arm and jerking her inside.*) You, Ester!

DON ANTONIO. Abel, have you noticed how much Lupita is like Doña Beca?

ABEL. I believe I told her that this afternoon, Father.

DON ANTONIO. Eh! And where were you this afternoon?

ABEL. Here at the house.

DON ANTONIO. Doing what?

ABEL (*easily*). I did a good many things. I learned a new song, and wrote a letter, and went to sleep.

DON ANTONIO. Didn't you do any work on the plans for the flour mill?

ABEL. But I just finished building the powerhouse. Surely I deserve one day's vacation.

DON ANTONIO. With the nearest flour mill two hundred kilometers away? Vacations are for the baby.

ABEL (*sulkily*). I had an important letter to write.

DON ANTONIO. And who is more important than a flour mill?

ABEL. Right now . . . Nancy Moreno.

DON ANTONIO. May the saints have patience!

ABEL. I wanted her to say on paper that she wouldn't marry me. I need it to show somebody.

DON ANTONIO. And all that is more important than flour-mill plans!

ABEL. To me it is.

DON ANTONIO. Sometimes I wonder if you are my own son. Does this valley mean so little to you that you can neglect it for something of no value?

ABEL. My happiness has value!

DON ANTONIO. The valley is your happiness.

ABEL. Father, do you realize what you are saying? I don't think you can, or you wouldn't say it.

DON ANTONIO. Am I to be constantly torn at by these little things? Why must I go on fighting when I thought my days of fighting were finished?

ABEL. I knew you loved this valley, but I didn't think you'd put it before . . . me.

DON ANTONIO. Abel, can't you understand? Helping these people has been my religion for thirty years. Now that I can help them, do you help me? No. You sit at home and write letters.

ABEL. I'm beginning to think Lupita is right.

DON ANTONIO. Lupita? What has she to do with it?

ABEL. She said this valley was a poison that seeped into a man's blood. *(He sits.)* It's in yours. I'd never realized it before. And it's beginning to get in mine.

DON ANTONIO. Lupita has fancies. They mean nothing.

ABEL. So I thought. But I'm seeing a little clearer now. What right have you to keep her here when every nerve in her body cries out against staying?

DON ANTONIO. What right has she to want to go?

ABEL. The right of every person to carve out his own life.

DON ANTONIO. You told her you couldn't go, didn't you?

ABEL. I told her I didn't want to go.

DON ANTONIO *(smiling with relief)*. There spoke my son.

ABEL *(with an abrupt change of tone)*. But I've changed my mind. I'm going to take her just as soon as I can.

DON ANTONIO (*unable to comprehend this*). You mean you would leave me . . . leave the valley?

ABEL. That's exactly what I mean.

DON ANTONIO. You can't do it. I forbid it. (ABEL *gets to his feet.*)

ABEL (*feeling as though he were trying to batter down a wall*). We don't want to stay!

DON ANTONIO. Your desires are childish.

ABEL (*still not believing it*). You'd keep us here against our will?

DON ANTONIO. Yes. (*As* ABEL *draws back, he tries to justify his answer.*) I've worked hard during my life, sacrificed much. I haven't very long to live. And when I die I want to know that you and Lupita are finishing what I can only begin. For centuries my people have been whipped down to the earth, first by the Spaniards and then by men like this Rufino. Protecting them is your duty. I place it upon you.

ABEL. Leaving us in bondage to set them free?

DON ANTONIO. What is your bondage compared to theirs?

ABEL. Are they goats that we must herd them to see they don't nibble on cactus and get thorns in their noses?

DON ANTONIO. They have been crushed down too long. They don't know how to help themselves.

ABEL. Let them learn. Lupita and I need to go back to the States and drink a little freedom of our own. (*He starts toward the house calling.*) Lupita!

LUPITA (*inside the house*). Yes, Abel?

ABEL. Start packing your things. We leave for the States tomorrow.

LUPITA (*inside the house, crying out ecstatically*). Abel. (*She appears in the door, an apron tied around her waist, and wiping her face with the back of her hand.*) Do you mean that?

ABEL. Ask Father. (LUPITA *looks at* DON ANTONIO *who is sitting in the chair, his head bowed, his eyes closed. Then she looks back at* ABEL.)

LUPITA. I can't believe it!

ABEL. It's true enough. I'm going downtown. Don't expect me home to dinner (*He goes past her into the house.*)

LUPITA (*calling after him*). Where are you going?

ABEL (*from inside the house*). Down to the saloon to get drunk!

(LUPITA *stretches out her hand and half starts toward the house when a moan from* DON ANTONIO *stops her.*)

DON ANTONIO. Abel!

LUPITA (*going over to him, and kneeling down beside him*). Father. What happened?

DON ANTONIO (*pushes her away and standing up*). Go back to the States with him. The two of you aren't fit to stay in my valley. Go back to the long exile. Until dust covers my eyes I shall weep because I am childless, and my tears shall make the ground fertile. (*His voice almost choked with his emotion.*) But I shall be at home, at home, while you will be homeless and far away. Because when you leave you shall never return.

LUPITA (*appealingly*). Father, this never could be our home.

DON ANTONIO. When the days crawl into other days, you will listen for voices laughing with the wisdom and joy of the earth. No air perfumed with orange blossoms and flowering thorn and night-blooming jasmine will be in your nostrils. No friendly heart will open to your smile. You will know then what it is to desperately long for something of home. (*She looks up at him a moment, then buries her face in her hands and begins to cry. He looks down at her for a moment.*) Weep all you can now. Afterwards there will be no tears. That is the last great tragedy. (*He turns and goes slowly into the house, no longer a fine straight figure, but bent and old. Inside the house* PEREZ *speaks heartily.*)

PEREZ. Your house is magnificent, Don Antonio . . . but magnificent. (*As he speaks,* LUPITA *hastily wipes her eyes. He comes into the patio looking back, puzzled, over his shoulder.*) Is your father ill, señorita?

LUPITA (*trying to smile*). No . . . no, he's not ill. He's just . . . tired.

PEREZ. I see. Myself, I never tire. I am as strong as John the Bear.

LUPITA (*trying to be polite*). Who was John the Bear?

PEREZ. Legendary figure of these mountains. He had a bear for a father. In a small way I am interested in the folklore of these simple people, just as you interest yourself in . . . (*He gestures towards her apron.*) in cooking.

LUPITA (*blankly*). Cooking? (*Realizing she is still wearing the apron, she hastily takes it off.*) It's just an amusement. Servants are so difficult to find in this remote valley . . . good servants, I mean.

PEREZ *(having examined the patio, he now wanders over to the patio gate)*. I know what you mean. Personally, I like perfection in all things, even the merest details. Strange. There seems to be smoke down by the river.

LUPITA. Fog, probably.

PEREZ. From your tone, señorita, I gather you have no interest in the valley.

LUPITA. Interest? I hate it. *(Suddenly bursting out.)* But now I shall be free . . . free! I can't believe that I'm going away . . . I'm going away . . . I'm going away tomorrow!

PEREZ *(frowning)*. You are leaving all this?

LUPITA. Back to New York . . . it's like a dream.

PEREZ *(thoughtfully)*. But I understood, señorita, that your father owned vast tracks of land here . . . that he is quite . . . ah . . . wealthy. Surely he wouldn't care to exchange this pleasant country living for the smoke and gray skies of New York.

LUPITA. Not my father! Abel . . . my brother . . . and I. We're going back to our old friends, our good friends, our talented friends.

PEREZ. Talented?

LUPITA. Oh, yes. One is Pierre Dumarque, the composer. He wrote "Song without Melody," a composition that will change all future music. He says so himself.

PEREZ. "Song without Melody." *(Obviously lying.)* I believe I have heard of it. Magnificent, really magnificent. Tell me, señorita. This Dumarque, is he a truly free spirit? I mean must he labor at some grubby little job and then compose in his pitifully few free hours?

LUPITA. Oh, no. He says that artists should be supported by the State. People like me, with very little talent, find it a real privilege to help Dumarque expand his . . . his great creativity.

PEREZ *(coming toward her, with real interest)*. Indeed? I . . . ah . . . entirely agree with Dumarque, but unfortunately Mexico has no soul for artists.

LUPITA. No wonder, with every candy vendor spouting silly folk songs.

PEREZ. You say you have a little talent. May I ask in which of the arts?

LUPITA. I write a little. I've even had a poem published! Under another name, of course.

PEREZ. But I adore poetry. Perhaps I know your creation.

LUPITA. You probably know the magazine. It's very small, very select, edited by my good friend Nancy Moreno. It's called *Nothing*.

PEREZ *(baffled)*. It's called what?

LUPITA. *Nothing*. Nancy calls it that because the writing she publishes is like nothing else in the world.

(ESTER *appears in the doorway twisting her apron into knots.*)

PEREZ. I can imagine. Tell me, señorita, is it so exclusive that contributors pay for their poems to be published?

LUPITA. Why, yes. How did you know?

PEREZ. I'm thinking of starting that type of magazine myself. May I ask what you paid this . . . this *Nothing?*

ESTER *(from the doorway of the house, in a loud whisper)*. Lupita! Ssst, Lupita!

LUPITA *(unaware of* ESTER*)*. It was just fifty dollars. But the poem was only worth that.

PEREZ. Fifty dollars. That would be . . . *(Suddenly smiling.)* four hundred pesos. Yes, I must start such a magazine.

ESTER *(louder)*. Please, Lupita!

LUPITA. Be quiet, Ester. *(To* PEREZ.*)* Why, that would be fascinating, Señor Perez. What are your plans for it?

ESTER *(nervously)*. Where is Don Antonio?

LUPITA. How do I know where he is? Go find him yourself. *(To* PEREZ.*)* Do tell me about it.

PEREZ. I think I shall call it *Tomorrow*. A simple title, but it embraces the entire future.

LUPITA. Oh, yes, yes it does.

PEREZ. As I visualize it, I see sections in Spanish, naturally, but also English, French, perhaps even Russian. Señorita! I have just had a magnificent idea. How would you like to be the English editor?

LUPITA. Me?

ESTER. It's important, Lupita.

LUPITA. Be quiet, Ester! *(Then.)* Me, an editor?

PEREZ. Naturally you realize that an editorship in my *Tomorrow* will be much coveted by all artists. Ordinarily I would have to charge quite a large sum for the privilege. But since you are really my inspiration in creating the idea . . . for you it would be a mere bagatelle . . . a mere two thousand pesos. (*He looks royally off to allow her to admire him.*)

LUPITA (*thrilled beyond speech*). Oh . . . oh, Señor Perez. Such an opportunity!

ESTER (*desperately*). Lupita! The powerhouse is on fire! (*Both* PEREZ *and* LUPITA *look at her blankly. Then, coming to, they rush to the patio gate.*)

PEREZ. That smoke I saw!

LUPITA. If that powerhouse burns down, it will break my father's heart! Ester! Try the back garden. You know he often sits there in the sun! (ESTER *hurries into the house.*)

PEREZ. I think I can see men rushing around.

LUPITA. I hope they save it. Oh, I hope so.

PEREZ. It must have cost a great deal of money.

LUPITA. What does the money matter? It's my father's whole life!

PEREZ. I do hate to see money burn. (DON ANTONIO *runs in from the house.*)

LUPITA. Father! How do you think it started?

DON ANTONIO. It was Rufino. (*He hurries past them to the patio gate.*) I should never have let him stay in the valley.

LUPITA (*trying to stop him*). You mustn't go down there!

DON ANTONIO (*hurrying out*). This is my work, and no one will stop it!

LUPITA. Father! Come back! (*She starts after him, but* PEREZ *catches her arm.*)

PEREZ. If you go down there, you might be injured. I wouldn't like anything to happen to you . . . not now!

LUPITA. Poor Father. I should hate to leave him with the powerhouse burned.

> (*As she sinks down, crying, the lights dim. Darkness holds for a moment, and then the lights come up again.* LUPITA *and* PEREZ *are seated at the table. He is intent on lighting a cigarette but her interest is fixed on the patio gate.*)

PEREZ. I am sorry that you are leaving tomorrow, I should have liked to have known you longer. You have a mind that would be very easy to mold.

LUPITA (*absently*). So Pierre Dumarque used to say.

PEREZ (*stiffly*). My dear girl, once in a while I say something altogether original.

LUPITA. I'm sorry. I didn't mean to . . . *(Voices can be heard laughing and shouting off left.)* Listen! What's that? *(She runs to the gate.)* There's a mass of people coming up the road, and . . . Father . . . and Abel!

PEREZ *(frowning)*. A crowd? I was hoping that we could plan my magazine together this evening.

LUPITA *(ignoring him)*. Abel! What have you done to yourself?

FATHER ZACAYA *(off left)*. He is a true hero, Lupita.

> (ABEL *comes through the gate followed by* DON ANTONIO *and a gay* CROWD *from the village including* FATHER ZACAYA, DON PABLO, DOÑA BECA, CARLOS BALDERAS, *and* CONCHA.)

DON ANTONIO *(proudly)*. He saved the powerhouse.

LUPITA. Look at your clothes!

ABEL *(glancing down at himself and laughing. His trousers are dirty and torn, he has lost his coat and tie. He catches her by the arms and swings her around in a circle.)*. What do clothes matter? Don't you understand? The powerhouse is saved!

CROWD. Viva! Viva!

FATHER ZACAYA. Luckily he passed the powerhouse just as the blaze started.

CARLOS. He put it out all alone.

ABEL. You pulled me out from under that blazing timber. *(He stops laughing, goes over and shakes CARLOS by the hand.)* Thank you for saving my life.

CARLOS *(embarrassed)*. You would have done the same for me.

VOICES *(off stage)*. Viva! Viva! *(More people pour into the patio from the house, bringing ESTER and DON PABLO's son, JULIO ROMERO.)*

NEW CROWD. Long life to this house, Don Antonio!

FULL CROWD. Viva!

DON PABLO *(excitedly quieting the CROWD)*. My son, Julio, was also a hero! Tell them what you did, Julio!

JULIO *(strutting a little)*. Personally I took Rufino to jail!

VOICE FROM CROWD. He should dance with a rope around his neck!

ANOTHER VOICE. Rufino has lighted his last cigarette! *(The CROWD laughs.)*

DON PABLO *(trying to quiet them)*. Did you lock him up safely, my son?

JULIO. If he can escape now, then my name is not Julio Romero.

CONCHA. Julio is so brave.

JULIO. And I left him a bottle of tequila to remember me by.

VOICE FROM CROWD *(laughing loudly)*. Let the tequila make him forget he was ever in this valley.

ANOTHER VOICE. We want no more long-eared goats among us . . .

CARLOS *(yelling)*. Who fed us tallow instead of good yellow wax?

CROWD. Don Rufino!

JULIO. But who saved the powerhouse?

CROWD. Abel!

ESTER *(excitedly)*. Oh Abel . . . *(Then, shyly.)* . . . I'm so glad.

ABEL *(standing in front of* ESTER*)*. Are you Ester?

ESTER *(fleeing to the safety of* DOÑA BECA*)*. I . . . I . . . *(The* CROWD *laughs loudly.)*

FATHER ZACAYA *(holding up his hands)*. Let there be peace on this house! *(The* CROWD *is silenced. The men remove their hats; the women draw their veils over their heads.)* Let the Lord bless us and keep us . . . *(He points to* CARLOS.*)* And fill our hearts with the beauty of music. *(The* CROWD *relaxes with laughter.)*

CARLOS *(jumping up on the table)*. Songs should come from heroes. And today our hero is Abel!

DON PABLO. Abel shall sing for us!

JULIO. A good song, Abel.

CROWD. The best song, Abel.

ABEL. I have a song for you. How do you like this one, Ester? *(He swings her up on the bench and sings triumphantly.)*

> Shadow of our Lord, St. Peter,
> The river lures me,
> The river lures me.
> And thus your love would my poor love allure,
> My love allure.

ESTER. Saints in Heaven!

VOICES FROM CROWD. He sings the rooster before he even walks around the plaza! And what a rooster! Be careful, Ester, that he doesn't bring you to the altar before he proposes!

ABEL. Does it not wring your heart with sadness? Have you no sorrow for my lonely state?

DOÑA BECA. You shameless one! What does this mean, Abel?

ABEL. What can it mean, Doña Beca? Will you speak for me, Carlos . . . Julio?

CARLOS and JULIO *(stepping forward)*. We will indeed. (*They turn to* DOÑA BECA *and make her a low bow, much to the delight of the* CROWD.)

CARLOS. Doña Beca, our friend begs the honor of your niece's hand.

JULIO. He brings money and land to the marriage.

CARLOS. A house.

JULIO. A trousseau for the bride.

ABEL. And she can have a thousand orange blossoms made out of wax, if she wants them.

CARLOS *(frowning)*. Silence, Abel. It is not your place to speak (*He turns to* DOÑA BECA.) He waits for your answer with a humble heart.

DOÑA BECA. And what do you say to this, Antonio?

DON ANTONIO. I have nothing to say. Abel leaves the valley tomorrow.

LUPITA *(going to* ABEL*)*. Abel, we can't take Ester. What would we do with her?

ABEL. I'm sorry, Lupita, but I didn't think about having to leave Ester when I told you I'd go.

ESTER *(looking down at* ABEL*)*. If you want to go, I won't hold you. Lupita is right. There is no place for me outside of the valley.

ABEL *(to* ESTER*)*. But I'm not going to leave you. (*He turns to* DON ANTONIO.) When I saw smoke from the windows of the powerhouse, I realized what you were trying to tell me this afternoon. I helped to build it, to create it out of nothing, and no one can destroy it. You were right. My place is here, guarding this valley. Can you forgive me . . . for what I said? (*They look at each other a moment, and then give each other the abrazo, while the* CROWD *claps loudly.*)

CROWD *(turning to each other occasionally)*. Viva Don Antonio! Viva Abel! Viva! Viva!

DON ANTONIO *(fairly glowing)*. We shall hold a wedding here on New Year's Day!

CROWD. A great wedding . . . a fine wedding.

LUPITA *(bitterly, to* ABEL*)*. I hope you'll be very happy in a little stone house down by the riverbank, with children in the front yard and orange trees in the back.

ABEL. I know how bitter you must feel, Lupita, but after awhile you'll come to love this valley, too, just as I love it.

LUPITA. I won't. I'll never love it, because I won't be here.

DON ANTONIO. What's that?

LUPITA. I'm going away . . . alone.

DOÑA BECA. And what will you use for money?

DON ANTONIO. You'll not get a cent of my money for such foolishness . . . that I promise you.

LUPITA. I don't need your money. Señor Perez has offered to make me the New York editor of his magazine. He'll help me.

PEREZ. Just a moment, señorita . . . one little moment! After all, the magazine is still just a dream!

LUPITA. Then I'll write to Nancy Moreno.

ABEL. Do you think Nancy would send you money? She squeezes every dollar until the juice runs out!

LUPITA. She believes in helping creative artists. Before today, I had nothing to offer. But now . . . (*She turns to* PEREZ). When she finds out you trust me enough to make me an editor, she'll help me. You'll see. You'll all see.

ABEL. She won't waste a stamp on an answer.

LUPITA. I know Nancy Moreno. She'll answer by return mail. And when her letter comes, I'm leaving. I won't stay in this valley a moment longer than I have to.

DOÑA BECA. And once you're gone, the valley will call you back . . . you'll return to us.

LUPITA. Never! I'll be free of this valley forever. And I'll thank God for it with every breath I draw. (*Turning on the* CROWD.) Have your party. Have your fun in your silly, stupid little way! I don't want any part of it! All I want is to get away from here, and to stay away . . . forever!

(*As she runs into the house, the curtains close.*)

Act 3

It is three-thirty in the afternoon on the twelfth of December. There is very little change in the patio, and the light is very brilliant. ESTER *is sitting at the table sewing, and* CONCHA *is seated on the stool at the left, her arms fastened about her knees.* DOÑA BECA *is standing in the gate looking down the path, her hand shading her eyes.*

ESTER (*to* CONCHA). Next we went to the store of the Three Brothers. They had the most beautiful wedding dresses, Concha. One of them had a veil of lace that went down to the floor.

CONCHA (*sighing*). It must be wonderful in Monterrey.

ESTER. It is . . . but the streets are so hard they hurt my feet. Lupita took me into the great market. It was on Saturday and a band was playing on a little platform right in the center of it. A man sang, but (*Proudly.*) he couldn't sing like Abel. There was pink netting on the grapes to protect them from the flies, and an old woman was making mats out of straw.

DOÑA BECA. Why doesn't Julio come with the sugar? He's doubtless sitting at the mill munching cane.

CONCHA. He will be here in a moment, Mamá.

ESTER (*looking at* DOÑA BECA, *then leaning forward confidentially*). I did something very wicked.

CONCHA. What?

ESTER. Lupita had given me a little money, and she left me by a pottery stall while she went to buy wool for her embroidery. Just across the way from me was a public letter writer.

CONCHA. You didn't . . .

ESTER (*giggling*). Yes, I did. He wrote a letter from me to Abel. It looked beautiful. He drew a dove at the top of the page with a heart in a net of roses dangling from its beak. And you should have seen the writing. All curves. (*She demonstrates in the air.*) The *A* in Abel was beautiful. It took up most of the page.

DOÑA BECA (*coming into the patio*). Stop your mumbling, Ester, and get to work. You'll never have those things finished by New Year's. You promised me you'd be done with them if I let you come this afternoon.

CONCHA (*sitting down on the bench*). Do you think Lupita will be pleased with the surprise?

DOÑA BECA. There won't be a surprise unless Julio returns with the sugar. People must be fed. Sometimes I think Rufino put a black-magic spell on him.

CONCHA. I heard Don Pablo say that he was going to let Don Rufino out of jail today. He's been in it a long time. June . . . *(She counts the other months rapidly on her fingers but silently moving her mouth.)* December. Seven months. Don Pablo said he ate more than any prisoner we've ever had.

DOÑA BECA. You shouldn't be listening to gossip. (LUPITA *comes into the patio, a subdued* LUPITA *with sad eyes and a listless manner. She wears a very modish silk dress.)*

LUPITA *(pausing for a moment at seeing them, then coming forward)*. Good afternoon. I didn't know you were here.

DOÑA BECA *(going to her and kissing her on either cheek)*. A happy Saint's Day to you, Lupita.

CONCHA. May Heaven smile on you, Lupita.

ESTER. And bring you joy.

LUPITA *(without interest)*. Saint's Day?

DOÑA BECA. Have you forgotten that this is the twelfth of December?

CONCHA. All the Republic worships Our Blessed Lady of Guadalupe today.

ESTER. It must be wonderful at the miracle shrine near Mexico City, with all the people climbing the long stairs on their knees and holding candles in their hands.

DOÑA BECA. Don't turn your eyes astray, girl. We have a miracle Virgin in this very patio. May she bless us all. *(They all cross themselves.)*

CONCHA *(standing)*. If you give me permission to leave a moment, Mamá.

DOÑA BECA. Go away, go away. *(As* CONCHA *starts into the house.)* And if you see that Julio Romero, tell him to hurry.

CONCHA. On the back of a swallow. *(She runs into the house.)*

LUPITA *(To* ESTER*)*. Has Carlos brought the mail yet?

ESTER. I've not seen his face since yesterday.

DOÑA BECA *(sniffing)*. So you've had no answer yet to all your letters to your fine friends.

LUPITA *(quickly)*. They will write just as soon as they have time . . . I know they will. There is so much to do in New York. It is hard to settle down to writing a letter.

ESTER. Why don't they go to a public letter writer? He could do it so quickly.

LUPITA. They don't have them in New York.

ESTER *(shaking her head)*. What a sad thing, because not everyone can write with flourishes

DOÑA BECA. How do you know so much about them, miss?

ESTER *(bending over her work)*. I've heard tales of them. (CONCHA *enters with a bouquet of flowers hidden behind her back.*)

CONCHA (*To* LUPITA). Guess which hand.

LUPITA *(wearily)*. I don't feel like playing games, Concha.

CONCHA *(teasing)*. Just this once, Lupita.

LUPITA. The right. (CONCHA *grins and shakes her head.*) The left. (CONCHA *giggles and shakes her head.*) Both of them, then. (CONCHA *draws forward the flowers and hands them to her.*) Are these for me?

CONCHA. For your Saint's Day.

LUPITA *(smiling a little)*. That was very sweet of you, Concha. Will you put them in water, Ester? Oh, no you're busy. I'll do it. *(She moves slowly toward the house.* CARLOS *is heard singing faintly off stage.)*

DOÑA BECA. Did you see the worthless Julio, Concha?

CONCHA. No, Mamá. Just Carlos Balderas riding up the trail on his old long-eared donkey. (CARLOS's *voice constantly gets stronger.*)

LUPITA *(with more animation)*. Carlos! Perhaps he has . . . *(She gives almost a sob and starts running toward the patio gate.)*

DOÑA BECA *(reaching out and catching her by the back of the dress)*. Not so fast, miss.

LUPITA *(trying to pull away)*. But I want to go and meet him.

DOÑA BECA. What conduct for a decent girl. He will come in here and meet you where others are present. That is only decent. (LUPITA *drops her hand and comes back.* CONCHA *takes the flowers from her.*)

CONCHA. I'll put them in water for you . . . (CARLOS *can be heard singing from far off left.*)

CARLOS *(off stage)*.

> The four cornstalks are left all alone
> On the ranch that was my own, ay-yay.
> The house that's so tiny,
> So white and so shiny,
> Is left very sad.

(DOÑA BECA *and the others continue to speak against the background of his song which comes closer and closer.*)

There're no deer on the mountainside gray,
Everything is withered today, Ay-yay.
For no birds are flying,
The roses are dying,
Since I've been away.

DOÑA BECA. There comes Carlos, singing as usual.

CONCHA. Has he sung the rooster to you yet, Lupita?

LUPITA *(laughing quickly and turning away, shaking her head)*. No.

ESTER *(wisely)*. Have no fear. He will. He's shy.

DOÑA BECA. Which no one can say about Abel . . . the more pity to him.

CONCHA. I'll see if Julio is coming, too. *(She runs into the house.)*

DOÑA BECA. Ay, it takes young eyes to see the tortoise move.

LUPITA *(calling through the patio gate)*. Carlos! Carlos, did you bring me a letter?

CARLOS *(calling off)*. O-la! O-la!

LUPITA. He knows how much I want it. Surely he'd call out if he had it.

DOÑA BECA. Ester, run down to meet Carlos.

ESTER. But, Aunt Beca, he'll be here in just a moment.

DOÑA BECA. Do as you're told, girl. *(She waits until ESTER runs through the gate, then turns on LUPITA.)*

DOÑA BECA. A fine one you are . . . making a good man like Carlos wait and wait . . .

LUPITA. I've told you a thousand times, Doña Beca . . . I've no intention of marrying Carlos.

DOÑA BECA. Oh, no! You'll spend your smiles on someone like that newspaper reporter . . .

LUPITA. I don't want to think about Perez and his promises . . .

DOÑA BECA. Ha! Sense at last! I've seen hundreds like that one. All he wanted was your money . . . and when he found out your father wouldn't give you any, he dropped you quickly enough. Personally, I think your friends in New York are exactly like him!

LUPITA. Stop it! You have no right to . : . .

DOÑA BECA *(sharply)*. I intend to see you happy if I have to slap you into good sense!

LUPITA. Don't you see? They're all I've got! They're all I've got! *(She bursts into tears.* DOÑA BECA *looks at her a moment, then puts motherly arms about her.)*

DOÑA BECA. There, there, child. Once I had dreams, too. I think every woman, at one time in her life, must love the flying birds. *(She strokes* LUPITA's *hair.)* In this valley there was a man with a dream . . . a great dream . . . so great that it pushed him out into the world. I was a fool, and fell in love with him. I thought he could love me, but . . . he flew away on the wings of his dream. I could have shut myself off from life, just as you are doing. *(She turns* LUPITA's *face up to meet hers.)* But I didn't. I married a good man . . . and if the wild abandon was not there, it didn't matter. I've had a fine life, and now that I am old . . . too old for dreaming . . . I have no regrets. Marriage to that wild dreamer would have destroyed me. My dreamer had his dreams . . . that was all he wanted. But a woman has to have more. She has to be needed . . . to fill a place in a man's life no other woman could fill. And Carlos Balderas really needs you.

LUPITA. Carlos needs a girl like Ester . . . sweet, simple, in love with a home.

DOÑA BECA. Carlos needs ambition! He needs a woman behind him to push him. He has great talent . . . he has courage, he's dependable, he's honest . . . every man in this valley would follow him if he chose to lead them. But he prefers to stand in his candy kitchen and watch the world pass by . . . when the world, his world, this valley, needs him. You could give him that push, Lupita. A girl like Ester would destroy him . . . make him even worse than he is now.

LUPITA. Doña Beca, you don't understand . . . you've never understood. I wouldn't be content with this valley. It isn't big enough for me. But it is big enough for Carlos . . . and that is the difference between us.

DOÑA BECA. There's a circle of mountains around this valley, but Carlos has climbed their peaks many times. He left them behind him when he went to fight with Pancho Villa. When Villa captured Mexico City, did you know he put Carlos in charge of the whole Republic?

LUPITA *(startled)*. Carlos? Carlos Balderas?

DOÑA BECA. Yes. Who knows? He might have been president, if Villa hadn't been driven out of the city . . . his army broken up. An ambitious man would have stayed and fought for his rights, but Carlos was sick of fighting, sick of political squabbles. He wanted to come home . . . to peace. But married to you, Lupita, he can always climb those mountains again.

CARLOS *(calling off)*. Who wants a present for a Saint's Day?

DOÑA BECA. Think about it. *(Then calling to CARLOS.)* Put your candy under your arm and walk through the gate. *(CARLOS, followed by ESTER, comes laughing through the gate. Under one arm is a box of candy.)*

CARLOS *(shaking hands)*. A good afternoon to you, Doña Beca.

DOÑA BECA. Um. If it doesn't rain.

CARLOS. As God wills.

ESTER. Did you bring almond paste?

CARLOS *(grinning)*. Perhaps. *(He goes to LUPITA, and shakes hands with her.)* A happy Saint's Day.

LUPITA *(rising)*. Thank you, Carlos. *(Anxiously.)* No letters?

CARLOS *(shrugging)*. Nothing of importance. *(Extending the box.)* This is for you.

LUPITA *(her sadness returned)*. Thank you. *(She manages a smile.)* I won't offer to pay for it this time.

CARLOS *(laughing)*. Do not mind. We forget easily in the valley.

DOÑA BECA. Room enough for one friend, there's room enough for two.

LUPITA. You are all so friendly, and I . . . you must hate me.

ESTER *(shocked)*. No, Lupita.

DOÑA BECA. A fool is known by the nose he wears.

CARLOS *(gently)*. We couldn't hate you, Lupita. *(He jerks his head.)* Aren't you going to see what kind of candy it is?

ESTER. It couldn't be better than almond paste.

DOÑA BECA. Unless it were cheese of pecans.

CARLOS. Open it. *(LUPITA looks up at him, then lifts the lid from the box. Her expression changes to surprise as she looks into it, and then to pleasure and then pure happiness.)*

LUPITA. Carlos!

DOÑA BECA. What is it?

ESTER *(excitedly)*. I'm sure it's almond paste.

The Singing Valley | 113

LUPITA. Oh, Carlos. *(She suddenly puts her hand to her face and begins to cry.)*

CARLOS *(anxiously)*. But what is there to cry about, Lupita?

DOÑA BECA *(pushing him away)*. You fool, what did you put in the box?

ESTER. Almond paste never made me cry like that.

LUPITA. It isn't almond paste. It's . . .

DOÑA BECA. The letter!

LUPITA. Yes! The letter! *(She flings her arms about DOÑA BECA.)* Oh, I'm so happy!

ESTER. The letter? *(Accusingly.)* Carlos! And you with your face behind a barn door.

CARLOS *(concerned)*. I didn't mean to make you cry, Lupita.

LUPITA *(wiping her eyes)*. I'm not crying, Carlos. I'm just . . . happy.

DOÑA BECA. Well, well, what does it say?

LUPITA. Oh . . . oh, yes. I ought to read it, shouldn't I?

DOÑA BECA. She waits seven months, and then forgets to read it!

CARLOS *(taking the box, lifting out the letter, and handing it to LUPITA)*. You open it.

DOÑA BECA. And why shouldn't she? Isn't it her letter? *(LUPITA looks at all of them, then turns the envelope over in her hands.)*

LUPITA. It's from Nancy Moreno.

DOÑA BECA. Do you think to read it through the envelope?

LUPITA. No, I . . . *(She rubs her hand over the envelope, looks at them again, then tears open the envelope and takes out the sheet of paper. They are all watching this intently.)*

ESTER. I had a letter once. My grandmother sent it to me.

LUPITA *(suddenly pushing the letter into DOÑA BECA's hands)*. Read it to me. I . . . I can't see the words.

DOÑA BECA *(with a disgusted glance at LUPITA, she opens the sheet, shakes it, looks down at it, then frowns)*. Am I a magician that I can read English?

LUPITA *(puzzled)*. I wonder why she wrote in English? She's as Mexican as we are.

ESTER. That comes of living away from the valley.

DOÑA BECA. Call Abel, Carlos. He reads English. *(CARLOS goes quickly into the house.)*

ESTER. Let me see it. (LUPITA *hands her the letter and she looks eagerly at it, then she makes a little face of disappointment.*) It has no doves drawn on it.

DOÑA BECA *(slowly)*. Ester!

ESTER *(hastily handing the letter back to* LUPITA, *her voice showing her guilty conscience)*. Yes, Aunt?

DOÑA BECA. When were you at a public letter writer's?

ESTER. Why, Aunt, I . . .

DOÑA BECA. When were you?

ESTER *(shamefully)*. In Monterrey.

DOÑA BECA. And to whom did you send it?

ESTER. To Abel.

DOÑA BECA. So! This is why I reared you! I took you, an orphan child, and reared you . . . so that you could write letters to a man!

ESTER *(all in one breath)*. But I'd been in Monterrey two weeks, and Abel was out here, and I hadn't seen him, and I thought . . .

DOÑA BECA. You think too much for a decently brought up girl!

LUPITA. Please! Don't scold her. Not today. I'm too happy today.

(ABEL *enters from the house with* CARLOS. *He waves mischievously to* ESTER.)

DOÑA BECA. I thank you to remember your manners, Abel Lozano.

ABEL *(in mock repentance)*. I'm sorry, Doña Beca.

LUPITA. The letter came from Nancy. But she wrote in English, and I haven't spoken English in so long, I'm all confused. I can't . . . I can't understand what she's saying.

ABEL *(taking the letter and, as he reads it, frowning)*. There's no need to understand it. *(He slowly folds it into the original creases.)*

LUPITA. What does she say?

ABEL *(bursting forth)*. What do you care about Nancy Moreno and her worthless crowd!

LUPITA *(frozen)*. She doesn't want me to come. *(Fiercely.)* I want you to tell me exactly what she says.

ABEL *(on a deep breath)*. All right. She says that she can't afford to support you . . . your talent isn't worth her time. Without your money, they don't want you.

LUPITA. Even Pierre Dumarque? He said he loved me!

ABEL. She wrote for all of them.

DOÑA BECA. Just like Fernando Perez! No money . . . no friendship.

LUPITA *(bursting forth)*. I don't believe it! Not a single word! It's a trick . . . a trick from all of you!

ABEL. Lupita! Be sensible!

LUPITA. You're trying to hold me here. That's it! You're trying to make me stay in this valley. But I won't stay! I won't!

CARLOS. Do you think we're that cruel, Lupita?

ABEL *(extending the letter)*. Translate it word for word for yourself! (LUPITA *turns her back on him.*)

CARLOS. Stay with us, Lupita, where you're safe.

LUPITA. Take your music to another house! *(She suddenly realizes what she has said.)* Oh, now I'm even speaking proverbs! This valley is destroying me! But I won't let it. I don't need Nancy . . . I don't need Pierre . . . I can depend on myself! I'll get away somehow! I'm not beaten yet!

CARLOS *(stretching out a hand toward her)*. Please, Lupita . . .

LUPITA. Don't touch me! *(She runs into the house.)*

ABEL. I'd like to wring the necks of every one of those New York devils. Why did they have to do this to her?

DOÑA BECA. The surgeon's knife is cruel but kind. It was better to take away all her hope than lead her on.

CARLOS. They didn't have to be that cruel! *(He turns, suddenly, and goes out through the patio gate.)*

ESTER *(looking after him)*. Poor Carlos. He sings to chase away sorrow these days.

ABEL. If he had the sense of a three-day-old crocodile, he'd hit Lupe over the head and make her listen to him. (CONCHA *enters from the house.*)

CONCHA. Mamá, Julio and I . . .

DOÑA BECA. Ay, so Julio has returned, has he? Did he forget that he was supposed to go for sugar? Or did he just take himself to the village and escort himself back?

CONCHA. He brought the sugar but . . .

DOÑA BECA. But what!

CONCHA. Well, we were trying to put planks on sawhorses to make tables in front of the house and . . .

DOÑA BECA. And Julio fell over the side of the mountain?

CONCHA. No, not Julio. One of the sawhorses!

DOÑA BECA. Into the house with you! What daughter of mine is this that rolls the eye so much that a man throws sawhorses down a mountainside? Am I a good mother, or am I the victim of Grandfather Devil? Into the house! *(She swoops down on* CONCHA, *who gives a shriek and dashes ahead of her. They both go inside.* ABEL, *who has been laughing at* DOÑA BECA'S *anger, now turns and looks at* ESTER. *She hastily goes over and starts to gather up her sewing.)*

ABEL. There was a postscript on that letter of Lupita's.

ESTER. Abel! You didn't . . .

ABEL. What?

ESTER. It really said for her not to come, didn't it?

ABEL. Oh, yes, it said that all right. The postscript was for me. I wrote Nancy Moreno, too, you know.

ESTER *(slowly)*. I remember. *(She looks down at her sewing.)* You still love her, don't you?

ABEL. How can you think that, Ester?

ESTER. Don't make the bad promises, Abel. If you do love her . . .

ABEL. Let me read it to you. *(He opens the letter and glances at the end of it.)* "Abel, why should I marry a man whose money is spent on a valley? I wasn't born to be a fool."

ESTER. Eh, but she is a woman and you are a man, and it is well known that rabbits are born for the fox to eat.

ABEL. Are you calling yourself a fox?

ESTER *(protesting)*. I don't write letters.

ABEL. No? Not even with the drawings of doves decorating the page?

ESTER. I don't know what made me do that. You must think me a very wicked, forward girl. Now you will go to New York and marry her. *(She nods toward the letter in* ABEL'S *hand.)*

ABEL. And who taught you such lies? I will make you pay for each one. *(He darts toward her, but she gives a startled shriek and runs around the table from him.* CARLOS *comes to the gate, but neither notices him as* ABEL *catches* ESTER.*)*

ESTER. I will call Aunt Beca!

ABLE *(lifting her up and swinging her around)*. Call her. And get a lecture for your pains. *(He sees* CARLOS *and puts* ESTER *down on the floor.)* But the rooster must not frighten the dove.

ESTER. Or else the dove will peck out both his eyes . . . so. *(She tosses him a kiss and runs into the house.)*

ABEL *(turning to* CARLOS*)*. I'm sorry, Carlos. I don't think Lupita wants to see anyone now.

CARLOS. I think she'll see me. I have a plan.

ABEL. Carlos, I like you. I think . . . I hope . . . we're good friends. You even saved my life. But Lupita is not the girl for you.

CARLOS *(stiffly)*. Good friends do not interfere in important matters. Please ask her to see me. *(*ABEL *shrugs and goes into the house.* CARLOS *stands at the gate looking out over the valley, and at first does not notice* RUFINO *peering in through the window. Then he turns and sees him.)*

CARLOS. You, Rufino, what are you doing here?

DON RUFINO *(suddenly)*. I didn't come to see you. *(He pushes* CARLOS *aside and comes into the patio.)* My quarrel is with Don Antonio. He stole my goats. I have come to revenge myself.

CARLOS *(following him)*. He stole nothing from you. It was your own stupidity that put you in jail.

DON RUFINO *(pulling out his knife)*. Do not try my patience, Carlos Balderas. I am not a squealer of words like you. I'm a man of action, me. Behold, a knife from Oaxaca, where they know how to make real knives, even to the motto. And mine has a great motto. *(He reads from the knife.)* It says, "Old hide, I need you to make my drum."

CARLOS *(pulling out his own knife)*. And mine is from the hand of Pancho Villa. This, too, has a motto.

DON RUFINO. Better than mine?

CARLOS. It says, "Scatter, chickens, here comes your hawk."

DON RUFINO *(laughing sarcastically)*. A fine, brave motto for a candy vendor.

CARLOS. Mottoes have no value. But days have value. And this is the Day of Guadalupe . . . the Saint's Day of Lupita. You're not going to spoil it.

DON RUFINO. And you think to stop me, candy vendor?

CARLOS. If I have to. You're drunk, Rufino.

DON RUFINO. Not too drunk to knock you down! *(He takes a sudden lunge at* CARLOS. *The next moment they are fighting, with* RUFINO, *at first, getting the best of it with his wild lunges. Then* CARLOS *settles down to real fighting, and in a moment he has* RUFINO *down on his knees with one arm pulled up behind him.)*

CARLOS. I've put up with your nonsense in my valley long enough.

DON RUFINO *(screaming)*. Your valley. It's mine! Mine!

CARLOS. And a find mess you've made of it! And the village let you do it . . . all the men were mush! And I have no more use for mush than for you! But upsetting Lupita is a very different thing! She is my business. *(He gives* RUFINO *a sudden push that sends the man sprawling.)* Now get out of this house and stay out of it.

DON RUFINO *(struggling to sit up)*. I'll get my revenge on this house. Never fear.

CARLOS. If you try it, you'll deal with me! Remember that! (RUFINO *stares sullenly at him as he rises.* LUPITA *enters from the house.)*

LUPITA. Abel said you wanted to speak to me, Carlos. I . . . *(She suddenly notices* RUFINO *and is silent.)*

CARLOS. Don Rufino is just leaving, Lupita. He came to give you his regrets that he can't stay for your Saint's Day party. A good day to you, Don Rufino. (DON RUFINO *glares at both of them, then tries to swagger out.)*

LUPITA *(going up to* CARLOS). What happened? You look as though you'd been fighting!

CARLOS. Oh that. It was nothing. *(He takes a small bag from his pocket and puts it on the table.)* Here, Lupita. This is for you. (LUPITA, *puzzled, opens the sack and pours some coins into her hand.)*

LUPITA. Why it's . . . it's gold!

CARLOS. I saved it over the years. But for what? A candy vendor needs very little. There's enough there to take you to the States, and keep you until you find a job.

LUPITA *(putting the money back into the sack)*. You'd give me your life's savings?

CARLOS. I'm going to speak to you with my hat on the back of my head. When I first saw you, I knew you were my woman. And the more I've seen you, the more I've wanted you.

LUPITA. Carlos, please . . .

CARLOS *(fiercely)*. Don't say anything! I must finish this now. I hoped in time, you'd come to love the valley. But you belong out there . . . beyond the mountains. To you they are a prison wall. To me they are protection and peace. Those who love the mountains never leave them . . . while you must voyage on strange seas.

LUPITA. Carlos, I don't know what to say, I . . . *(Clutching the gold to her, she runs into the house, nearly colliding with DOÑA BECA.)*

DOÑA BECA. That was a fine bit of politeness. What has happened between you?

CARLOS. Forgive me, Doña Beca. This is a great feast day, and I have many orders for candy. *(He goes quickly out through the gate. DOÑA BECA follows him.)*

DOÑA BECA *(calling off)*. I don't like secrets, Carlos Balderas! It won't take me long to find out what happened!

    (CONCHA, pursued by JULIO, runs in from the house. JULIO is carrying a pulley and rope. Not seeing DOÑA BECA, he catches CONCHA and aims a kiss at her cheek, which CONCHA, with a dainty shriek, manages to evade.)

DOÑA BECA. I'll thank the two of you to behave with dignity! *(They both swing around, embarrassed.)*

JULIO. We didn't see you, Doña Beca.

DOÑA BECA *(dryly)*. That was quite obvious.

CONCHA. Oh, Mamá, such a scandal! We passed Lupita's room and we could hear her crying.

DOÑA BECA. Lupita's tears are private to Lupita.

JULIO. But she cries all the time. No one can escape noticing.

CONCHA. She needs friends, Julio. She's very lonely.

JULIO *(winking at her)*. So am I. Of course, if we were to get married tomorrow . . .

DOÑA BECA. You'll get married when I set the date. *(She goes into the house.)*

CONCHA. Mamá is right, Julio. Now put that pulley up there on the rain trough, and quickly! Everyone will arrive before we're through.

JULIO *(standing on the bench, and attaching the pulley to the rain trough)*. What is to be the piñata?

CONCHA. A beautiful crepe paper watermelon. I made it myself.

JULIO *(bending toward her)*. Then it should be in the church, for it was made by an angel.

CONCHA *(laughing)*. Ay, Julio. Put your hat on the back of your head.

JULIO. Why should I lie? To me you are a true angel. *(Yanking on the pulley.)* Will it have candy inside?

CONCHA. Carlos Balderas has been making it these two days.

JULIO. Now there's one who will be singing the rooster up here in the nights to come.

CONCHA. Ay, and " Shadow of Our Lord, Saint Peter" will be one of his songs, I can tell you.

JULIO. I like Lupita. I don't know why I do . . . but I do.

CONCHA. We all like Lupita. Perhaps, someday, she'll like us.

JULIO *(stepping down from the bench)*. How does that look?

CONCHA *(examining it)*. It will do. I wonder who will break the piñata?

JULIO. If I run the rope up and down, you can break it.

CONCHA. You will run no rope. Are you Don Antonio that you are filled with your own importance?

> *(DOÑA BECA now enters the patio with FATHER ZACAYA, DON PABLO, DOÑA AMPARO, and a CROWD of men and women.)*

DOÑA BECA *(to FATHER ZACAYA, as they enter)*. Did you meet Carlos Balderas as you came up the trail?

FATHER ZACAYA. No.

DOÑA BECA. That stupid fool!

FATHER ZACAYA. Is there something wrong?

DOÑA BECA. For the first time in my life, good priest, I have no answer! *(She suddenly bears down on JULIO.)* Did you fix the pulley?

JULIO *(pointing)*. There it is.

CROWD. This will be a fine piñata . . . Lupita should like this . . . Hush, I hear her coming.

> *(The CROWD opens to leave a free path for LUPITA to enter. ESTER, however, comes in. She looks as though she had seen a ghost.)*

ESTER. She is coming, and . . . wait until you see her!

DOÑA BECA *(anxiously)*. What is it?

ESTER *(flinging out her arm)*. Look!

(LUPITA *comes slowly into the patio. She has changed her clothes, and now wears the colored skirts and the gay blouse of a village girl. She really is pretty now. She stops in surprise at seeing all of the people.)*

LUPITA. Why . . . what . . .

DOÑA AMPARO *(bearing down on her)*. A happy Saint's Day, Lupita. We have bought you a piñata.

LUPITA. You have bought me . . . what?

DOÑA BECA. A piñata. You will find out what it is soon enough. But here is Father Zacaya.

LUPITA *(going up to him and kissing his hand)*. A good afternoon to you, Father. To all of you. This house is yours. (*To* DOÑA BECA.) Isn't Carlos . . . ? I . . . I mean . . .

CONCHA. He's busy as usual, making candy.

LUPITA. Oh . . . yes, of course.

DOÑA BECA *(sharply, to* CONCHA*)*. Silence, miss. (*To* LUPITA.) This piñata is a surprise for you. Are you surprised?

LUPITA. I . . . I don't know what to say.

DOÑA BECA. Silence is the best speaker.

FATHER ZACAYA. Shall we wait for Don Antonio?

DOÑA BECA *(sarcastically)*. He's probably with Abel, gazing with delight on the new flour mill.

FATHER ZACAYA *(holding up his hands)*. No matter. We can proceed without them. Will you please kneel? *(Everyone kneels except the priest.* LUPITA *hesitates just a moment before she goes down on her knees. The men remove their hats and the women cover their heads with their veils.)* This house stands in the shadow of Our Blessed Lady who has worked miracles.

CROWD. Amen.

FATHER ZACAYA. She wears many names, Our Lady of Sorrows, but her most beautiful name is Guadalupe.

CROWD. Blessed is her name.

FATHER ZACAYA *(turning and facing the niche)*. May peace dwell in this house forever . . . we, your servants ask it.

CROWD. Amen. *(He kneels down, and* DOÑA AMPARO, *rising, comes up to* LUPITA *and puts both hands on the girl's head.)*

DOÑA AMPARO. On her I put the ancient prayer.

CROWD. Amen.

DOÑA AMPARO. With the blue mantle of Our Lady of Guadalupe and with the white robe of Her Beautiful Son may you and all of yours be enveloped. May not storm, nor fire, nor heathen enemy, whether Moor or Comanche or those who are privileged to ride with spurs, ever touch you. May you never thirst in the desert, suffer from drought, feel the trembling of the earth, or be struck by lightning. May you be delivered from dangerous roads and swollen rivers and from Grandfather Devil and all small devils. May you never fall into mortal sin. May your enemies have no eyes to see you, nor feet to overtake you, nor hands to lay hold of you, nor tongues to bear false witness against you. May you be secure from poisonous serpents, from the guile of traitors, and from sudden death. Mary and Joseph accompany you at all hours. May you be hidden in the wounds of the Holy Ribs. May you marry with joy and bear many sons and two daughters. Jesus, the sweet name. Amen!

CROWD. Amen. *(They all rise quietly to their feet, crossing themselves.)*

FATHER ZACAYA *(beginning to sing and the others taking it up).*

> My Lord Jesus smiles on me,
> And on the house where I was born. Amen.

(The women remove the shawls from their heads.)

CONCHA *(suddenly breaking the spell).* And now the piñata!

CROWD. The piñata! The piñata!

CONCHA. Ester! *(They run into the house together to get it.)*

> (LUPITA *has stood all this time as though dazed. Now she abruptly turns to* DOÑA AMPARO *and kisses her on the cheek.*)

LUPITA. You are too good to me.

DOÑA BECA *(patting* LUPITA's *shoulder).* You have been in exile, Lupe. Will you come home to us?

LUPITA *(turning away).* I wish . . . oh, I wish . . . *(She breaks off as* DON

ANTONIO *and* ABEL *enter, each of them with a firm grasp on the arms of* CARLOS BALDERAS.)

ABEL. We found this fool sitting on top of the powerhouse gazing down into the river.

DON ANTONIO *(jovially)*. He tried to make excuses . . . but no excuses for Lupita's Saint's Day. Eh? (CARLOS *and* LUPITA *are careful not to look at each other.* DOÑA BECA *stares thoughtfully at both of them, then waves her hand to* DON ANTONIO.)

DOÑA BECA. Lupita has had her blessing. Now it's time for the piñata.

(ESTER *and* CONCHA *enter, bearing the watermelon piñata between them.*)

CROWD *(yelling)*. Viva! Viva!

CONCHA *(excitedly, to* LUPITA*)*. The first to break it will be married first!

ABEL. Then that will be me. Eh, Ester?

ESTER. Abel, have you no shame?

JULIO. I'll be the first. And to hasten the wedding . . . (*He bows in front of* DON ANTONIO.) Don Antonio, may I offer my services to help hang the piñata?

DON ANTONIO *(jovially)*. I am honored, friend Julio. *(They both take the piñata from the girls and fasten it to the pulley.* ESTER *and* CONCHA *link their arms around* LUPITA'S *waist.)*

CARLOS *(suddenly)*. Lupita should be the first. It's her Saint's Day.

LUPITA *(quickly)*. Ay, no! *(She looks quickly away from him.)* You be first. I know nothing of this game.

ESTER *(excitedly)*. Yes, Carlos! You try!

CARLOS. I resign the honor to Don Antonio.

DON ANTONIO *(taking the stick from* JULIO, *he bends over so that* CONCHA *can blindfold him)*. I warn you, I'm very good at breaking piñatas. Remember, Beca? (DOÑA BECA *takes up the rope.*)

DOÑA BECA. That was when my father was pulling the rope. I have a better technique! (DON ANTONIO *laughs and swings the stick, but the piñata whirls up out of his reach. The* CROWD *laughs.*)

DON ANTONIO *(laughing also, and pulling off the blindfold)*. Here, Carlos. This game needs a steadier hand than mine. You try it. *(While* CONCHA *blindfolds an unwilling* CARLOS, DON ANTONIO *takes hold of the rope.)*

DON ANTONIO. I'll do this now.

DOÑA BECA (*grinning*). You've been away too long. You don't know how to do it.

DON ANTONIO (*grinning*). The swallow may leave the nest, Beca. But it always can find its way home. (*He takes the rope while she moves reluctantly out of the way.* CARLOS *comes up and takes a swing, but again the piñata flies out of reach.*)

VOICES FROM CROWD. Show your strong muscles, Carlos . . . Beat the air, Carlos . . . Be a man and break it, Carlos! (CARLOS *tries again and misses again. He laughs and pulls off the blindfold.*)

DOÑA BECA (*disgusted*). Sometimes the swallow gets in the wrong nest!

DON ANTONIO (*laughing*). Well, Lupita, do you think you can break it now?

VOICES FROM CROWD. Yes, yes! Let Lupita try . . . Break it, Lupe . . . Remember it's your Saint's Day! (CARLOS *comes up to* LUPITA *with the handkerchief. They are both embarrassed. He ties it around her eyes, and presses the stick into her hands, then suddenly whirls her around three times.*)

LUPITA (*crying out*). That's not fair!

CARLOS (*as the* CROWD *laughs*). It's your Saint's Day. You'll have to find the piñata alone.

LUPITA. I'll find it. (*She swishes the air, entirely the wrong direction.*)

DON ANTONIO (*laughing with the* CROWD). You'll never find it that way, Lupita.

LUPITA (*sharply*). Ester. Is it true that the one who breaks the piñata first will be married first?

ESTER (*laughing*). That's the promise, Lupita.

LUPITA. Very well! (*Suddenly she pulls off the blindfold and, before they realize what she's doing, she stalks over and breaks the piñata, candy cascading all around her.*) There! (*She turns to face* CARLOS, *and stares straight at him. He stares at her in complete surprise.*)

ABEL. That wasn't fair, Lupita!

LUPITA. I'm a woman. I don't have to play fair! Do I, Doña Beca?

DON ANTONIO (*disturbed*). What's wrong with you, my daughter?

DOÑA BECA. I think she's just come to her senses.

LUPITA. I want to hear singing. I want to hear the songs of this valley. Will you sing for me, Carlos Balderas?

CROWD. Yes, Carlos, a song . . . a good song . . .

CARLOS. What kind of a song do you want, Lupita?

ABEL. Why don't you try "Shadow of Our Lord, St. Peter"?

DOÑA BECA. Keep your mouth shut, Abel, on the outside of your teeth!

DON ANTONIO. Lupita . . . my little daughter . . .

LUPITA. I want this house . . . and this valley . . . and . . . and . . . *(She suddenly breaks off and turns away.)*

DON ANTONIO *(putting his arms around her)*. Oh, welcome home, my daughter . . . my dear, dear child.

DOÑA BECA. And what is the third thing you want, Lupita?

ESTER *(walking up to CARLOS)*. I would say it's something for Lupita to want, and . . . and . . . *(Shyness suddenly overcomes her, and she hastens back to ABEL.)*

CONCHA *(convulsed with laughter)*. And someone else to guess!

> *(Someone in the CROWD suddenly laughs. In a few moments everyone, looking at CARLOS, also laughs.)*

CARLOS *(suddenly laughing at himself, jumping up on the table)*. You want a song, Lupita? I'll give you a song, if you promise to walk three times around the plaza with me Sunday night.

DOÑA BECA. Carlos Balderas! You have no more shame than Abel!

CARLOS *(ignoring her)*. Well, Lupita?

LUPITA *(tossing her head)*. And who says I'll even be on the plaza Sunday night?

CONCHA *(delighted)*. You've learned to talk like a real valley girl!

> *(LUPITA, head lowered, moves away from them and, at the patio gate, gazes out over the valley.)*

FATHER ZACAYA *(holding up his hands)*. There's only one song for this moment.

ABEL. You're right, good priest. *(He takes DON ANTONIO's hand and the two go up to join LUPITA with DON ANTONIO in the center. He puts his arms about both of his children.)*

CARLOS *(singing)*.

My Lord Jesus, smile on me . . .

And on the house where I was born. Amen.

(While they are singing, the curtains close.)

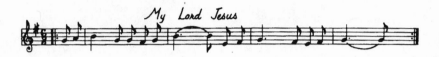

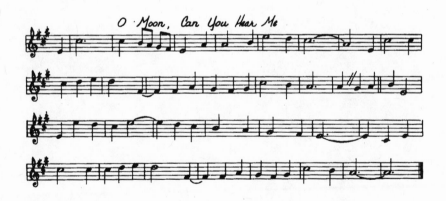

The Cry of Dolores

1936

Author's Foreword

This is the story of a miracle . . . a miracle that aided a small band of patriots to free Mexico from the bondage . . . not of Spain, but of Napoleon Bonaparte.

The situation, the characters, the scene, and even the speeches have been lifted directly from the pages of history. In this instance, at least, history is stranger than fiction.

Synopsis

Lolita cannot understand the patriotic feeling governing not only her family but her fiancé as well. To her, revolution means only death and destruction, so she demands that Allende choose between herself and Revolution. To her horror, he chooses the Revolution.

When she turns to her mother for help, Doña Josefa tells her that there are times when a man puts his duty to his country above everything else. As proof of this, Lolita's father, feeling the strength of his duty to Spain, orders the arrest of Allende. By some miracle, a Mexican patriot is within reach of Doña Josefa's voice, and with his aid, tragedy is averted.

Characters

LOLITA DOMINGUEZ, engaged to
IGNACIO ALLENDE, a captain in Her Majesty's dragoons

DOÑA JOSEFA DOMINGUEZ, mother of LOLITA

DON MIGUEL DOMINGUEZ, husband of DOÑA JOSEFA and mayor of Querétaro

FATHER MIGUEL HIDALGO Y CASTILLO, the father of Mexican independence

DON CARLOS VARA, warden of the city prison

NIMFO, servant

The Scene

The living room of the house of the mayor of Querétaro, DON MIGUEL DO-MINGUEZ, *on the evening of Saturday, 15 September 1810.*

It is a pleasant room, a bit stiff, a bit unhomelike, but one has the feeling that people of character and individuality live here.

There is a large barred window in the wall back center, and a door in the right wall. For furniture, there is a sofa down left with a chair near, and a table right, flanked by three chairs.

When the curtains open we see LOLITA DOMINGUEZ *sitting by the window embroidering. She is a sweet, pretty girl, about twenty, dressed in a soft pink gown of the period. She would be beautiful if it were not for the stubborn line of her chin.*

In a moment the servant enters. He is quite a young boy, dressed all in white with a red sash about his waist, and is pure Indian in type.

NIMFO. Captain Allende asks your permission to enter, señorita.

LOLITA *(standing excitedly).* Admit him, immediately. And tell my mother and father that he is here.

(NIMFO *bows and goes out.* LOLITA *runs to the mirror to pat her curls into place, and while she is doing this,* IGNACIO ALLENDE *enters. History calls him a "proud young captain, very handsome, in the uniform of Her Majesty's dragoons," which consists of a short red coat held in by a gold sash, white trousers, tall black cavalry boots, a cocked hat, and, hanging from his shoulders, a sky-blue cape. At this time he was thirty-one years old with a certain charming boyish enthusiasm and was only lately engaged to* LOLITA. *He flings his cape and hat on a chair and stands beaming at her.)*

ALLENDE. Lolita!

LOLITA *(starts toward him, then pauses shyly and extends her hand)*. Good evening, Captain Allende.

(He goes to her and kisses her hand.)

ALLENDE *(with an effort at poise)*. I hope that you have passed a pleasant day.

LOLITA *(sits on the sofa)*. Very pleasant, thank you, Captain. Will you be seated? My mother and father will be here in a moment.

(He gazes at her in admiration, then sits beside her . . . which rather startles her, as she had naturally expected him to sit as far across the room from her as possible . . . and takes her hand in his.)

ALLENDE. Lolita, I have a surprise for you.

LOLITA *(shyly pulling her hand away)*. Have you?

ALLENDE. I brought a very dear friend of mine to meet you this evening. For many months now I have been anxious for him to know the girl who is so soon to be my wife. *(At his words a strange change comes over her. She turns her face from him, touching her mouth with her handkerchief in agitation. Unable to control her feelings, she rises suddenly and crosses to the table where she stands gazing down at it. He stares at her in amazement, then goes to her.)* Lolita! What is wrong?

LOLITA *(gives him a trembling smile)*. Nothing . . . I . . . *(She puts her hand on his arm.)* Captain Allende . . . Ignacio . . . *(Then she shakes her head and turns her back to the table.)* I am afraid that I am a very foolish creature. I beg of you, do not concern yourself with me.

ALLENDE *(turns her face to him)*. You are my promised wife, Lolita. When you are with me, you should fear nothing. *(He kisses her.)* Now tell me what is troubling you.

LOLITA *(clinging to his hands)*. You're so changed, Ignacio. For over a year now . . . Ever since that day when it was feared that we were to fight the English . . . It is as though you were another man. And all these new friends of yours . . . They frighten me. And then these meetings here, at night. This strange Literary Society, with the members coming so late after I am in bed. And finally this dream that I have had night after night . . . Oh, Ignacio, it is more than I can bear.

(She sits down on a chair and he kneels beside her.)

ALLENDE. Tell me about your dream.

LOLITA. I dreamed that there was a battle, and that men were killing you . . . men in uniform . . . Men in . . . *(She touches his shoulder.)* . . . in this uniform. Please, Ignacio, tell me what it all means.

(He stands and walks to the window. Abruptly he comes back to her and draws her to her feet.)

ALLENDE. If I were a superstitious man . . . But, no. They say dreams always mean the opposite, don't they?

LOLITA *(helplessly)*. I don't know . . . I don't know anything. That is the trouble.

ALLENDE. I suppose the time has come to tell you the truth. *(He leads her to the sofa and they sit down.)* We will start with a year ago, after the mobilization of the troops when we feared war with the English. I was riding toward the barracks, when I realized that I had no idea of the military strength which we possess. Never had we seen so many soldiers united at a single instance under the command of one general. In reality we were strong, but this strength belonged to Spain. Now here is the great question. If all Mexican soldiers were united by a single thought the strength would be ours . . . We could overthrow the Spaniards.

LOLITA *(horrified)*. You mean . . . Revolution?

ALLENDE *(firmly)*. Revolution. Freedom at last. Freedom from oppression, from slavery.

LOLITA. And this Literary Society?

ALLENDE. Is really a meeting of the friends of liberty, the leaders of our cause.

LOLITA. No! No, Ignacio. Don't you realize what this means? Death and disgrace for all of us. My dream, my horrible nightmare of a dream, was no dream at all, but the truth. They are going to capture you . . . They are going to kill you.

ALLENDE. Let them . . . Let them kill all of us. What is the difference if Mexico is freed from the chains of bondage that have bound her for over two centuries.

LOLITA *(pleadingly)*. Ignacio, does my love mean so little to you?

ALLENDE. It means everything, Lolita.

LOLITA. Then for my sake, I beg of you, give this up. These are idle hopes. Spain is all-powerful. It will crush you down, and Mexico will be more pitiful than ever.

ALLENDE. Spain no longer exists. Napoleon has driven Fernando from his throne. To be bound to Spain is misery. But to be bound to France would be disgrace. We have gone too far, Lolita. We can't turn back now.

LOLITA *(frantically)*. You must turn back, Ignacio, for my sake. I love you. If you were dead . . . If they killed you . . . Life would end for me. Ignacio, Ignacio, have pity on me.

ALLENDE *(putting his arms about her)*. Poor child. Poor frightened child.

> *(The door opens and* DON MIGUEL DOMINGUEZ, *mayor of Querétaro, enters. He is a nice little man, with a large nose, a weak mouth, and a tendency to be foppish in his dress. He is at this time about fifty years old. Preceding him is his wife,* DOÑA JOSEFA. *She is a matronly, kindly woman of forty-five. The portraits of her, made at this period, show an aggressive nose, a firm chin, a stern but gentle mouth. In her neatly plaited hair is a low Spanish comb. Her dress is simple and modest with a white fichu for relief.)*

DOÑA JOSEFA *(startled at the tableau in front of her)*. Ignacio! Lolita! What is the meaning of this?

LOLITA *(running to her and throwing both arms about her neck)*. Mother! Don't let him do it. Don't let him do it!

DOÑA JOSEFA *(puzzled)*. Don't let him do what?

ALLENDE *(quietly)*. Good evening, Doña Josefa . . . Don Miguel.

DON MIGUEL *(gives* ALLENDE *the traditional embrace, and then shakes hands)*. Good evening, my boy. What miniature tempest is this?

ALLENDE. I have been telling Lolita about our plans.

DOÑA JOSEFA *(disapprovingly)*. Telling our plans to this child.

LOLITA *(draws back from her)*. I am not a child. After all, I'm old enough to be married, and I have a right to know what my . . . *(She draws a deep breath and sets her chin.)* . . . my husband's plans are.

DOÑA JOSEFA *(laughs and goes to sofa; she holds out her hand to* ALLENDE, *who goes and kisses it)*. That is right. I forget she is no longer a child.

DON MIGUEL *(teasingly)*. Then why does she weep like a baby?

ALLENDE. She dreamed that I was captured and executed.

DOÑA JOSEFA. To die a martyr to our cause? Who could wish for a more beautiful death?

LOLITA. I could. *(Scornfully.)* To die a martyr! I don't want him to die at all. Mother, how can you be so cold? If it were Father you would feel differently about it.

DON MIGUEL. Lolita! I will not have you speak so to your mother.

ALLENDE. Lolita, calm yourself.

LOLITA. Lolita this! Lolita that! *(Covers her ears with her hands.)* I won't listen to anything you have to say. You can make your choice between me and this absurd idea of Mexican independence. I will not marry a martyr. *(She flings herself on her knees beside her mother, and buries her face in* DOÑA JOSEFA's *lap. As* ALLENDE *and* DON MIGUEL *start to speak,* DOÑA JOSEFA *smiles gently and places her finger against her lips, then strokes her daughter's hair.)*

DOÑA JOSEFA. You are perfectly right, Lolita. I think we have forgotten about human beings in the rhythm of our beautiful fine words.

ALLENDE *(horrified at* DOÑA JOSEFA's *about face)*. I protest, Doña Josefa . . .

DOÑA JOSEFA *(stopping him with a frown and a quick gesture of her hand)*. In the days that are coming you will not be the only young girl to weep as she sees the man she loves marching off to battle.

LOLITA *(wailing)*. Why does there have to be a battle or a war?

DOÑA JOSEFA *(gaining her point)*. Ah! Now you see! You don't really understand what this is all about, do you?

LOLITA. I don't want to know.

ALLENDE. There is one person who can make you understand. I am going down to get Father Hidalgo.

DON MIGUEL *(startled)*. He is coming . . . here?

DOÑA JOSEFA *(flustered)*. But where is he? Why didn't you tell me that?

ALLENDE. He is down in the room of Don Carlos Bravo.

DON MIGUEL *(laughingly)*. What a magnificent jest on the Spaniards. The great revolutionary leader in the room of the warden of the city prison.

DOÑA JOSEFA. Fetch him immediately, Ignacio.

ALLENDE. Lolita, he will explain.

DOÑA JOSEFA. Don't bother about Lolita now. Go and bring this sainted patriot . . .

ALLENDE. Yes, yes, of course . . . *(He goes to the door where he pauses.)* I . . . *(He sees* DOÑA JOSEFA *looking at him.)* Yes, immediately. *(He goes out.)*

DON MIGUEL. What a great man Hidalgo is. I remember the first night I met him. He . . .

DOÑA JOSEFA. No reminiscences, please, Miguel. Stand up, Lolita. (LOLITA, *still pouting, stands.*) In a few moments, you will see the greatest man in Mexico today.

LOLITA. I don't want to meet him . . . All I want . . .

DOÑA JOSEFA *(sternly).* You said yourself, that you are a woman now, and not a child. Try to act like a woman. Now, go and wash your face. Your eyes look as though you have been crying for days. And when he comes, try to behave with proper dignity. You don't want Ignacio to be ashamed of you, do you? ·

LOLITA *(slowly).* No.

DOÑA JOSEFA *(rises and kisses her on the cheek).* That's a sweet daughter. Run along now, and hurry. We mustn't keep Father Hidalgo waiting.

LOLITA *(turns and goes out of the room, and then sticks her head back in).* But I still don't want to marry a martyr. *(With a final jerk of her head she disappears.)*

DOÑA JOSEFA *(looks at* DON MIGUEL *and sighs).* It is in moments like these that I realize that she is your daughter.

DON MIGUEL *(smiles).* On the contrary, my love. No one could ever call me a stubborn man.

DOÑA JOSEFA *(laughs softly and takes his hand in hers).* You are a kind soul, Miguel. I know that my impulsive spirit has often caused you much sorrow. Spain has given you so many honors. And now you are mayor of Querétaro, with an ardent revolutionist for a wife. Believe me, I realize what a difficult situation I have made for you.

DON MIGUEL. Do you remember that first day I saw you standing among your friends at the convent? I thought at the time, "There stands the rose I shall wear in my heart." A man cannot be angry at a rose, Josefa.

DOÑA JOSEFA *(nods wisely).* But he can be angry at the thorns.

(NIMFO *enters.)*

NIMFO. His Reverence, Father Miguel Hidalgo y Castillo. His Excellency, Don Carlos Bravo and Captain Allende.

DOÑA JOSEFA *(moving forward).* Ask them to enter. (NIMFO *bows and goes out.* DOÑA JOSEFA *turns to* MIGUEL.) If only your conscience would allow you to be really one of us.

DON MIGUEL *(flings out his hand).* I am mayor of Querétaro. As long as I hold that office, my duty binds me to Spain.

> *(The three men now enter.* FATHER HIDALGO *is a delicate, slender man, not very tall, with beautiful white hands. His nose is prominent, and his soft white hair falls in silky profusion to his shoulders from the sides of his head, as he is quite bald on top. He wears a long black coat, belted with a red sash. At this time he is fifty-seven years of age, and he possesses to a marked degree that personality of leadership which made men follow him and his ideals long after the man, himself, was dead. The man next to him is* DON CARLOS VARA, *warden of the city prison. A large, red-faced, hearty man, he walks with a limp from an old wound,* DOÑA JOSEFA *kisses the priest's hand.)*

DOÑA JOSEFA. Our house is yours, Father; and yours, Don Carlos.

FATHER HIDALGO *(makes the sign of the cross).* A blessing on this house. Don Miguel, we meet again.

DON MIGUEL *(bows).* Our house is always open to you, Father. Don Carlos, your servant.

DON CARLOS *(kisses* DOÑA JOSEFA's *hand).* Your servant, Doña Josefa. And yours, Don Miguel.

DOÑA JOSEFA. Please be seated.

FATHER HIDALGO *(peering about him nearsightedly as he sits down near the table).* And where is the little Lolita? Has she run away from shyness at seeing this big captain of ours?

> (ALLENDE *gives a forced laugh, which ceases as* DOÑA JOSEFA *looks sternly at him.)*

DOÑA JOSEFA. Young girls are often shy, Father. She will be here presently. Miguel, perhaps the gentlemen would care for a little wine.

DON MIGUEL. Of course, of course. A glass of sherry, Father. For you, Don Carlos, a drop of good Spanish muscatel?

DON CARLOS. As a servant of Spain, I should drink her wines, but as a revolutionist, I prefer good Mexican mescal.

> *(They all laugh . . .)*

FATHER HIDALGO. For me, a little wine. I am very tired. This business of
    revolution is a weary work.

DON MIGUEL. And you, Ignacio?

ALLENDE *(who has been watching the door for* LOLITA, *is jerked back to con-
    sciousness)*. Wine, sir.

DOÑA JOSEFA *(as* DON MIGUEL *serves the drinks)*. We have missed you at our
    Literary meetings, Father.

FATHER HIDALGO. I have been baptizing converts. Ay, we have gathered
    about us a fine large army. Soon we shall be ready to strike.

DON MIGUEL *(jesting)*. As mayor of Querétaro, I should report this to the
    viceroy.

DOÑA JOSEFA *(with mock sternness)*. And as my husband, you will do noth-
    ing of the sort. *(She sees* LOLITA *enter.)* There you are, Lolita. Come and
    ask Father's blessing.

FATHER HIDALGO *(as* LOLITA *comes up to him)*. So this is Lolita. *(She kisses his
    hand.)* Blessings on you child. Ignacio, she is even prettier than you
    said, and I have always learned to discount a lover's word.

ALLENDE. Father, Lolita says that she won't . . .

DOÑA JOSEFA *(interrupting)*. What manners are these, Lolita? Have you no
    word of greeting for your godfather?

LOLITA *(goes to* DON CARLOS). Good evening, Godfather.

DON CARLOS. Good evening, child. You should have been with us this
    afternoon. Father Hidalgo staged a *rodeo* for us out at Dolores. Our
    young captain here proved himself the hero of the hour.

LOLITA *(without enthusiasm)*. Did he?

FATHER HIDALGO. It was a fine sight. As easily as though the bull were a
    stuffed doll, he forced its shoulders to the ground. If all Mexicans were
    like him, there would be no Spaniards left in New Spain.

LOLITA *(turns to* ALLENDE). Have you forgotten that your father is a
    Spaniard?

ALLENDE *(quietly)*. My mother is a Mexican. I was born and reared here. I
    owe my allegiance to Mexico.

FATHER HIDALGO *(peering at* LOLITA). What is this? Have we a loyalist in the
    camp?

LOLITA (*goes to* FATHER HIDALGO). Father, this would mean war. I am afraid. If Ignacio should be killed . . . and he will be killed . . . I know it, I had a dream . . . a terrible dream. *(She starts to cry.)*

ALLENDE. I told you about her dreams as we were coming up the stairs, Father.

FATHER HIDALGO. Yes, yes . . . Listen to me, my child. Would you rather be married to a loyal patriot or to a coward? His country needs Allende. You must let him go.

LOLITA. I am a woman; I would rather be married to a live husband than to a dead patriot.

DOÑA JOSEFA *(sternly)*. Then you are no daughter of mine! I only wish that I were a man, but since I am a woman, then with my blood I shall mold a patrimony for my sons.

ALLENDE *(pleadingly)*. If you would only listen to me, Lolita. You are thinking of the old days, when a man could be proud to call himself a subject of Spain, but the old days are gone. Napoleon Bonaparte rules instead of Fernando.

FATHER HIDALGO. The native Mexicans will not permit New Spain to fall into the hands of the French.

ALLENDE. By no means. And if the Spaniards have such an intention, it is the duty of every good Mexican to disillusion them.

DON MIGUEL *(cautiously)*. It appears to me that if the Mexicans could assume control of the colony, then it would be returned to Fernando VII when he comes again to the throne.

FATHER HIDALGO. No. The independence of New Spain must be bought at any price.

ALLENDE. Mexicans must be aroused! And how easy it is, since the Spaniards see us only as degenerates, imbeciles, incapable of exerting the smallest sign of volition.

DON CARLOS. You are right. Only today, Don Diego de la Cerda was put into my charge with orders to place him in my most desolate cell because he refused to pay the viceroy the gold demanded of him. Don Diego has broad lands, but he is really very poor. To pay what was demanded of him was impossible, and so he has to rot in prison.

ALLENDE. If we could only convoke a Mexican Congress to give just laws to our country, to use its vast resources for good instead of lining the pockets of dissolute men.

DOÑA JOSEFA. Yes! Yes! Now is the time to free our country! I dedicate myself to the Revolution although it may cost all of us our lives.

DON MIGUEL (*with a worried frown*). My dear, you are an impulsive woman. You must remember that I . . . (*He breaks off as the door opens and* NIMFO *enters.*) Well, what do you want?

NIMFO. There is a messenger here from the superintendent of Guanajuato. He says his business is urgent.

DON MIGUEL. Tell him I will be with him immediately. (NIMFO *bows and goes out.*) Gentlemen, your servant. Josefa, I beg of you . . . Don't be too impressionable.

DON CARLOS (*sighs*). If only Don Miguel could be made to see our side of the question. He is a wealthy man, and revolutions need money.

FATHER HIDALGO (*shaking his head*). At least our good Don Carlos does not pride himself on being a man of tact.

DOÑA JOSEFA. But he is right. If only we had money to help the cause. It is bad enough for us, but it is really the poor who need the freedom. There are nights when I cannot sleep for weeping over their sorrows. No one who has not seen them can ever understand how much they need our help.

FATHER HIDALGO (*gently*). A coin of gold weighs less than a tear from the heart.

DON CARLOS. Unfortunately tears won't buy ammunition.

FATHER HIDALGO. No, but the poor are used to helping one another. In Dolores, in all the small towns of my parish, it is amazing how many guns are hidden under piles of hay; how many swords are being beaten out on blacksmiths' anvils.

DOÑA JOSEFA. It is this waiting . . . This waiting for the moment to strike that I cannot bear. We have waited so long, so very long.

ALLENDE (*anxiously*). May I tell her, Father?

FATHER HIDALGO (*indulgently*). Tell her.

ALLENDE. The time is almost here. The cry of freedom has been set for the second of October.

LOLITA. So soon!

DOÑA JOSEFA (*triumphantly*). So soon! At last! You have the plan, the names of the leaders, everything?

FATHER HIDALGO. Everything. Think of it. On the second of October, the cry of Dolores: Long live the true religion . . . Long live our sacred Mother of Guadalupe . . . Long live America and death to false government.

DON CARLOS (*standing*). And speaking of false government, I must get back to the prison. Poor Don Diego has to be fed, along with a hundred other prisoners.

DOÑA JOSEFA. You can take him a message of hope. After October the second, no more dark cell, no more misery for any of them.

FATHER HIDALGO (*rises*). Señora, you are our mast of courage. Do not fail us. Good night, my daughter. (*Turns to* LOLITA.) And you, my child. You have heard great news tonight. Remember, one slip of your tongue, and we are all lost.

LOLITA. I will remember. Good night, Father. (*She kisses his hand.*)

(FATHER HIDALGO, DOÑA JOSEFA, *and* DON CARLOS *go out into the hall.* ALLENDE *goes up to* LOLITA *who turns away from him.*)

ALLENDE. Can't you understand, Lola?

LOLITA. You are the one who doesn't understand, Ignacio.

ALLENDE. You are right. I can't understand this loyalty of yours to Spain. If you had ever been there, or if your family were Spaniards . . . But they are not. They are Mexicans, and so are you, and so am I. Do you think that I don't want to have a hand in freeing Mexico from the power that has oppressed us for so long? You know Don Diego. Do you think it's right that he should be in prison because a viceroy wants more gold than he has to give?

LOLITA. What do I care about Don Diego? Or Spain, or Mexico, or anything else? I am a girl engaged to a man. I want to be married, to have children, to grow old with the man I love. All I can see in this war is the fact that you might be killed. That means something to me . . . Your living. I thought you loved me as I love you . . .

ALLENDE (*interrupting*). But I do love you.

LOLITA. No you don't. I found that out. I gave you your chance tonight, and you chose . . . Mexico instead of me. Well, that seems to be all there is to it.

ALLENDE *(irritated)*. But it's not the same thing. There are times when a man has to put his duty to his country above everything else, and this is one of those times.

LOLITA *(in a dead voice)*. Very well then, there is nothing more for us to talk about is there? Good night.

ALLENDE *(pleadingly)*. Lolita . . .

LOLITA *(almost at the end of her strength)*. Good night!

(He turns dejectedly, and as he reaches the door, DOÑA JOSEFA *enters. She looks curiously from him to* LOLITA, *and he shakes his head. She pats his cheek, he catches her hand and kisses it and then goes out. She walks thoughtfully over to her daughter.)*

LOLITA *(turns and looks at her)*. Mother, his cape when he went out. It looked like a shroud.

DOÑA JOSEFA. My child, you must get over these morbid notions.

LOLITA. I can't help it. If only just one of you could understand how I feel.

DOÑA JOSEFA. I do. I remember when your father was first appointed mayor of Querétaro. I begged him on my knees not to accept it.

LOLITA *(surprised)*. You did? Why?

DOÑA JOSEFA. Your father was a Mexican, and these Spanish viceroys are not in the habit of honoring Mexicans through pure goodness of heart. I was afraid they wanted to use him and his transparent honesty as a tool. Every morning I have awakened with the same thought, "Today will be the day." So far it hasn't come, but it will come. I know it will, and when it does his cape will look like a shroud, too.

LOLITA. Then why have you let him do it all these years? Why have you let him do it?

DOÑA JOSEFA. Because he felt it was his duty to his country, and when a man feels patriotic there is nothing a woman can do about it. So, if I were you, I would sit down and write Ignacio a little note and tell him that you understand at last.

LOLITA. If only I hadn't had that dream.

DOÑA JOSEFA *(nods)*. Unfortunately we can't rule our lives by . . . (DON MIGUEL *enters, a very worried man.)*

DON MIGUEL *(curtly)*. Josefa! How long have our guests been gone?

DOÑA JOSEFA. I really don't know, my dear. Why? You look worried. What is the matter?

The Cry of Dolores | 141

DON MIGUEL. I have just received a message from Riano, superintendent of Guanajuato, a sergeant from Ignacio's regime, by the name of . . . *(He consults the paper in his hand.)* . . . of Gariedo, has betrayed the revolutionary plans to the viceroy, along with the names of the leaders. I have them here on this paper.

LOLITA. What made him do a thing like that?

DON MIGUEL. Fear of being caught, himself, I suppose.

DOÑA JOSEFA. Miguel, is my name on that paper?

DON MIGUEL. No, luckily this Gariedo seemed to know only men's names.

LOLITA. What . . . What does this mean?

DON MIGUEL. It means imprisonment, disgrace . . . Perhaps exile . . . perhaps even death . . .

LOLITA *(afraid to ask the question in her mind)*. Father . . . The names . . . Is Father Hidalgo's there?

DON MIGUEL. It lists all of them.

LOLITA. Is . . . Don Carlos . . . ?

DON MIGUEL. No, not his . . . Luckily.

LOLITA *(frantically)*. Father, I can't . . . Oh, why don't you tell me? Is . . .

DON MIGUEL. Yes, Ignacio's is here too. They are all here . . . Abasolo, Balleza, Aldama . . . They are all here save yours, Josefa, and our good friend, the warden downstairs.

DOÑA JOSEFA. How does it involve you, Miguel?

DON MIGUEL. Naturally, I must order their arrest at once.

LOLITA *(flings her arms about her father's neck)*. No, no, . . . Father, please . . . Ignacio means everything to me. You can't do it.

DON MIGUEL. My child, do you think I want to do it? I must. It's my duty.

LOLITA. Duty! Duty! I shall hate that word all my life.

DON MIGUEL *(beckons to DOÑA JOSEFA to draw LOLITA away)*. What I do now is the hardest thing that I have ever done.

DOÑA JOSEFA. Miguel, I have asked so little of you during all our years together. Will you this once . . .

DON MIGUEL *(holds up his hand)*. Do not put it into words, please, Josefa. If I had been a loyal subject, I would have revealed the truth to the viceroy long ago. Instead, I allowed myself to be swayed by you. But this is a direct order. If I refuse to carry it out, it would only put us under suspicion and would not help them.

DOÑA JOSEFA. I see, I understand.

DON MIGUEL. Of course I must take our servant with me to make certain that you send them no word, and Josefa, forgive me, but I am going to have to lock the door. I know your impulsive nature.

DOÑA JOSEFA. Yes, Miguel.

DON MIGUEL *(takes her hand)*. My dear, if there were anything I could do . . . But you can see for yourself. I have no other alternative.

DOÑA JOSEFA. I know.

DON MIGUEL. Good-bye, my . . . *(He forces a smile.)* My children.

(He goes out and the door closes securely behind him. LOLITA *is crumpled upon the floor, weeping.)*

DOÑA JOSEFA *(more to herself than to* LOLITA*)*. This is the hour for which I have been waiting so long. What a magnificent joke it must be for the viceroy to send a Mexican to capture loyal Mexicans.

LOLITA *(sobbing)*. Ignacio! Ignacio!

DOÑA JOSEFA *(closes her eyes in pain and then goes to the door and tries it)*. He *did* lock it. *(For a moment her old sense of humor flashes clear.)* Your father is a very thorough man, Lolita.

LOLITA. We must do something. We must.

DOÑA JOSEFA *(thoughtfully)*. If there were only some way by which I could get a message to them. *(She goes to the window and peers out.)* There is no one in the street I can trust. *(Impatiently.)* Stop weeping, Lolita, and pray. If ever we needed a miracle, we need it now.

LOLITA *(who has been lying prone on the floor, now stiffens and listens acutely to sounds below her)*. Mother! Mother!

DOÑA JOSEFA *(goes to her)*. What is it?

LOLITA. I hear someone moving around downstairs in Don Carlos's room. Do you think he is still home . . . that he hasn't gone to the prison?

DOÑA JOSEFA *(efficiently)*. We shall soon find out. *(She beats a brisk tattoo on the floor with her heel.)* Lolita, if he really is there, I will believe in miracles all the rest of my life.

LOLITA. Do you think he can reach Dolores ahead of Father? After all, Father has had a few minutes start. Don Carlos is so slow with that limp of his. And if he gets there, what can he tell them? Oh, it's no use, it's no use. My dream is coming true. *(Her voice rises hysterically.)* It's coming true! Ignacio will be killed, I know it!

The Cry of Dolores | 143

DOÑA JOSEFA *(gives her a resounding slap).* Time enough to weep afterwards. *(There is a knock at the door.)*

DON CARLOS *(in the hall).* Doña Josefa, what is it? What is the matter?

DOÑA JOSEFA *(runs to the door).* Are you alone?

DON CARLOS. But naturally. I had to return to my room for some documents. Señora, I am in a hurry. If you will open the door . . .

DOÑA JOSEFA. I can't . . . I am locked in.

DON CARLOS *(startled).* What?

DOÑA JOSEFA. Listen to me, and ask no questions. Just do as I tell you. A traitor has revealed everything to the viceroy and Miguel has gone to arrest our leaders.

DON CARLOS. Saints in Heaven!

DOÑA JOSEFA. You must send someone to Dolores to warn them.

DON CARLOS. I will go myself.

DOÑA JOSEFA. That is better still. On the way tell the villagers to stop Miguel and his soldiers some way; any way, but stop them. When you reach Hidalgo, tell him not to wait until October second. Tell him to give the cry now, tonight! The period of waiting is ended.

DON CARLOS. But we dare not strike now.

LOLITA. We must take that chance. Tell Ignacio that it is better to die fighting, than to die without a shot fired. Tell him that all my love goes with him to the battle.

DOÑA JOSEFA. Hurry, Don Carlos. Hurry!

DON CARLOS. Don't worry, Doña Josefa. By daylight Mexico will be fighting her first battle for freedom. *(His voice grows fainter as he leaves the door.)*

> (LOLITA *and her mother stare at each other, then both run to the window.)*

LOLITA. There he goes! Oh, do you think he will reach them in time?

DOÑA JOSEFA. He must reach them. *(She catches the girl's arm.)* What is the date, Lolita?

LOLITA. I think it's . . . It's the fifteenth of September.

DOÑA JOSEFA. Then by midnight Don Carlos will be with Hidalgo. Think of it. Sometime between midnight and dawn of September sixteenth, Hidalgo will give the cry that will bring Mexico to arms. Up with the true religion, down with false government. The sixteenth of September! What a glorious day for all of us.

(Quick curtain.)

The Fair God
Malinche

1936

Author's Foreword

Guarding the Museum door were the portraits of the seven boys who had protected Chapultepec from the Americans in 1848. They had protected the castle and gave their lives to it. The oldest was sixteen, the youngest no more than twelve. The portraits showed the stern young faces, duty bound, quiet, impassive. Dead faces that had once lived. Or tried to live. One doesn't have much chance to live when one dies at twelve, gun in hand, bullets in the heart.

Poor boys, poor babies, dead for nearly a century, but still on guard in front of the door to that long narrow room in which the government had cradled the relics of Mexico's great.

Guides showed tourists through that room. Tourists, ignorant mostly, of what those relics meant. The sword of Morelos. Who was he? A priest protecting his tonsured head. What difference that the great Napoleon had said, "With Morelos beside me, together we could conquer the world." A priest with a gun in his hand, a child with a gun in his hand. Who was there to care now? They had died so long ago.

There was the death mask of Juárez, the northern fox. Oh yes, Juárez, the Abraham Lincoln of Mexico. Had something to do with the French,

---

Editors' note: *The Fair God* is an excerpt from a longer play by Niggli called *Maximillan.* The play was never finished and exists in several typescript forms in the Josephina Niggli Papers at Western Carolina University.

didn't he? Pure Indian of forehead, cheekbones, chin, molded now in the white plaster.

All these memories of great dead men. The gold chair of Díaz, that poor old man who died in exile in Paris, desperately longing for "something of home," "*algo de Oaxaca,*" the saddest phrase in Mexican history.

There at the end of the room the portrait of a man on horseback, the horse pawing the ground, the man's delicate face, half hidden by a golden beard, Mexican hat on his head, Mexican leather shielding his body. Living, this man had been an emperor. Dead, he was a portrait hanging on the wall at the end of this long narrow room.

Emperor. Magic word. The tourists clicked their tongues and walked away through that child-guarded door, forgetting him as soon as possible. Why not? He was dead. So were the rest of these venerable men. All of them . . . dead.

But a child turned back to look at that portrait, came to look at it again and again. Why his portrait here in this room? The portrait of this Austrian interloper here amongst these men who had loved Mexico so much? Ghost of Maximilian, ghost of Juárez, enemies in life, together in this room? Why? It puzzled the child. I know. I was the child.

Years later in the market of Saltillo a clever salesman had me buy a book I didn't want: the life of Maximilian by his secretary. Maximilian was a figure on a horse to me, and nothing more. I'd seen his flag, the crowned flag of Mexico, here in Monterrey in the governor's palace. I'd seen the guns that shot him and his two generals that tragic day on Querétaro's hill. Just an image caught out of history.

One day, having nothing else to do, I started to read that book. In the last few pages I found the conundrum. Why was Maximilian shot? Sentenced to death, yes, by the little northern fox, he of the pale death mask. Yet Juárez himself had helped to plan Maximilian's escape. The Emperor refused. Three times he had a chance to go. The Princess Salm-Salm, once a circus bareback rider, went on her knees to him, but he showed her to the door, gently, kindly shut it after her, shut his lie out with her. Why?

I began to read other books. Austrian authors, German authors, English, American, yet none could answer the riddle. They didn't try to answer it. What was the use? The answer was in Maximilian's mind, and now, sixty years later, Maximilian was only a painted figure on a pawing charger.

One day, re-reading Blasios, I came to a description of Maximilian in the saddle. A quirk of memory threw my mind back to that day in the Museum. Once more I saw those dead boys' faces patiently guarding the door, once more the sword of Morelos, the golden chair of Díaz, the Juárez plaster mask of forehead, cheek, and chin. All men who had loved Mexico enough to die for her. Maximilian's portrait was there, too. Maximilian's portrait . . . there! I knew the answer to the riddle. I should have guessed it long ago.

The answer I have put into this play. No need to speak about it any-more. It's caught here in the speeches of Maximilian, in those of Marina, the woman he loved, in those of Carlota, the woman who despised him.

For the purposes of drama I have telescoped time, used some incidents, tossed away others, invented still others. But to this I have been true. To Maximilian, the man. However the other characters are drawn, to this man I have been true as I see it.

As far as Carlota is concerned, my treatment of her is rather revolution-ary. According to Blasios, she was a "cold elegant whiner, but so beautiful that no man could really hate her." Daughter of Leopold of Belgium, she was too haughty, too proud for the warmly affectionate Mexicans. Her own cousin called her "an ambitious shrew." There are legends about her, of course. Some say she went mad after she reached the Vatican, others that she was fed a slow dangerous poison by the Indians of this western empire . . . a poison so horrible that Mexicans themselves will barely whisper the name. I say again, these are legends. I think she poisoned herself out of the vial of her own ambition. Her mother had been a queen, but Carlota was wild to be an empress . . . not of Mexico, never of Mexico. That was but the stepping-stone. Empress of Hungary. That was the title of her ambition.

Unfortunately for her, Maximilian was an idealist, a dreamer. Her own tremendous personality pushed him on. From the day she sailed for France, his was a lost cause. Her ambition had over-reached itself. But she left her stamp on him. His enemies painted him in her colors. So do most of the authors who draw his portrait in better words. Perhaps I am wrong, and they are right, for Brutus said he was ambitious, and Brutus was an honorable man.

The Cast in the Final Scene

MAXIMILIAN, Emperor of Mexico	Bedford Thurman
MARINA, an Indian girl	Madeline Haynsworth
GRILL, valet to MAXIMILIAN	John Graff
CARLOTA, Empress of Mexico	Nancy Schallert
BARON SAILLARD, envoy of Louis Napoleon	Eugene Langston
GENERAL BAZAINE, commanding the French forces in Mexico	Douglas Langston
COUNT STEFAN VON HAGLENSTEIN, lifelong friend of MAXIMILIAN	Lubin Leggette

The Scene

Dawn flooding across the jasmine-scented balcony into the tall-ceilinged room with its gold French furniture and its Mexican plaster walls; light touching the golden hair of an emperor, the black hair of an Indian girl. But there is no light in the eyes of MAXIMILIAN, *no light in the eyes of* MARINA. *An empire is ended. In northern Mexico, Juárez, the Indian fox, is president of the republic by the grace of God and the United States government. In France, Louis Napoleon sighs over the ill-fated Mexican venture. But in Mexico an emperor who had been, grieves for the empire he might have created. To* MARINA *he is still the re-incarnation of the ancient fair god who had once brought glory to her country. To* MAXIMILIAN, *this man, himself, is a triumphant failure.*

Through the long night he has worked and worried. What was best for Mexico? That was the important thing to him. He had listened quietly to BARON SAILLARD *as this French messenger offered him the abdication paper written by Louis Napoleon's own hand. He had heard the Empress* CARLOTA'S *ambitious personal demands to keep the empire; his French general's dreams of war; his friends' pleading with him to go or stay as it suited their own ambitions. Not one word for Mexico, the country* MAXIMILIAN *loved beyond and above a country. A country that in his mind had somehow become personified in the body of* MARINA, *an Indian girl who had crossed battlefields to see this emperor whom the priests of the ancient religion, the old dead gods, had told her was the Malinche, the fair god. Loving him, she knew, and she alone, that Juárez would kill him. Out of her love for him she had begged him to leave, to save her country as that other fair god had done so long ago.* MAXIMILIAN, *not knowing that Juárez would dare to kill him, realizing that he is too weak to carry on alone, has finally decided to abdicate.*

MAXIMILIAN *sinks down on the sofa. He rests one elbow on his knee and presses his face against his hand. Vitality has ebbed out of his body leaving him bent and broken.* MARINA, *kneels beside him, her hands folded listlessly in her lap. After a moment* MAXIMILIAN *speaks, and his voice is the voice of an old man.*

MAXIMILIAN *(sadly and wearily)*. You are right Marina. It is better that I should leave . . . much better for Mexico.
> *(The girl gazes up at him for a moment, anguish shadowing her face, then she droops her head and begins to weep silently.)*

MAXIMILIAN *(speaking his thoughts aloud to this girl, who will never understand the words, and yet who so fully understands the man)*. So ends another chapter in this book of me. *(Bitterly.)* How shall we title this book, Marina?

MARINA *(speaking his name imploringly, almost as though she wanted to tell him something, yet did not have the courage)*. Malinche.

MAXIMILIAN *(smiling faintly, for he is still capable of appreciating the irony of this girl's worship of himself, the failure)*. No, Marina, not Malinche. You were wrong, you and your priests. I am not a god.

MARINA. You are to me.

MAXIMILIAN *(shaking his head)*. I am not even an emperor any more. I have failed, Marina. There is nothing left now but for me to go away.

MARINA *(hopefully)*. You are going?

MAXIMILIAN *(whispering)*. Yes.

MARINA *(moving closer to him, rests one arm on his knee and peers up into his face)*. Will you take me with you?

MAXIMILIAN *(smiling sadly at her)*. No, Marina. You'd never be happy away from Mexico.

MARINA *(rises and goes to the desk, her back to him)*. But after you leave, where shall I go?

MAXIMILIAN. You must return to Juárez.

MARINA (stubbornly). No! I won't go back to Juárez. Never!

MAXIMILIAN (gently). You must, Marina. He loves you as much as I do. He will take care of you.

MARINA (turns to him). But he hates you.

MAXIMILIAN (turns away from her with a sign). Yes, I know. (Then he smiles up at her.) Perhaps you can teach him to be my friend.

MARINA (with conviction). No one can do that. (Trying to make him understand Juárez's hatred.) Juárez has cursed you!

MAXIMILIAN. The gods cursed me, Marina, long before Juárez ever heard my name.

MARINA (with passionate hatred). That Juárez! I put on him the seven curses.

MAXIMILIAN (sharply). Marina!

MARINA. And the eighth curse! May worms feed on his brain. May eagles tear out his tongue . . . (Crying out.) May serpents wind about his bones!

MAXIMILIAN (catches her shoulders and shakes her). Stop! Enough of this!

(MARINA stops speaking. Flinging back her head she gazes steadily at him. There is a pause, then she sinks to the floor, hiding her face in her hands.)

MARINA (whispering). Forgive your servant.

MAXIMILIAN. Why do you curse him so bitterly?

MARINA. He is like the jealous war god who sent the Malinche from us long ago.

MAXIMILIAN (goes to the window and gazes across the great Mexican valley). How can any man ever hope to understand you, with your symbols, and your strange, weird mysteries?

MARINA (follows him to the window, her hands clasped, her eyes fixed pleadingly on his back). No man could, Malinche. No one but you. You are kind, and patient. You are wise, Malinche. Some day you would have brought us the glory of Mexico, just as you did so long ago.

MAXIMILIAN. Now Juárez will take my place. He is the stronger god, Marina.

MARINA. Strong with blood and sacrifice. (Bursts out against what is to her Juárez's stupidity.) Why should he want to kill you? Why can't he see you as you really are?

MAXIMILIAN *(surprised. It has never occurred to him that Juárez might want to kill him.)*. Juárez would kill me, Marina?

MARINA. Yes. I tell you he hates you . . . he's afraid of you.

MAXIMILIAN. No, Marina. He might kill Count von Haglenstein. He might kill my French general. But he wouldn't kill me. I am an emperor, Marina.

MARINA *(stubbornly)*. The war god killed the Malinche. Juárez will kill you!

MAXIMILIAN. This is life, not a legend. Juárez would not kill me.

MARINA *(with conviction)*. He will kill you.

MAXIMILIAN *(frowning)*. Say that again, Marina.

MARINA *(her voice quivering with fear of Juárez)*. I heard him say it. He said that if he killed you, no other foreign emperor would ever dare come here.

MAXIMILIAN *(slowly)*. No other foreigner would dare to come again.

MARINA. He said that was the only way to free Mexico.

MAXIMILIAN *(with growing comprehension)*. To free Mexico.

MARINA *(wildly)*. He will kill you. I know he will! That is why you must go away.

MAXIMILIAN *(seeing the truth at last)*. Yes, of course. *(He stretches out his hand to the valley, the valley he loves so much. His mind has encompassed the truth. With his death, this country would be free of foreign invasion forever.)* Free you forever. No more dead men rotting in the sun. No more tears. No more slavery.

MARINA *(sinking to her knees, pleadingly)*. I can't go back to Juárez now.

MAXIMILIAN *(not hearing her, and sure in his own mind of what he must do at last)*. Laughter again. Women singing as they grind the corn. Men singing as they build their roads. Children singing as they go to school.

MARINA. Take me away with you, Malinche. Please take me away.

MAXIMILIAN. No more sickness, no more oppression. All the things that I wanted to do for you, to give you, if you were free at last.

MARINA *(desperately)*. You said you could never refuse me anything.

MAXIMILIAN. End of failure! *(Slowly, as though trying to comprehend the immensity of death.)* End of life. *(Then triumphantly.)* But it doesn't matter. Nothing matters if Mexico is free!

MARINA. Tell me that you'll keep me with you.

MAXIMILIAN *(turns toward her, his body no longer broken but proud and straight, and a new light burns in his face; the light of duty seen and understood. He goes to the bell cord and pulls it, his voice lighter and gayer than it has been for two years.)*. Yes, Marina. You will stay with me.

MARINA *(joyfully)*. Always?

MAXIMILIAN *(goes to her and slips his arm about her as a father slips his arm about a favorite child)*. Always. I shall never leave you now.

(The door opens and GRILL, *the Austrian valet, enters. He is startled to see this exultant* MAXIMILIAN.*)*

GRILL. Good morning, sir. Are you ready for your coffee?

MAXIMILIAN *(beaming at him)*. Good morning, Grill. Have you been out in the sunshine?

GRILL *(blankly)*. Yes, sir.

MAXIMILIAN. It's a beautiful morning. No shadows, no darkness.

MARINA *(delightedly)*. He said I could stay with him . . . always!

MAXIMILIAN. Hand me the paper of abdication, Grill. *(GRILL gets it from the desk and brings it to him.* MAXIMILIAN *looks down at it and laughs.)* It's a very little paper to be so important, eh, Grill?

GRILL *(anxiously)*. You are going to sign it, aren't you, sir?

MAXIMILIAN *(in amazement)*. What is this, Grill? I thought you liked Mexico.

GRILL. I do love it, sir. But I am homesick for Austria.

MARINA. Will I see Austria?

MAXIMILIAN *(walks down to the sofa, his eyes seeming to gaze into the future)*. Who knows, Marina? Who knows what we will see together? *(He turns his head slightly toward* GRILL.*)* Ask the Empress and the others to come here.

GRILL. Her Majesty and the others are waiting in the anteroom.

MAXIMILIAN. Bring them in. The Empress must wait no longer for her answer.

GRILL *(peers up into his face, then smiles)*. Immediately, sir. *(As he starts toward the door, he pauses, then goes to the desk, dips a pen in the ink and brings it to* MAXIMILIAN.*)* The pen is ready, sir.

MAXIMILIAN *(taking it with an amused smile)*. Thank you, Grill. You think of everything, don't you?

GRILL *(to whom every sentence of praise from his Emperor is like the smile of God)*. I try to, sir. *(He hurries to the anteroom door, swings it wide open, then announces stentoriously.)* The General Bazaine. The Count von Haglenstein. The Baron Saillard. *(The French general, the Emperor's Austrian friend, and Napoleon's messenger enter as their names are called and bow to the Emperor.)* Her Imperial Majesty, the Empress!

    (CARLOTA sweeps into the room. The men bow to her.)

CARLOTA *(seeing the pen in MAXIMILIAN's hand, stops short, her eyes fixed on it in horror)*. The pen!

SAILLARD *(joyfully)*. You're going to sign, sir? That is a very wise decision.

BAZAINE *(thankfully)*. This finishes my games of handball with the enemy.

VON HAGLENSTEIN *(dejectedly)*. The end of an empire.

MAXIMILIAN *(going to SAILLARD)*. The end of an empire . . . *(Extends the pen to him.)* . . . and the beginning of a new freedom.

    (A change comes over the court. They are all dazed by this sudden reversal of what they had taken for granted. SAILLARD takes the pen as a man in a dream. He steps back, his eyes fixed in wonder on MAXIMILIAN's face. CARLOTA covers her mouth with the back of one hand, joy struggling with doubt on her face.)

SAILLARD *(bewildered)*. But your answer. Your answer to the King of France.

MAXIMILIAN *(rips the abdication paper and extends it to SAILLARD with a smile)*. To the King of France with my compliments. *(On a sudden impulse he hands it instead to CARLOTA.)* Or perhaps you would prefer to give it to him yourself, my dear.

CARLOTA *(still not quite sure of him)*. You mean . . . we stay?

MAXIMILIAN. Yes, Carlota. We stay.

MARINA *(sobbing)*. No. No! Juárez . . .

MAXIMILIAN *(goes to her and smiles down at her)*. Juárez and I will meet some day, Marina, and when we do, Mexico will be free.

MARINA *(stares up at him fascinated)*. Free! You would do that for Mexico?

MAXIMILIAN. Mexico is my country . . . forever.

MARINA *(sinks to her knees, her eyes worshiping him)*. Thus spoke the Malinche.

CARLOTA *(with triumphant joy, she faces the court)*. Gentlemen, the Emperor!

VON HAGLENSTEIN *(saluting)*. The Emperor!

(BAZAINE *slowly follows suit,* SAILLARD *bows and* CARLOTA *sinks into a deep curtsy. But* MAXIMILIAN, *his hand resting gently on* MARINA'S *head, does not see them. Instead he is gazing forward to that day, a year later, as he stands on Querétaro's hill, and the soldiers of Juárez raise their guns at their colonel's quiet command. Curtain.*)

Soldadera
A Play of the Mexican Revolution

1936

The Cast

As originally produced by The Carolina Playmakers at Chapel Hill, North Carolina, on 27, 28, and 29 February 1936.

THE RICH ONE, a prisoner	Robert du Four
MARIA, the sentinel	THE AUTHOR
THE BLOND ONE, the ammunition guard	Christine Maynard
CRICKET, soldadera	Phoebe Barr
TOMASA, soldadera	Jessie Langdale
ADELITA, a young girl	Barbara Hilton
THE OLD ONE	Mary Lou Taylor
CONCHA, their leader	Gerd Bernhart

The Scene

A soldier's camp in the spring of the year 1914 in the Sierra Madre Mountains near the capital city of Saltillo in the northern state of Coahuila, Mexico. It is really a mountain pass, and there is a path that begins at the rear right and leads up and out left.

The rocks are rugged spikes of stone against the dark blue sky. Here is no flowery green softness, no delicacy of outline, but a grim fortress built by nature against the valley below. What vegetation exists is sparse and scattered. Perhaps a yucca palm stands aloof from the organ cactus that rears its head above its two vertical bent arms. A maguey thrusts up its pointed leaves here and there, while small round cacti, studded with thorns, wear scarlet flowers for crowns.

In daylight the rocks are gray, but the early morning mist turns them to sapphire, brushing the tips with bronze and gold.

It is that hour just before dawn, that hour when even nature itself seems to be asleep, and the only moving thing in all that silence is the figure of a woman standing on the high rock that shields a part of the path from view. Her name is MARIA, *and she is a sentry. In her hand, the butt resting on the ground, is her gun. Her clothes are dirty and ragged, and as a protection against the cold mountain air she has drawn over her head and shoulders a fringed shawl. As a further protection she wears a man's sombrero.*

The stillness of the hour seems to have placed her, too, under a spell, and she stands there like a bronze image, gazing off into the distance at the left.

Below her in the pass are the sleeping figures of other women, the tousle-headed BLOND ONE *stretched out in front of the cave's opening on the left, and the woman known as* CRICKET *bundled up in what was once a blanket, in front of the built-up fire. The middle-aged woman named* TOMASA *is sitting there with her back against the sentry rock at the back. Sleep has toppled her body sideways, but her arm is curved in her lap as though to protect the head that rests there, the head of the youngest of them all,* ADELITA. *She is the poetry of the Revolution, and the beauty, and she who has seen almost nothing of death finds life very gay.*

After a moment, MARIA *looks down at the women she is guarding, and then after a glance up at the sky to see the first pink wisps of dawn draped across the mountains, she allows herself a little moment of rest. Slowly lowering herself to her haunches, she rests her gun across her lap and dares to snatch at forbidden sleep.*

Again there is silence, as though MARIA'S *movements had desecrated a holy service, and then, out of the shadows to the right, steals a figure of a young man . . . a man whose shirt, once white, is now dirty and torn, whose trousers look as though they had been slept in for days.*

He moves slowly, cautiously, seemingly fearful of disturbing the women. As he approaches the path the reason for his caution is revealed. His hands are tied behind his back. Every step he takes forward is a new adventure. Now and then he pauses to look over his shoulder toward the right, about him at the women, above him at the motionless MARIA. *Very quietly he moves up the path, holding his breath as he creeps past her, and with his head turned toward her he works his way up, and so out of view.*

He is hardly gone from sight before MARIA *begins to raise her head, a grim smile on her face. In a single movement she rises to her feet, and her gun swings up to her shoulder. Carefully sighting down the barrel, she calls out suddenly, raucously.*

MARIA. Look behind you, tenderfoot! *(The echo of her words and the shot come at the same time. She turns her head and spits.)* I can't even shoot a Rich One in the back!

> *(Instantly there is confusion in the path. The women, startled into consciousness, are swaying back and forth, almost as though they were drugged. Their voices come in confused shouts.)*

THE BLOND ONE. A shot. I heard a shot! Get up you . . . Cricket!

CRICKET *(still dreaming, the only one who has not moved)*. Kiss me again, you brown-eyed devil, or I'll break my knife off in your stomach.

TOMASA *(excitedly to the sentry)*. Is it Concha coming home at last, Maria?

MARIA. No. I just shot our little wealthy pig. You, Cricket and Adelita, go down and get him. He's all crumpled up on the path.

ADELITA *(crying anxiously as she runs up to* MARIA*)*. You didn't kill him!

MARIA *(patting her on the shoulder)*. No. I only shot him in the shoulder. Didn't I promise Concha not to kill him until she came back from taking the ammunition to Hilario? You run down and help bring him in.

ADELITA. Oh, the poor man. *(She runs off up the path.)*

MARIA *(shrugging her shoulders)*. Our Adelita has the heart of a young hen. Blondie, wake up the Cricket.

THE BLOND ONE *(goes over and looks down at* CRICKET, *then kicks her)*. Wake up. Dream about your lovers some other time. *(Kicks her again.)* Wake up I tell you.

CRICKET *(starting up)*. What in the name of . . . He was just buying me a bottle of mescal.* A whole bottle.

---

*Mescal is a colorless liquor made from the sap of the maguey cactus.

THE BLOND ONE. Maria's just shot the Rich One. She wants you to help Adelita bring him in.

CRICKET *(shaking herself awake)*. Why does she have to shoot him when I'm having a pleasant dream? *(She goes muttering up the path and disappears at the left.)*

TOMASA *(coming down to the fire)*. If we'd killed him when Concha first brought him in we could have slept for another hour this morning.

MARIA. Tomasa, you go find out if he slit the Old One's throat for her.

TOMASA. Why don't you send Blondie? I'm an old woman, I am.

THE BLOND ONE *(who has gone back to the mouth of the cave)*. That's a fine way to talk. Didn't Concha tell me to guard this ammunition? What if one of the bombs should fall out of the box? Do you want to be blown to hell before we shoot all the Federals? *(She spits.)* The mangy blood-drinking dogs.

TOMASA *(whining)*. I'm an old woman, I tell you. *(Nevertheless she goes off into the shadows at the right.)*

THE BLOND ONE *(digging down into her loose dirty blouse and pulling out a package of cigarettes. As she takes one out she shows the pack to* MARIA.*)*. Look what he gave me yesterday. He wanted me to help him get away. I told him all right, and then I tied him up tighter to his tree. *(Both the women laugh.)*

THE BLOND ONE *(as she lights the cigarette, she asks curiously but without much concern)*. I wonder if he did kill the Old One?

MARIA *(shrugs)*. What is the difference? All she did was grumble anyway. If Hilario didn't have such a kind heart he'd have gotten rid of her long ago. (CRICKET *and* ADELITA *now come into view. They are supporting* THE RICH ONE *between them. Although he possesses a name, he is called* THE RICH ONE *by the women, since he represents the hated upper-class which has held them in subjection for so long.)*

ADELITA. You almost killed him, Maria.

MARIA. Rich Ones have as many lives as a monkey. Why don't you roll him down the hill? It would be easier. *(She steps in front of them.)* The next time, Rich One, I'll put a bullet through that piece of black liver you call a heart.

CRICKET. He's heavier than the hand of God.

ADELITA (*gently, to* THE RICH ONE). Put more weight on me.

(TOMASA *has entered, and she is watching the procession from beside the glowing fire.*)

TOMASA. He'll be all right, Adelita, if you let him look at his pretty face in the mirror Cricket got for him. (*All the women think this is a great joke . . . all but* ADELITA.)

CRICKET. Adelita will wash your shoulder for you, Rich One. You won't feel the pain then.

(*She reaches out and slaps him across his wounded shoulder.* THE RICH ONE *gives a sharp moan of pain and flinches back.* ADELITA *swings around in front of* CRICKET.)

ADELITA (*angrily*). What are you doing! You let go of him; I'll take him.

(*She pushes* CRICKET *out of the way, and, putting* THE RICH ONE'S *unwounded arm over her shoulders, she supports him off into the shadows at right.*)

CRICKET (*after a pause*). Our little Adelita is angry with us, my pigeons.

THE BLOND ONE. Perhaps she thinks we ought to give our prisoners a bed made of feathers, and a gay, striped blanket from the factory down in Saltillo.

(CRICKET, *her hands on her hips, strolls to the right and stares after* ADELITA *and* THE RICH ONE.)

MARIA. Well, Tomasa, is the Old One dead?

TOMASA (*putting an iron kettle on the fire*). Not unless the dead can snore. I tried to wake her up, but she had too much mescal last night.

THE BLOND ONE (*indifferently*). Oh, well, it keeps her from thinking about her son.

TOMASA. I had a son, too, but I don't want to forget him.

MARIA. You don't let us forget him either.

CRICKET. What do we care about your son?

THE BLOND ONE. Why don't you let our memories alone? We don't want to think of them.

TOMASA (*clutching* THE BLOND ONE'S *arm*). I want to think of him all the time, and every moment I think of him, I want to have a Rich One between my hands.

MARIA (*sharply*). You keep away from this Rich One until Concha comes back. You know what a temper she's got if she finds we haven't done what she told us to do. Why, she'll beat up the lot of us.

TOMASA (*sullenly*). I haven't touched him, have I?

THE BLOND ONE. Anyway she told us we could have this Rich One, and Hilario would never do that when he was here.

(THE OLD ONE *shambles in from the right. She is a very old woman who has seen too much of death, but still she clings to life with the hope burning in her . . . the same hope that burns in all these women . . . that this time the Revolution must succeed.*)

THE BLOND ONE. Who woke you up, Old One?

THE OLD ONE (*wiping her face with the back of her hand*). Adelita threw water in my face. These young girls don't know how to respect age any more. (*Looks up at* MARIA.) Well, do you see anything? Maria! You, Sentinel! Do you see anything!

MARIA (*behind whom the sun is spreading a warm red light*). Nothing. Nothing but cactus and yucca trees . . . and the mountains across the valley.

THE BLOND ONE (*to* THE OLD ONE). When do you think Hilario will come back?

THE OLD ONE. When he wins a battle.

CRICKET (*wanders down to the fire*). When he wants to see Concha . . . the hellcat.

(*All women laugh.*)

THE BLOND ONE. Cricket is jealous. She would rather have Hilario than the common soldier she's got.

CRICKET (*disdainfully*). And perhaps you think I could not have Hilario if I wanted him.

MARIA (*laughs*). Roll the eye at him and Concha would tear out every hair in your head.

THE OLD ONE (*holding up her thumb*). Not our Concha. She has no need to fight for her men. One shrug of her shoulders, one swirl of her skirt as she dances, and even Cricket's common soldier would slit his own gullet for her.

CRICKET. I can dance too.

THE BLOND ONE (*sneers*). Perhaps you can dance better than Concha.

CRICKET. The men would be slitting each other's gullets for me.

MARIA. You never could dance.

CRICKET. I'll show you.

(Her foot slaps the ground, her fingers grasp the folds of her skirts, and as she begins to dance MARIA *mockingly sings "La Cucaracha.")*

MARIA.

> One thing always gives me laughter,
> Pancho Villa* the morning after.
> Ay, there go the Carranzistas . . .
> Who comes here?

(The other women joining in the chorus.)

> Why the Villistas.
> Ay, Pancho Villa, ay Pancho Villa,
> Ay, he can no longer walk.
> Because he lacks now, because he has not
> Any drug to help him talk! Ay-yay!

(CRICKET finishes triumphantly in front of THE OLD ONE.*)*

---

*Pancho Villa was the leader in the north of the Agrarian Revolution of 1910. His followers were called Villistas. He was opposed to the government of Venustiano Carranza whose followers were known as Carranzistas.

THE OLD ONE (*grinning with tightly closed mouth and nodding her head*). When Concha returns, perhaps she will teach you how to really dance. (CRICKET *spits at her, goes back to the fire, and flops down on the ground*.)

TOMASA (*pointing toward the cave left*). What does Hilario care about women? He'll come back when he needs bullets.

THE OLD ONE. Ay, there's the answer. He won't let us fight any more, but we're good enough to mold his bullets for him.

MARIA. And guard his ammunition for him.

CRICKET. And keep a prisoner for him.

THE BLOND ONE (*meaningly*). Leave that to Adelita.

THE OLD ONE (*startled at* THE BLOND ONE'S *tone*). What's that? What did you say about Adelita?

MARIA. Nothing, nothing at all. They were just talking. Words as large as a barn door and full of holes as a cheese.

THE OLD ONE. Has she been talking to that wealthy pig? (*Spits and wipes her mouth with the back of her hand.*)

MARIA. The joke of it is that he doesn't like being called a wealthy pig.

TOMASA. He wears silk next to his skin, doesn't he?

THE BLOND ONE (*holding up a package of cigarettes*). And smokes paper cigarettes.

CRICKET (*teasing* THE OLD ONE). And kisses a lady's hand. You ought to see him kiss Adelita's.

THE OLD ONE (*shuffles up to* CRICKET). What did you say?

MARIA (*raises her gun*). You, Cricket, down there. Keep your mouth shut, or I'll shut it for you

CRICKET (*whiningly*). I'll talk if I want to . . . about any rich corn rustler.

THE OLD ONE (*goes to* THE BLOND ONE). What about Adelita and this man?

THE BLOND ONE. Well, what can you expect in five days? Is she not the youngest in the camp? Yes, and the prettiest, too? And he's a very handsome young man. For them to stay apart would be against nature.

TOMASA. He reads to her, too. And he's teaching her her letters. Oh, our Adelita will soon be a fine lady in silks and in laces . . .

CRICKET. And will turn up her nose at the camp.

TOMASA. Imagine. He told Blondie over there she ought to teach the rest of us to talk like ladies.

THE BLOND ONE *(slaps her knee)*. He thought his sweet words would buy his freedom from me.

MARIA. Perhaps he feels it is not manly to be captured by a woman.

CRICKET. But it took courage, you must admit that. I feel proud of myself.

MARIA *(laughs)*. You. You! When all the world knows that Concha brought him in.

TOMASA. With the point of her knife in his back.

THE OLD ONE *(disregarding the others and looking to the right where* ADELITA *and* THE RICH ONE *are. Swaying back and forth, she is moaning to herself.)*. Adelita . . . with a Rich One . . . a Rich One.

CRICKET *(to the others. No one is paying any attention to* THE OLD ONE.*)*. You needn't worry. This louse won't live long after Concha gets back *(She sighs.)* It is a sad thing, too. He has a lively eye in his head.

MARIA *(slowly)*. If Concha gets back. She's been gone five days. Hilario wouldn't keep her this long.

TOMASA. Perhaps he's showing her the new way of hanging.

THE BLOND ONE. I'd like to see one of those hangings. I've only heard about them.

TOMASA. They tie their ankles together with the same rope that makes a noose around their necks, and then dangle them from a tree limb. As long as they keep their feet pulled up, they live . . . but once they straighten out . . . *(Draws her finger across her throat, then points to heaven and laughs.)*

CRICKET. I heard one of them stayed alive three days.

MARIA. It's still too easy a death for them.

THE OLD ONE *(shuffling back to the fire, her shawl wrapped around her. Her voice is dead.)*. A thousand years in hell would be too easy for them.

CRICKET *(slaps* THE OLD ONE *on the back)*. Listen to the Old One. Hilario should have you on his staff to tell him how to get rid of these rich bastards.

THE OLD ONE *(jerking away from her)*. Who has a better right than I? Who has suffered more than I have?

THE BLOND ONE. Now, Old One, we all know the story.

THE OLD ONE *(her voice rising to a crescendo as the mere thought of* ADELITA *being attracted to a Rich One is too much for her)*. Sometimes in the night I wake up and hear him crying for me . . . small mother, small mother! . . . until I have to cover my ears and scream to God. *(Rocks back and forth.)* When those Federals took him away I ran after them until I fell to the ground, and then I crawled on my knees for miles and miles until the dear Virgin sent sleep to cover me. Oh, Holy Angels . . . Oh, Blessed Child of God!

TOMASA. They took my son, too.

THE OLD ONE *(as if she were seeing enacted in front of her this story out of the past. The spell of common suffering has bound the women's attention to her.)*. When I had reached the place, they had crucified him . . . put nails through his hands and fastened him against a door. He was looking up at heaven . . . I closed his eyes, and then his head drooped down as though he were hunting for my breast. Like a little baby he was . . .

TOMASA *(laughs grimly)*. They were good to my son. They gave him ten paces ahead of a starved pack of dogs. When I found him there was nothing left but the bones. The little rich squirts told me to make soup out of them.

CRICKET, THE BLOND ONE, and THE OLD ONE. Oh, Holy Virgin . . .

MARIA and TOMASA. Oh, Mother of God.

ALL. Have pity on us.

THE OLD ONE *(shaking her clenched fist above her head)*. If Adelita wants a Rich One . . .

> (ADELITA *comes in from the right. As she walks, her skirt swings from side to side and she is lightly humming the "Adelita."*)

THE OLD ONE. Ay, so here you are, my pretty. Was it hard to tear yourself away from his arms?

ADELITA *(startled)*. What are you talking about? Why are you all staring at me?

CRICKET. It is not every woman who can boast of a wealthy lover.

ADELITA. He's not my lover!

> (*They glare at each other,* MARIA *suddenly jerks her head and yells at* ADELITA.)

MARIA. Where is the Rich One?

ADELITA. He's asleep.

MARIA. And you left him unguarded?

ADELITA *(flinging out her hands)*. He is wounded. He cannot escape. And, besides, the cliffs are too high around him. There's no way for him to escape except through here.

MARIA *(relaxing)*. I don't trust these Rich Ones, even when I'm looking at them. Old One, you go and watch him.

THE OLD ONE. Why does it always have to be me?

MARIA *(raises her gun)*. You heard me.

THE OLD ONE. I'm going. I'm going. *(She disappears right.)*

ADELITA. Can't you give the man a moment's peace? After all, he's human.

THE BLOND ONE. No Rich One is human. They are beasts, all of them.

ADELITA. This man is different. He believes in the Revolution. Why, he even knows the words of the "Adelita" . . .

TOMASA *(sneers)*. What does he know about the great song of the Revolution?

ADELITA. He's crazy about the Revolution and he wants to know all about us, what we think about, how we live, everything.

MARIA. And I suppose you tell him everything, eh? Not that the news will do him any good, when he's dead.

ADELITA. He says that if he hadn't sworn an oath to the Federals, he'd like to join Hilario.

THE BLOND ONE. So he tells you that, eh? That eater of cow's meat.

MARIA *(jibingly)*. And she believes him.

ADELITA. Why shouldn't I believe him? What do you know about him? Any of you? You've never spoken to him . . . not seriously you haven't.

CRICKET. Didn't I capture him?

ADELITA. You? It was Concha.

THE BLOND ONE. Even the infant knows the truth of that story, my Cricket.

CRICKET *(defending herself)*. Well, I found him . . .

MARIA. So you say . . .

CRICKET. He was standing by a tree in our territory.

TOMASA. And you went up to him, I suppose, and said, "Rich One, you are my prisoner."

CRICKET. I shot his hat off his head.

TOMASA *(laughs)*. I wish I could have heard our Cricket squeak for help when he turned to face her.

CRICKET *(springs at her)*. I'll teach you to watch your tongue.

   (They begin to fight.)

THE BLOND ONE *(seizing hold of* CRICKET *and pulling her back)*. You can't fight on an empty stomach.

ADELITA *(trying to hold* TOMASA*)*. Now, Tomasa, remember, you are an old woman.

CRICKET *(spitting at* TOMASA*)*. You cross-eyed shrew!

TOMASA. You monkey's wench!

CRICKET. I'll scratch out both your eyes!

   (Her surging movement forward is arrested by the sound of a woman's voice in the far distance to the left, singing. It is CONCHA *returning.)*

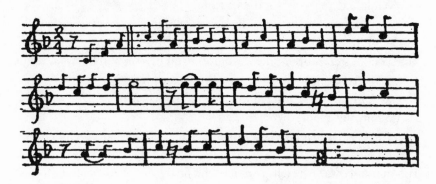

CONCHA *(off left)*.

   If Adelita should go with another,
   If Adelita should leave me all alone,
   I would follow in a boat made of thunder,
   I would follow in a train made of bone.*

MARIA *(raising her gun)*. Concha comes! Back to your post, Blondie! If Concha finds out you left those bombs unguarded, she'll tear out your

---

*"Adelita" was one of the great songs of the Revolution and has over one hundred known verses. It holds the same place that "Annie Laurie" did to English soldiers during World War I.

heart to see it wiggle *(Turns to the left and waves her arm above her head.)* Concha! Concha!

CONCHA *(still off left, but coming nearer, she calls).* O-la! O-la!

ADELITA *(calls joyfully as she runs up the path).* Concha! *(She runs off to meet her.)*

MARIA *(looking down at the woman).* The first one that opens her mouth to Concha about Adelita and that Rich One will get a bullet through her head . . . from this gun.

THE BLOND ONE *(sullenly).* We won't say anything. *(Putting some beans from the pot on a plate.)* You, Tomasa, take this food to His Highness . . . the son of a three-legged goat.

TOMASA. That's Adelita's work, not mine.

THE BLOND ONE. You heard me! Or would you rather I threw the plate in your face?

TOMASA. All right. *(She takes the plate with poor grace and goes out right.)*

(There is a moment's silence, during which THE BLOND ONE *goes over and squats in front of the cave, then* ADELITA *and* CONCHA *enter down the mountain path at the left.* MARIA *has stepped back to make way for* CONCHA. *As dirty as the rest of them, there is strength that flowers in her body and sets her above and beyond them. Born of the earth, it is the earth's pulse that she has for her heart. She is the one who keeps these fighting, snarling women together . . . who can punish with a sure, cold hand, but at the same time can heal their wounds. As merciless as the wind and rain, she is as warm and healing as the sun.)*

MARIA. Thanks to our Lady of the Mountains for your return, Concha.

THE BLOND ONE and CRICKET. May the saints pour blessings on your head, Concha.

CONCHA *(her arm around* ADELITA'S *waist, smiles at the women as a mother smiles at her children).* Hilario sends you many greetings and the news that he has killed a hundred Rich bastards.

ADELITA. Now the Revolution will soon be over.

CONCHA *(as she comes down the path).* Perhaps today, perhaps tomorrow . . . perhaps a hundred years from now. Ay, the Revolution is a glorious thing. But these bones of mine are weary. *(Looks about her.)* Where is the Old One? Has she no food for me?

THE OLD ONE (*coming out of the shadows at right*). Beans and rabbit stew. Cricket has had good hunting since she found the Rich One. He has put courage in her. (*She starts to fill a plate for* CONCHA.)

MARIA. I killed the rabbit.

CRICKET (*wrathfully*). Is all the world going to credit from me? Can't I even kill a rabbit?

CONCHA. Enough of this snarling. Get out of here, all of you. I want some rest.

THE OLD ONE. But how about the Rich One? Aren't we going to kill him?

ADELITA. Oh, no!

THE OLD ONE (*the plate in her hand, she faces* ADELITA). Why don't you weep for your pretty golden lover?

THE BLOND ONE (*sharply*). Shut your mouth on the outside of your teeth!
(*All of the women but* CONCHA *and* ADELITA *freeze into silence.* MARIA, *who has raised her gun, quietly drops it.*)

CONCHA (*looks at all of them, her eyes darting suspiciously from person to person, then she relaxes slightly*). Do I have to speak twice to you carrion crows?
(*As though a magic wand had brought them back to life again, the women relax and start moving about.* ADELITA *takes the plate from* THE OLD ONE *and hands it to* CONCHA.)

CONCHA. Thank you, Adelita. The rest of you get out of here.

THE OLD ONE (*sullenly*). But we cannot keep the Rich One much longer. He eats more than we do.

CONCHA. You can come back after a while. We'll talk about it them. Cricket!
(*The women start out.*)

CRICKET (*turning back*). What do you want?

CONCHA (*eating*). Your soldier told me to tell you that if you went again to the saloon in Saltillo he would nail your face to its door.

CRICKET (*startled*). How did he know I'd been there?

CONCHA. Knowing you, he probably guessed it. It wouldn't be hard.

CRICKET. But I only went down to Saltillo to find a mirror for our Rich beauty. What harm was there in slipping into the saloon for a minute?

CONCHA. At how many men did you roll the eye?

CRICKET. A woman has to have some fun. That soldier of mine isn't wasting his minutes, I can tell you. I've got as many rights as he has.

CONCHA. Were they Federal soldiers, or our men?

CRICKET. I don't remember. But they had gold, and they knew how to spend it.

CONCHA (*stares at her, mouth curling*). So you don't remember. For a twopeso gold-piece you would forget the road to heaven. Get out!

CRICKET (*shrugs her shoulders as she passes* ADELITA). Perhaps the Rich One is awake now and my hand is as soft to hold as yours.

(ADELITA *draws away from her, and* CRICKET *laughs as she goes out. This by-play has not been lost on* CONCHA *who pretends that she has noticed nothing and speaks lightly.*)

CONCHA. Thank the saints, Adelita, you don't snarl. (*She smiles up at the girl.*) I have a message for you, too.

ADELITA (*with the interest of a child*). What kind of a message?

CONCHA (*handing* ADELITA *her plate*). From the young Rubén. He wants to know if you still love him.

(MARIA *is standing at the high left end of the rock and takes no notice of this conversation.*)

ADELITA (*sniffs*). He has been gone a month and not one letter from him. I don't call that love.

CONCHA (*laughs and sings teasingly*).

So farewell my beloved Adelita,
So farewell to all that I hold most dear.
Do not sigh if I write you no letter,
I'll not change you for any girl here.

(ADELITA *squats down beside her, and* CONCHA *brushes the girl's hair back.*)

CONCHA. Anyway, you couldn't read it if he sent you one.

ADELITA (*proudly*). I can now. See, I can write my name. (*She writes it in the air as she pronounces the syllables, A . . . de . . . li . . . ta! As she crosses the t and dots the i, she laughs up at* CONCHA.)

CONCHA (*with mock surprise*). Who taught you such magic?

ADELITA (*gestures with her thumb*). He did. He said that in the towns all the girls know how to read and write.

CONCHA (*suspiciously*). What else has he told you?

ADELITA. Oh, he uses a lot of words. I don't know what they mean, but they sound so beautiful. He said I made him think of red wine in an amber glass. What is amber?

CONCHA. I don't know. *(Narrows her eyes.)* So he talks about you a lot, does he?

ADELITA. Ay, yes. He says I'm the symbol of the Revolution. What is a symbol?

CONCHA. Why . . . it means when people look at you they think of the Revolution. What made him say that?

ADELITA. It was my name. He says that when all the soldiers sing the verses of my name, they think of me. *(She laughs.)* But that is foolish. I don't know all the soldiers.

CONCHA. He seems to be a very clever young man. I think I had better have a little talk with this Rich One.

ADELITA. But he isn't like all the other Rich Ones.

CONCHA *(raising her brows)*. No? Imagine that. Did he tell you that, too?

ADELITA. Oh, yes. He says he believes in the Revolution. He wants to know all about us . . . everything we do, and everything Hilario does . . .

CONCHA. Fancy! All about us. *(Bending toward ADELITA.)* And you tell him?

ADELITA. Of course I tell him. I told him a lot about you, too. He thought you were very brave to take the ammunition all alone to Hilario. He seemed surprised that Hilario would let you go back and forth all alone.

CONCHA *(looking over her shoulder to the right, her sarcasm lost on the girl)*. I suppose that he was surprised when I arrived back here this morning all alone, too. Very much surprised.

ADELITA *(laughs gaily)*. You should have seen his face when I told him about all the ammunition we keep hidden, in that cave over there, and especially about the bombs.

CONCHA *(laughing without mirth)*. Yes, I imagine that was funny, Adelita. He sounds very amusing indeed. Do you think that he could make me laugh?

ADELITA. He could make even a sad fox laugh.

CONCHA. Then you run and get him. But don't run back with him until I call you. I must talk to Maria first. *(Her mood shows irritation.)* I leave this camp for a few days, and when I come back everything is wrong. You're no better than children.

(ADELITA *laughs and runs out right. The moment she is gone,* CONCHA's *air of light good humor is lost and she is again a worried woman. She hesitates a moment, looks up at* MARIA, *then making up her mind she goes halfway up the path and calls.*)

CONCHA. Maria!

MARIA *(turns and moves toward her).* What do you want, Concha?

CONCHA. There are Federal soldiers in the mountains. *(At* MARIA's *surprise, she shrugs her shoulders.)* They almost caught me two days ago. I've had to dodge around them like a rabbit. From the way they acted anyone would think they knew I'd been to Hilario.

MARIA *(intently).* How could that be? No one here would tell them but the Rich One and we've kept our eyes on him I can tell you.

CONCHA *(doubtfully).* Cricket might have told them when she was in that saloon in Saltillo. For a handful of gold Cricket would sell her own right arm.

MARIA. If she had told them anything, she would have been afraid to come back. She hasn't the courage of a flea.

CONCHA *(turns jerkily away and folds her arms).* I know it. It's the Rich One who told them if anyone did. But how? He's a thin cord,* that one. If he is sending messages to the Federals, I must find out how he does it.

MARIA. Why worry about it, Concha? The Federals will never find this hiding place.

CONCHA. If he sent them a message about me, he can tell them how to find the way here.

MARIA *(thoughtfully).* How many Federals were there?

CONCHA. It was a scouting party . . . just five or six. I don't think they were able to follow me. *(She turns and comes down to the fire.* MARIA *follows her a short distance.)* But I don't know. *(She faces* MARIA.) If they do come here . . . if they find this ammunition . . .

MARIA. It will be the end of Hilario . . . yes, I know. *(Sharply.)* If the Federals know about this place, they'd know how important this ammunition is to us. They'd send a company to get it, not just a scouting party.

---

*"Thin cord" is a typical Mexican phrase which is the equivalent of "city slicker" in English.

CONCHA. If they know that much, they know only women are guarding it. *(With bitter humor.)* And the Federals are clever. Surely only five or six men are needed to deal with women.

(Both the woman laugh, but without mirth.)

MARIA *(pats her gun).* I'd like to stand them up in front of me like mescal bottles and practice shooting their ears off.

CONCHA. You could practice on the Rich One if I knew he told them . . . or . . .

MARIA. Or what?

CONCHA *(starts pacing up and down).* Oh, I don't want to believe that Cricket had anything to do with this. If I could only be sure!

MARIA. You could find out. *(As* CONCHA *looks up at her . . . startled.)* There's more than one way of getting straw into a barn.

CONCHA *(rubbing her mouth).* Yes, I could find out, couldn't I, Maria? There are times when you are almost as clever as I am. *(They smile at each other, then* CONCHA *is again businesslike.)* But first of all I must find out about these Federals. Are they hunting the ammunition . . . or . . . me?

MARIA. It would be a grand thing for them if they could capture the great Concha.

CONCHA. They would shoot me dead before I could blow my nose. They would shoot any of us . . . even the little Adelita.

MARIA. You are the only one of us whose face is known.

CONCHA *(snaps her fingers).* Precisely. That is why I want you to do something for me. *(Looks over her shoulders toward the right, then goes up to* MARIA *and drops her hands on the woman's shoulders.)* You are a brave woman, Maria.

MARIA *(quietly).* What do you want me to do?

CONCHA *(very quietly).* Pretend that you are hunting for firewood. If they ask you about us . . .

MARIA. I will tell them nothing.

CONCHA. You will tell them the truth.

MARIA *(startled).* But then they will come here. They will take Hilario's ammunition and us, too. And what will Hilario do then?

CONCHA. Hilario will not miss one bomb, especially if it blows six Federals to hell, the wealth . . . *(She turns her head and spits.)*

MARIA. They're not easy to trap I can tell you. They've got brains . . .

CONCHA. Leave all that to me. You're just the bait. They'll follow you all right. They'll trust you. They'll have to trust you. But at the foot of the trail you dodge into the rocks and lose them. I don't want you between us and the Federals when we throw the bomb at them.

MARIA *(grasping* CONCHA's *arms)*. Who will throw the bomb?

CONCHA. What is that to you?

MARIA. Whoever does will blow to hell with them. We're in the mountains, Concha. It will start a landslide. There wouldn't be a chance of escape . . .

CONCHA. Better one woman in hell then to lose Hilario's ammunition.

MARIA. I know what you're thinking. But you mustn't do it, Concha. Not you. We need you . . . Hilario needs you. He hasn't anybody to trust but you . . .

CONCHA. Don't be a fool, Maria.

MARIA. Give me the bomb now. When the moment comes. I'll throw it. There isn't so much danger in the valley. I might escape, and if I don't . . . *(She shrugs.)* I'm not much use. A woman with a dead heart never is.

CONCHA *(puts her hands on* MARIA's *shoulders, then kisses her on both cheeks)*. A beautiful plan, Maria, but not a good one. I have to find out who is sending those messages, you see. And the only way to do it is to trick him . . . or her . . . into warning them. Now go, and may God walk with you.

MARIA. Promise me first that you won't throw it. Please, Concha.

CONCHA *(smiles gently)*. I will choose when the time comes. Good-bye, my friend.

> *(They look at each other, then kiss each other on both cheeks and shake hands. Handing* CONCHA *her gun,* MARIA *turns and walks quickly up the path to disappear down the mountainside.* CONCHA *stares after her, then waves her arm at her. Finally she turns and comes down the path to the fire. She looks down at it, then, with grief almost too great for her to bear, she crosses her wrists above her head and her body droops forward. In a moment she straightens, goes up right, and calls softly.)*

CONCHA. Cricket! Cricket! Come here. *(She returns to the fire and squats down as* CRICKET *enters.)*

CRICKET (*half to* CONCHA, *half to herself*). That Tomasa and the Old One! All they can talk about is their sons. What's a poor woman who never had a son going to say? The only thing that ever happened to me was when the Rich Ones carried me off on my fourteenth saint's day. They brought me back quick enough, I can tell you. (*She sighs.*) One of them used soap that smelt like violets. Every time I smell a violet now I can remember the feel of my knife going into his stomach. Oh, well, the poor sinner's getting more rest than I am . . . be damned to him!

CONCHA. Stop your grumbling and get up there on the path. Take Maria's gun and hide behind that rock. If you stick your head up before I call you, I'll shoot it out between your ears.

CRICKET (*whining*). I hear you.

(*She hides behind the rock on the path. Not until she is hidden does* CONCHA *call.*)

CONCHA. Adelita! You can bring in the Rich One now. (*There is a brief pause, then* ADELITA *can be heard laughing off right. In a moment she enters with* THE RICH ONE *whose left arm is in a sling made of a red bandanna handkerchief. He walks with a bravado air as though he would show the world how brave he is.*)

ADELITA. Here he is, Concha.

CONCHA (*without raising her head*). Do not try to escape, Rich One. I have only to raise my voice and my women will shoot you before you run two feet. Come around here where I can get a look at you.

THE RICH ONE (*shrugs and comes down to her*). You said you had seen enough of my dirty face the day you captured me.

CONCHA (*raising her head*). I never look at Rich Ones unless I have to. What happened to your arm?

THE RICH ONE. One of your mosquitoes stung me this morning.

CONCHA (*stands*). If they have been sticking cactus thorns into you . . .

THE RICH ONE (*holds up his head*). They did not like the direction in which I was running.

CONCHA. Oh, so you tried to escape? (*Walks up to him.*) You do not like us, perhaps?

THE RICH ONE. As individuals, señora, you are magnificent . . . but in a crowd? (*He bows slightly.*) Forgive me, señora.

ADELITA *(proudly)*. Didn't I tell you he used big words? And, oh, you should hear him sing. Sing the "Adelita" for Concha.

THE RICH ONE *(shrugs and turns away)*. With my poor voice, I am afraid . . .

CONCHA. What is the matter? Are you afraid of the mountain air?

THE RICH ONE *(meaningly)*. On the contrary. I find that it gives me a zest . . . for life.

CONCHA. Really? And this new joy does not make you want to break out into song?

THE RICH ONE. I prefer not to sing.

CONCHA. You hear, Adelita? I am afraid our find gentleman is too proud to sing for us. After all, if there were no Revolution, perhaps we should be his servants.

THE RICH ONE *(looking insolently at* CONCHA*)*. I am glad the señora realizes that even the Revolution does not change . . . blood.

CONCHA *(walks up to him, her head very high)*. Precisely. Pigs remain pigs. You will sing for us.

THE RICH ONE *(coldly)*. But I do not care to . . .

CONCHA *(harshly)*. I said that you will sing. Sit down, Adelita, while the . . . gentleman . . . gets his breath. *(Both the women sit down.)*

THE RICH ONE *(looking at* CONCHA *for a moment as though he would like to kill her, he smiles sarcastically and bows)*. Always at your service, señora. *(He quite obviously sings to* ADELITA.*)*

And Adelita's the name of my loved one,
She's the girl whom I never shall forget.
In the world I have found a fair flower,
I remember the night we first met.

If Adelita would say she would wed me,
If Adelita would only be my wife,
I would buy her a fine dress of satin,
She could wear it the rest of her life.

CONCHA *(flings up her arm)*. Stop! You have no heart! What do you know of the song of the Revolution? It has fire! It has life!
(She flings back her head and sings it for him. The magnetism, the

vitality of his woman attracts THE RICH ONE *so that for a moment he loses his air of superiority.)*

I'm a soldier and now I must leave you,
For my country has called on me to fight.
Adelita, Adelita, my loved one,
You must not, dear, forget me tonight.

So farewell once again, Adelita,
So farewell to all your grace and all your charms,
Now I go with the hope of returning,
To come back once more to your arms.

(As CONCHA *finishes singing she faces him triumphantly.)*
THE RICH ONE *(with enthusiasm).* But you are magnificent, señora!
CONCHA *(turns away).* Thank you. And now . . . leave us, Adelita.
ADELITA *(plaintively).* But, Concha . . .
CONCHA *(almost sharply).* Leave us, child.

> (ADELITA *looks at both of them curiously and then walks out right. Both* CONCHA *and* THE RICH ONE *look after her until she is gone, then he moves toward* CONCHA. *It is obvious that this woman attracts him, doubtless because he has never seen anyone quite like her before in his life. The face she turns toward him, however, is so bitter and cold that it stops his forward movement.)*

CONCHA. We might as well do this the right way, not that I love talking. But if Hilario asks me questions, I have to answer him, don't I?
THE RICH ONE *(looking at her intently, but his voice is once more sarcastic).* You know him better than I do, señora.
CONCHA *(harshly).* I don't want any sneers from you. And take off your hat. I'm no common soldier's woman.
THE RICH ONE *(taking off his hat and bowing).* Great ladies have always frightened me. You will have to excuse my poor manners.
CONCHA *(seeming to grow nervous under his scrutiny).* You won't need manners where you're going. But one thing at a time. What's your name?
THE RICH ONE. Will I need that where I'm going?
CONCHA. I asked you a question. Answer it.

THE RICH ONE. For what it's worth to you, my name is Mario Galicia. I'm a lawyer by profession.

CONCHA. And what is a lawyer doing in these mountains?

THE RICH ONE. I'd been in Saltillo. Although I'm a Torreón man myself, there aren't many mountains in that direction. I thought I'd look at one close to while I had the chance.

CONCHA *(thinks this over, then glances sideways at him).* What do they raise around Torreón?

THE RICH ONE *(smiles with assurance).* Wheat.

CONCHA. That's right. What else do they raise?

THE RICH ONE *(no longer smiling).* Why . . . oranges.

CONCHA *(easily).* That's a lie. They raise cotton. What's the biggest factory?

THE RICH ONE *(breathing quickly).* Soap.

CONCHA. Excellent. And what is the name of the factory?

THE RICH ONE. Señora, I object . . .

CONCHA *(smoothly).* What is the name of the factory?

THE RICH ONE *(turns away slightly, then to her triumphantly).* The Mariposa.

CONCHA. That's the name of a brand of soap.

THE RICH ONE *(angrily).* I'm a lawyer, not a dealer in soap. How should I know what the name of their factory is?

CONCHA. I thought perhaps your office might be close to it.

THE RICH ONE. A distance I believe of two blocks. Perhaps three. I don't know. What is the difference?

CONCHA. Hilario likes to know these little details. Now let me be sure that I have the details correct. Your name is Mario Galicia, you are a lawyer, and your office is two blocks from the famous soap factory in the city of Torreón.

THE RICH ONE *(easily).* Precisely.

CONCHA *(looking at him thoughtfully).* You know, I have a feeling that Hilario isn't going to believe that.

THE RICH ONE. Why not?

CONCHA. Well, Hilario used to work in that factory and those two blocks must be awfully long blocks.

THE RICH ONE. What do you mean?

CONCHA. Nothing. Only the soap factory is in the town of Gómez Palacio in the state of Durango, while Torreón is in the state of Coahuila . . . three miles away. What part of the south are you from? I want the truth now.

THE RICH ONE *(sullenly)*. Cuernavaca.

CONCHA. And you had to come up here to see a mountain, eh? All the way from Cuernavaca that's fifteen hundred meters above the sea. Pah! We of the north know more about the south than you southerners know about us. And the next time you pretend to come from Torreón, use a Torreón accent. If there is a next time.

THE RICH ONE *(sharply)*. What do you care where I come from, or why I came? I'm here and you're going to shoot me, and that's the end of it.

CONCHA *(laughing softly)*. Shoot you? Yes, we *could* shoot you.

THE RICH ONE. I don't see what all this talk amounts to anyway. They promised me a fine execution when you got back. Well, you're here.

CONCHA. This killing doesn't seem to worry you.

THE RICH ONE. Would my weeping make you more merciful?

CONCHA. It might give us all a good laugh.

THE RICH ONE *(starts to light a cigarette, remembers his manners and offers one to CONCHA)*. Do you want a cigarette?

CONCHA *(startled at this unusual courtesy)*. Why . . . thank you. *(As she takes one.)* Of course you understand I've not got anything against you myself.

THE RICH ONE *(as he lights her cigarette)*. Yes, I realize that. But for a man . . . to die is easy.

CONCHA *(blowing out a puff of smoke)*. Is it?

THE RICH ONE *(stares at her)*. Why not? A bullet through the heart, blackness, and then . . . *(He blows out the match.)*

CONCHA. Precisely. If we shoot you, but we won't. *(She explains the situation as though she slightly regretted it, as between adults, but what can you do with children who get out of control?)* It's Tomasa and the Old One. They've suffered a lot from your kind, and Hilario never would let them play with any of his prisoners, so they've been looking forward to you.

THE RICH ONE *(to whom this idea is very new)*. You mean . . . you mean they want to torture me?

CONCHA. Why not?

THE RICH ONE. But you are women . . . not hardened soldiers.

CONCHA *(more to herself than to him)*. Are we women? Sometimes I wonder.

The Old One who cooks our food . . . she saw her son crucified by men of your kind . . . another one saw her son hunted down by dogs for the sport of it. That doesn't make women, my friend. That makes something worse than the devils in hell.

THE RICH ONE. But I had nothing to do with their sorrows. Why do they want to torture me?

CONCHA. You called Adelita a symbol of the Revolution. Well, you're a symbol to us. You're a symbol of all the hate and horror that the Rich Ones have made for us. There are no men here to tell us what to do. We stand alone. You are merely the victim. That is not our fault.

THE RICH ONE (looking down at his clenched hand). You do not seem very anxious for me to die. You've kept me alive for five days.

CONCHA. We wanted you to look forward to dying. We wanted you to wake up each morning and think, "This is the last time I shall ever see the dawn . . . the last time I shall ever hear a bird sing . . . the last time I shall ever feel the heat of the sun."

THE RICH ONE (laughing harshly to cover a growing fear). Señora, I am not a sentimentalist. My thoughts were quite different, I assure you.

CONCHA. Yes, I know they were, but the women didn't know that. I saw no reason to keep them from enjoying your agony.

THE RICH ONE. You are very wise. Perhaps you know what I was thinking.

CONCHA (softly). Perhaps I do. Perhaps you were thinking, "Today the Federals will be here. Today they will come and save me and capture all of this ammunition." Do you think I don't know a spy when I see one? Aye! Your face of ashes stinks like rotten meat.

THE RICH ONE (blustering). So now I am a spy. What a magnificent imagination you have. I let you capture me, I suppose, and then I send messages out to the Federals to tell them what you are doing. I am guarded night and day but still I find a means to send messages. Señora, I am no fool!

CONCHA (gravely). That's the trouble. For once you are too smart for me. I don't know how you send the messages . . . (She looks up toward the rock where CRICKET is hiding, then back at him.) . . . but you send them just the same.

THE RICH ONE. Since you are so clever, señora . . . suppose you work your brain over that, too.

CONCHA. Adelita had something to do with it. You weren't wasting all that fine talk on her for nothing. First you found out everything you wanted to know from her, the innocent child.

THE RICH ONE. Perhaps I got her to carry my messages for me . . . *(Pauses and adds climactically.)* . . . if I sent them. You see, I admit nothing.

CONCHA. But Adelita isn't foolish enough to carry news from you to the Federals. No, you used her . . . or someone . . . in a way without her knowing it, but how? (THE RICH ONE *laughs.*) You needn't laugh. I'll find out.

THE RICH ONE *(sneering)*. I suppose you women think you can stop the Federals, now you know so well they are coming.

CONCHA. I'll stop them, never fear. They'll be making a nice warm nest for you on the tail of Grandfather Devil.

THE RICH ONE. It has been five days. You are too late to stop them now.

CONCHA *(tossing away her cigarette)*. Then you admit that you are a spy?

THE RICH ONE *(flings out his hand. The sense of the Federals' nearness has overcome his fear of these women.)*. Why not? They are too close now for you to go running to Hilario for help. And if you shot me down here and now, what good would it do? The Federals might make it easier on you if you had a live prisoner to give them. They know I'm here. They'll hunt for me. My dead body won't help you any.

CONCHA. Are you trying to make a bargain with me?

THE RICH ONE. You're smarter than those other women. Come over to the Federals while I'm giving you the chance. *(Walks closer to her.)* I like you. I'm no small change with the Federals, I can tell you. Those soldiers will do as I say.

CONCHA. And if I say no?

THE RICH ONE *(puts his unwounded hand around her throat)*. My fingers are strong. I have only to press a little, and there would be no voice left in your throat to call for help. I would be up the path and away before your women could reach you. And then it would be too late.

CONCHA *(as his fingers start to close, she calls faintly in a strangled voice)*. Cricket!

CRICKET *(straightens behind the rocks and points her gun at THE RICH ONE)*. Drop your hand.

THE RICH ONE *(swings around and stares up at CRICKET, then turns back to*

CONCHA *and speaks with honest admiration).* You are worth two generals, señora.

CONCHA *(looks at him and smiles faintly, then goes to the base of the rock on which* CRICKET *is standing).* Did you hear what we said, Cricket?

CRICKET. Every word.

CONCHA. What do you think?

CRICKET *(looking cautiously at her).* I don't know. What do you think, Concha?

CONCHA *(laughs).* Always the cautious one, our Cricket. She jumps out of danger as easily as her namesake.

THE RICH ONE. It's the Federals who have the money.

CONCHA. Good clothes again . . . good food. The way it used to be.

THE RICH ONE. The little things that women like. Perfume, jewelry, holy medals like this one. *(He pulls the medal that dangles on a cord about his neck out of his shirt and shows it to her.)*

CONCHA *(touching it lightly, then bending forward to kiss it).* To go to Church again. I haven't been to Church in almost a year.

THE RICH ONE. The safety of a sheltered life. The Federals can give you safety.

CONCHA *(shakes her head).* I don't know. Hilario has given me excitement . . . danger. I love danger. A sheltered life doesn't mean very much any more.

THE RICH ONE. But think of how amusing it would be . . . learning to live all over again.

CONCHA. I . . . I don't know what to say.

CRICKET *(still watching* CONCHA). What has happened to you, Concha? I never saw you sway back and forth before . . . like a straw in the wind.

CONCHA. What if I tell you I'm sick of all this . . . of the dirt and the filth, of sleeping on the ground in rain and cold? . . .

CRICKET *(puzzled at this new* CONCHA). But what about Hilario?

CONCHA. Yes, and I'm sick of him, too. Every peso he gets he spends on ammunition.

THE RICH ONE. The Federals know how to spend their money on women.

CRICKET. I saw one of their generals down at the saloon the other night. He was plastered all over with gold like a statue in the Church . . .

THE RICH ONE. This Revolution can't last. Your men are good men, but they need money. And they don't know how to fight. They waste their energy chasing around all over the map trying to keep out of our way. And after the fighting is all over what have you got left but some burned-down houses, and some black clothes for mourning?

CRICKET. He's right, Concha. It's the Federals you see spending money in the saloons. And what have we got against the Rich Ones . . . you and me?

CONCHA. Years ago on the great ranch when my father was foreman for old Don Ramón, there used to be dances and flowers and music. Then Don Ramón died, and the ranch was sold, and the new owner came. I was young and pretty then. (*She looks up at* THE RICH ONE.) Would you think I had ever been young and pretty? (THE RICH ONE *smiles and kisses her hand, but she draws her hand away, seeming not to notice the gesture.*) The new owner thought so. He shot my father when he tried to . . . when he tried to protect me . . .

CRICKET (*interrupting what to her is a very boring recital*). But now his soul's in paradise with the Blessed Angels. He won't be burning in hell like you and me.

CONCHA. I don't know. I don't know what to do. Hilario has been good to me. He trusts me, and so do the women.

CRICKET. Tomasa and the Old One would groan and complain whichever side they were on. They're too old to be living anyway. But you and me, we could find plenty of rich soldiers. There was one Federal with a gold watch, and the prettiest black mustaches.

THE RICH ONE. There's plenty of Federal soldiers who would give three gold watches to slip his arm around Concha's waist.

CONCHA (*laughs sharply*). Three gold watches.

THE RICH ONE. Perhaps four. And plenty of tequila* to drink. No cheap mescal for them.

CONCHA (*almost hysterically*). All right, I'll do it. Let them take Hilario's ammunition. What do I care? I'm tired of this Revolution. I'm tired of fighting. I want to sing again, and dance again . . . dance!

(THE RICH ONE *with a triumphant laugh puts his good arm around*

---

*Tequila is a refined mescal.

her waist and they swing in gay circles while CRICKET *claps her hands; but abruptly* THE RICH ONE *lets go of* CONCHA *and catches his wounded shoulder.* CONCHA *half supports him.)*

THE RICH ONE. I'm all right. If your women make love as well as they dance and shoot . . . *(His light tone ends in a gasp of pain.)*

CONCHA. I forgot. *(She glances right, cautious again.)* The women will be suspicious if we are not careful. I'll have to stall them off. We can't do this too suddenly. We can't have them suspecting anything or they'll blow us all up, too.

THE RICH ONE. I knew you'd see the right thing to do.

CONCHA. We'll have to hold a trial to see which way we are going to kill you, Rich One. *(As he draws back, she adds persuasively.)* That's the only way I can make time. And you, Cricket, you think up just as good ideas as they have. They mustn't suspect anything.

CRICKET *(still delighted at the idea of future wealth)*. You can trust me.

THE RICH ONE. When the Federals arrive, you let me handle them.

CONCHA. Why not? You know them better than I do. *(Puts her hand on his arm.)* You are sure that they will come, aren't you? I won't feel safe until I know that they are climbing that mountain.

THE RICH ONE. Don't worry. They're coming.

CONCHA. Perhaps . . . you should send them another message.

THE RICH ONE. I sent them one this morning. *(He looks up at the sun.)* They should be here in . . . in another hour.

CONCHA. You know, you have courage. I don't think I could have waited as patiently for certain death as you have.

THE RICH ONE. That's the beautiful joke. I knew the Federals were going to save me. There was nothing to be brave about.

CONCHA *(looks at him a moment in contempt)*. I see. *(Jerks her head up and looks at* CRICKET.) Call the women, Cricket.

(CRICKET *goes to the edge of the rock, claps her hands together twice, then beckons with her arm.)*

CONCHA *(to* THE RICH ONE). There's only one thing. Keep Adelita away from them.

THE RICH ONE. Don't let that worry you. She's mine, I picked her out the minute I saw her.

CONCHA (hard for a moment). Did you? (Instantly gay again.) Now remember, Rich One, whatever happens don't get nervous. (She goes down to the fire, as THE OLD ONE enters.)

THE OLD ONE (muttering). So much talking when we could be killing him.

CONCHA. Bring me a bottle of mescal.

THE OLD ONE. Always wanting something new. Never wanting what you've got. (Goes into the cave left.)

CONCHA. You heard me! Get a move on you.

TOMASA (talking to THE BLOND ONE as they enter). I say the ants are better than a maguey* plant.

THE BLOND ONE. There aren't enough ants around here.

TOMASA (pulling a small bottle out of a pocket in her skirt). I've been catching them. I've got enough in here to eat him, and they're hungry, the little darlings!

THE OLD ONE (who has entered with a bottle of mescal, and hands it to CONCHA). Here you are. I've had to hide it in the box of bombs to keep it from these crows.

CONCHA. Salt and lemon, you old fool.

THE OLD ONE (behind the fire). I'm getting them . . . I'm getting them.

TOMASA (inspecting THE RICH ONE as though he were a piece of dried beef). A little honey on the eyelids and under his armpits and these little babies will soon make some pretty holes in him. They're nice large red ants. (As THE RICH ONE, a little sick, shuts his eyes and turns his face away from her.) Look at him, shaking already. He'll be screaming by tomorrow morning, like my son did when the dogs were after him, bless his sweet soul in heaven!

CONCHA (takes lemon and salt from THE OLD ONE and pours a little salt in the palm of her hand, then runs the cut lemon across her tongue, takes a drink from the bottle, and finishes by licking the salt from her palm† and spitting to one side). Where is Adelita?

ADELITA (coming forward out of the shadows to the right). Here I am, Concha.

---

*Maguey is a type of cactus found extensively in Mexico. It grows exceedingly fast—three feet in a night. The sap of the maguey is used as an inebriating drink, called mescal.

†This is the traditional Mexican method of drinking mescal.

CONCHA. Stand here beside me. *(She looks at the women who are spread out in front of the mouth of the cave, all but* CRICKET, *who is on the sentry rock.)* Women, we have to do with the death of a Rich One.

(There is a general unrest here, not so much of nervousness as hidden excitement.)

CRICKET *(enjoying this).* May he roast in the devil's own mouth!

CONCHA. Silence! You, Cricket, watch the trail for Maria. The moment you see her coming, tell me.

(This startles THE RICH ONE. *He looks up at* CRICKET *then at* CONCHA *and then back to* CRICKET *again. He knows that these women are no more to be trusted than mad dogs.)*

CRICKET. I have as much right to say how he will die as any of the rest of you. After all, I saw him first.

THE BLOND ONE. Look out, Cricket. Somebody will win the lottery ahead of you.

*(*THE BLOND ONE, TOMASA, *and* THE OLD ONE *laugh loudly.)*

CONCHA *(sharply).* You heard me. Watch the trail.

CRICKET. When the time comes, may I tie him up?

CONCHA. Yes, if you want to.

CRICKET *(to* THE BLOND ONE). Chew that in your gullet, you blond daughter of a seasick spider.

CONCHA *(as* THE BLOND ONE *snatches up a stone to throw at* CRICKET). To your place, you blond fool! (CRICKET *laughs and disappears up the trail.)* Now remember, you will talk one at a time as I call your names. And the first two that get into a fight I will beat until they can't stand up. You, first, Old One.

THE OLD ONE *(moves to center).* I say nail him to a tree, like his kind nailed my boy, and then let me slit his stomach from side to side . . .

CONCHA. Remember that, Adelita. *(Turns her face slightly toward* THE RICH ONE.) One, to crucify him.—Oh, Rich One, you may sit down.

THE RICH ONE *(who is beginning to grow more nervous).* Thank you, señora. *(He sits down, all the women staring at him.)*

CONCHA. And now you, Blondie.

THE BLOND ONE. I say the cactus plant. We have lots of maguey around here. They grow three feet in the night if you put a little water in the roots. Why the sharp point will grow right through that nervous, white heart of his.*

CONCHA. Adelita, the second is the maguey plant.

(ADELITA *is drawing slowly away from the circle toward* THE RICH ONE.)

TOMASA. It's my time to speak and I say the ants, the red ants eating through his flesh. I have them right here waiting for him . . . hungry for him, the little darlings. *(Flourishes her bottle.)*

CONCHA. And the third, Adelita, is the little red ant.

THE OLD ONE. What do you say, Concha?

CONCHA. I am the judge here, and my thoughts do not matter.

THE BLOND ONE. We've all spoken, haven't we? Which way do we finish him off?

(THE RICH ONE, *his eyes fastened on* CONCHA, *half rises to his feet, then sinks back down again, slipping* CRICKET'S *mirror from his pocket. He runs his hand over it again and again as though trying to shine its surface, while pretending to shape his mustache.)*

CONCHA. Adelita hasn't spoken.

THE BLOND ONE. What does the baby say about her pretty Rich One?

ADELITA *(moving forward).* I say you are animals, all of you . . . worse than animals. All you can think of are terrible things . . . things you shouldn't think about . . . devil's things!

TOMASA *(whining).* You shut her up, Concha. She's got no right to talk like that.

CONCHA. She's got as much right as any of the rest of us. Leave her alone. I want to hear what she has to say.

ADELITA. You are making something ugly and horrible out of the Revolution. And it isn't ugly . . . it's beautiful! What if the Rich Ones did kill your son, Tomasa? Will killing him bring your son back to life? Will the wrong they did to your son, you Old One, be made right if you do the same to him? I don't know what you're all thinking about. It isn't human . . . it isn't the Tomasa and the Blondie and the Old One and

---

*Death by maguey was a common mode of execution during the Revolution. The prisoner would be spread-eagled above the plant, and his body would be left as an example to the enemy.

the Concha that I have always known. And Cricket up there looking forward to tying him up! Oh, you are horrible, horrible!

THE BLOND ONE. You don't know what you're talking about. Why shouldn't we hate him and his breed? They took my man, didn't they, and hung him from the door of his own house. And Maria. How about Maria? They made her stand and watch while they tore her man's eyes out, didn't they? We can't do anything to them that's worse than what they've done to us! We're human, aren't we?

ADELITA. But that's over . . . that's finished. Nothing we do now can change that. Because they were brutes and animals, does that make us brutes and animals, too?

CONCHA. Adelita! Come here, child.

ADELITA. I don't want to touch you. I don't want to touch any of you. You're not the women I used to know . . . you're not the women who used to carry me around on your backs when my mother died. You've changed, all of you, horribly changed! Why, you're just like you're dead to me. All of the goodness and sweetness that used to be in you . . . it's dead! *(Crouches on the ground, crying bitterly.)*

TOMASA. This is the Revolution, not a nursery.

ADELITA. What do you know about the Revolution? It's beautiful, it's glorious, it's heroic. It's giving all you've got to freedom. It's dying with the sun in your face, not being eaten to death by little red ants in a bottle. If this is your Revolution, I don't want to see it . . . I don't want to see it!

CONCHA *(standing)*. Yes, this is the Revolution. We had to forget how to weep, and how to be kind and merciful. We are cruel, because the Revolution is cruel. It must crush out the evil before we can make things good again.

TOMASA. Crush it lower than the earth.

CONCHA. Adelita, Adelita, for you there is tomorrow, but for us there is only yesterday. The Revolution is a fire that flames up and destroys, and we are the fire.

THE BLOND ONE. Burning, burning, let us burn them all.

CONCHA. We are the flame, calling to flame, and we are the earth calling to earth, and we are the tempest blowing across the sky!

THE OLD ONE. Blowing us like dead leaves in the wind.

CONCHA. Your Rich One and his kind have crushed us down to ashes, but we are the spark that has kindled a new, a roaring blaze. If we have learned how to be cruel, he has taught us our lesson. Look at him sitting there, winking at his face in a mirror, Adelita, and we with his death in our hands!

CRICKET *(running down the path)*. I see Maria coming. She's almost at the top of the trail! And below her are men in uniform crawling up the mountain. *(She sees* THE RICH ONE *who is standing now, and quite openly trying to make the sun reflect from his mirror.)* Ay, the Rich One is flirting with the sun again. And what pretty words is he telling you today?

TOMASA. Is he telling you that tomorrow you will be ant's meat? Is that what he has been telling you all the week long?

CONCHA *(slowly)*. A mirror and the sun. A mirror to shine in the sun! *(Snatches it from him.)* So that is how you talked to your friends!

THE RICH ONE *(catching her wrist)*. Silence, you fool. Do you want to spoil everything?

CONCHA. Blondie, bring me . . .

THE BLOND ONE. I can guess what you want. *(She runs into the cave, left.)*

ADELITA. What are you going to do?

CONCHA. I am going to catch some rabbits and use the Rich One for bait!

MARIA *(running in, down the path)*. I got away from them at the foot of the path but they are already climbing it. There are five of them.

CONCHA *(freeing her wrist)*. And this one makes six.

THE RICH ONE. So you thought you would trick me, eh? Well, trick plays to trick. Listen to me, women. She was going to sell you out . . . sell you out to me for the price of three gold watches.

TOMASA. As though we would believe your lying tongue.

THE RICH ONE *(runs up the path to* CRICKET*)*. If you don't believe me, ask the Cricket here.

CRICKET *(frightened)*. I don't know anything. I don't know what he's talking about.

THE RICH ONE. How about the Federal general you wanted . . . the one plastered over with gold . . . like an image in the Church?

CRICKET *(haltingly)*. He's making it up. Out of his head, he's making it up.

THE RICH ONE. You're not women, any of you. You're vultures . . . flying around to see what dead bodies you can pick on.

THE BLOND ONE *(entering from the cave with a bomb in her hands).* Here's the bomb, Concha.*

CONCHA *(not looking at her).* Light the fuse.

THE RICH ONE *(screams).* You're not going to blow me to hell with your bombs.

> *(He tries to run up the path but* TOMASA *and* THE OLD ONE *catch his arms, one on either side. As* TOMASA *drops to her knees, her weight on his wounded arm makes him stop struggling and he drops his head, biting his lips with pain.)*

THE BLOND ONE *(who has been lighting the long fuse with a twig from the fire).* Here is the bomb. *(Hands it to* CONCHA.)

MARIA. You mustn't throw it, Concha. Not you.

TOMASA *(holding out one arm, the other arm still clutching* THE RICH ONE). You belong to us, Concha. We need you. Not you!

MARIA *(running down the path to* CONCHA). What will we do without you? You belong to us!

CONCHA *(laughs sharply).* You throw it, Cricket. You love the Rich Ones and their gold braid.

CRICKET *(screams).* No! Not me! *(Runs down, flings herself on her knees and throws both arms about* CONCHA's *knees.)* I wouldn't have a chance in a landslide. I don't want to die. Not me! I was only fooling. I didn't mean what I said. Please, Concha, not me, please. I don't want to die.

CONCHA. Choose quickly, my friend. Would you rather have Tomasa's red ants eating out your eyes?

> (CRICKET *screams and flings both arms up over her face.)*

ADELITA *(running toward them).* Wait. I will throw it. *(She snatches the bomb from* CONCHA.)

CONCHA *(horrified).* No!

ADELITA *(strikes* CONCHA *with her free arm and knocks her to the ground).* This is the Revolution! The sun will be in my face!

---

*During the Revolution bombs were made of bottles filled with explosives.

(She flings back her head after the triumphant cry and THE RICH ONE, *seeing the path free, gives a desperate pull, dashes past the women and up the path.)*

THE RICH ONE *(screaming to the Federals)*. Back, you fools, back!

ADELITA *(running up the path after him)*. Long live the Revolution! *(There is a stunned silence, then* CONCHA *springs to her feet, jerking herself free from the clutching hands of* CRICKET, *and runs to the path.)*

CONCHA *(screaming)*. Adelita! Adelita! *(As she reaches the great rock the sound of an explosion* stops her. She stops as though frozen, and there is a silence, followed by the awful sound of a landslide. As the echoes die away she turns dully, and looks down at the women below her.)*

CONCHA. Well, she got to them in time. The ammunition is safe. Aren't you glad? Aren't you happy? Hilario can fight on for the Revolution. You should show how happy you are. You should sing. Yes, sing, you devil's vomit, *sing!*

> If Adelita should go with another,
> If Adelita should leave me all alone . . .

(As the women slowly join in the song, CONCHA *stops singing, and her out-flung arms drop slowly to her side.)*

> I would follow in a boat made of thunder,
> I would follow in a train made of bone.

(The curtains close.)

Production note: The explosion is made by firing a shotgun down a flight of stairs. The landslide is produced by a large trough filled with gravel, which is tilted, slowly at first, then with increasing speed. To this is added the noise of a thunder-sheet.

This Is Villa!

1938

For Bob Nachtmann

The Characters in the Order of Their Appearance

THE PROFESSOR

LOPEZ

FIERRO

PANCHO VILLA

ROSITA

ANTONIO

CARMEN

SCENE: VILLA's headquarters at Ciudad Juárez
TIME: Afternoon in the Spring of 1917

Author's Foreword

This portrait of a general . . . or, if you like . . . this portrait of a sentimental man is not drawn from the idea of Villa that is so popular in the United States.

That he was a murderer and a looter of homes I cannot deny. That he was a military genius no one can deny. But for some reason people seem to forget that there was another facet to his character which did much to shape the course of his life.

The most important thing about Villa was that he came from the people, and the Mexican peasant, due, I think, to his close association with the ground and the simplicity of life, retains until death an essential childlike quality that no amount of adult problems can ever eradicate.

It is this very essential childlikeness . . . not childishness . . . that people forget when thinking about Pancho Villa. There is no man in the history of the Mexican people who so clearly represents both the best and the worst qualities of the race than does this moon-faced man with the yellow eyes of a jungle cat.

Scene

VILLA's *headquarters at Ciudad Juárez in the Spring of 1917. The room has whitewashed walls, dirty and peeling, that are pierced by an iron-barred window at the center back, a door leading directly outside on the right, and another door leading into a bedroom on the left. Pushed back between the window and the left wall is an army cot, covered with an old Mexican woolen blanket. A little to the right of center is a table surrounded by boxes and one chair. Near the bedroom door is a box turned up on one end. Only the most brilliant imagination could see this room as anything but what it is: a bare enclosed desolation, not scrupulously clean.*

When the curtains part a large stout man is rolled up on the cot, his face turned to the wall, his hat over his head, asleep. Through the door comes THE PROFESSOR *who is on his way to the table to get the pipe that he had left there that morning. He looks what he obviously is: a Mexican gentleman of letters from the top of his neat head to the bottom of his neatly polished shoes. A dried-up shell of a man, of indeterminate age between thirty-five and fifty, with his pince-nez balanced delicately on his thin, ascetic nose. Here is a philosopher who rarely exhibits emotions, and translates every human act into the reasons that caused it, out of which he evolves a logic of the idea which excludes reality.*

As he picks up the pipe he sees the sleeping man. Slowly and cautiously he goes to the foot of the bed and stares down at him. Like a tempest caught out of chaos, hatred wells up in him. His clenched hands raise, then he relaxes, weary from the unfamiliar display of emotion, and turns back to the table as LOPEZ *and* FIERRO *enter from the back room.*

LOPEZ *is a small, delicate man with the manners of a rat. He has all of a rodent's characteristics: the slyness, the nervous twitching of the face, the cupidity of a small animal. He is deceptive in that he does possess a certain amount of courage, brought out through his desire for money, which is greater than his fear.* FIERRO, *the man of iron, is the devil of the Revolution. His emotions, if they exist at all, are purely primitive. He eats, he sleeps, he drinks, he wants a woman. The major urge of his life is centered on solely one thing: to kill. Neither mercy nor justice were ever seeds in his soul.*

All of the men are dressed in high laced boots, khaki trousers and shirts, brilliant bandanas are tied about the throats of the men on the couch, FIERRO *and* LOPEZ. THE PROFESSOR *wears a neat black string tie.* FIERRO *and* LOPEZ *wear large straw hats well pushed back on their heads.* THE PROFESSOR *is hatless. The hat covering the face of the sleeping man is a stiff-brimmed Texan.*

THE PROFESSOR *after a brief disinterested glance at the two men, goes to the outer door.*

FIERRO *(suddenly and suspiciously).* What were you doing over by Villa?
PROFESSOR *(casually).* Looking at him. Just looking at him.
FIERRO. He doesn't like to be watched while he's sleeping.
LOPEZ *(with a nervous giggle).* A knife is easier to push into a sleeping man, eh?
PROFESSOR *(with a faint tinge of sarcasm).* Do you think I want to put a knife in Villa?
FIERRO *(slowly).* I don't know.
LOPEZ *(picking up a pack of cards from the table and shuffling them between his hands).* Death lives in your mind, Fierro. Forget it, forget it. Come and play the cards with me.
FIERRO *(moving toward the table and putting his foot up on the box seat).* You owe me money now. *(He takes the cards from* LOPEZ *and gives them an extra shuffle.)*
LOPEZ *(wetting his mouth with an eager tongue).* Ten pesos. You cut about a five.
  *(*FIERRO, *without looking at the cards, cuts them and extends one pack.)*
LOPEZ *(irritably).* You have the luck of your father, the devil.

FIERRO *(smiling slightly).* Then why do you play with me? *(Flings down a card).* Five pesos that your next card is above a seven.

LOPEZ *(draws a card from the extended pack. They both lean forward to look at it, and* FIERRO *laughs, then draws the bet money toward himself.).* May you roast in the devil's own mouth! *(He stalks sulkily across the room and sits down on the upturned box near the door.)*

FIERRO *(softly).* Children must weep in corners.

LOPEZ *(sullenly).* Your voice is as greasy as your face.

FIERRO *(his own hand on his gun, takes a step forward).* So, my little one? And you the son of a pink-nosed rat?

PROFESSOR. Love follows the unlucky, Fierro.

> *(Outside the window a soldier is singing the doleful chant of the northern soldiers, the "Valentina.")*

SOLDIER *(outside).*

> Valentina, Valentina.
> Oh why do you act like the rest?
> If Fate says I die tomorrow,
> Let them kill me and finish the jest.
> If I should drink down tequila
> I should still keep my head;
> For if they kill me tomorrow
> Then I would die and be dead.

LOPEZ *(laughs sneeringly).* Even the singer knows the truth of that . . .

> *(His voice is cut by silence as* FIERRO, *his eyes liquid with hate, jerks out his gun. Seeking an escape in action from the frustrated anger in his body, he springs across the room and shoots through the window. There is a cry of pain outside, followed by silence. Startled into wakefulness the man on the couch lets out a roar like a bull in agony and swings to his feet. He is a medium-sized man who gives the impression of tremendous height and strength. His round moon-face is gentle and soft; it is the eyes that are cruel. He has a strength in him that is above normal strength, not so much of the body but of the spirit. This is, of course,* PANCHO VILLA. *Half child, half cruel savage, quick to cry, quick to anger, no one knows from one moment to the next what the humor of the Chief may*

be. Philosopher, military genius, almost illiterate, he resembles nothing so much as the desert cactus, which possesses life in its sap for the wanderer dying of thirst, and festering death in its stinging nettles.)

VILLA. By the roar of God! Can a man not sleep in his own bed?

PROFESSOR *(mildly)*. I am afraid our little man of iron has lost his temper again.

VILLA *(stamping over to the window and peering outside)*. Eh, who did you shoot this time? *(Recognizing the man.)* So . . . the holder of horses. Luckily for you, Fierro, he wasn't one of my best soldiers.

PROFESSOR *(slowly)*. Even a holder of horses can desire to live.

VILLA. The Professor is whistling words again. What is your melody this time, my little one?

PROFESSOR. I was talking to God, but I don't think He heard me.

VILLA. Perhaps it is as well that I am deaf also. *(Turns to LOPEZ.)* Go and find out if the fool is dead. If he is, send fifty pesos to his widow.

LOPEZ. Yes, Chief. *(He starts out through the bedroom door, when VILLA stops him.)*

VILLA. Make it a hundred and get the money from Fierro.

FIERRO *(stubbornly)*. I won't pay it, Chief.

VILLA *(flatly)*. You'll do as I say. We must be polite in these affairs.

PROFESSOR. Do not grieve, Fierro. Perhaps the man isn't married.

VILLA. Of course he's married. *(Jerks his thumb at LOPEZ.)* I told you to get out, didn't I?

LOPEZ *(hastily)*. Yes, Chief. *(He goes into the bedroom.)*

VILLA *(as though he had never been interrupted, turns back to THE PROFESSOR)*. All my men are married. Even the young Antonio takes a bride today. It puts more guts into a man's fighting to know he's got a woman behind him.

PROFESSOR. Yes. The human animal protecting the home . . . the butcher making sure there are more calves to kill.

VILLA *(to FIERRO)*. There he goes, spouting wind again. And he as thin as a cactus thorn. By rights he ought to be puffed out as large as an Easter Judas.

LOPEZ *(through the window)*. This eater of cow's meat is still living, Chief. Fierro only broke his shoulder for him.

VILLA (*to* FIERRO). You're a menace to the Revolution. From the number of my men you shoot any one would think you were a liver-breasted Federal spy.

PROFESSOR. Perhaps he nourishes the great dream of ending the Revolution by getting rid of all the fighting men. (*Shrugs.*) Fierro isn't married. He has no home to protect.

> (*Through the bedroom door comes* ROSITA. *She is a luscious creature of soft delicate curves that are very evident beneath her loose red muslin skirt and white low-cut blouse. Wrapped around her shoulders is a long, narrow, fringed shawl of bright green. She is said to be the only living thing who isn't afraid of* FIERRO. *In some ways as cruel as he is, she is like a beautiful cat ready to spring at anyone who might show the slightest inclination to harm her. Her chief delight is herself, and her chief interest is whatever she most particularly wants at the moment.*)

ROSITA (*lounging into the room, hands buckled on her hips*). Perhaps no woman would have him.

VILLA. Why not? He has a pretty face.

ROSITA. He smells like a dead man.

FIERRO (*furiously*). Your fine tastes don't keep you from taking my money.

ROSITA (*shrugging*). Your money is as good as the next man's. And I wanted some blue silk stockings.

VILLA (*shouting with laughter*). Did she kiss you for it?

ROSITA. I let him hold my hand for it. Two little fingers.

VILLA (*suddenly angry*). You flirt with another man, eh? And you my woman! (*He gives her a shove in the face, which knocks her to the ground. With a cry like a cat, she comes to her feet, a knife gleaming in her hand.* THE PROFESSOR *catches her arm up her back and twists her wrist, forcing her to drop the knife which he returns to her with a bow.*)

PROFESSOR. You dropped this, Rosita.

ROSITA (*thrusts the dagger into her skirt band while she mutters to* VILLA). Some day I'll cut out your heart and serve it to you in red pepper sauce.

VILLA (*takes out a large bandana and mops his forehead*). Thank you, friend Professor. A she-leopard is worse than the Devil's stepmother. (*Goes to* THE PROFESSOR *and shakes the man's hand vigorously. When it is released,* THE PROFESSOR *holds that hand away from him stiffly, the fingers outspread. Not noticing this,* VILLA *turns to* ROSITA.) I give you permission to sit on his lap. But no kisses!

 (ROSITA *insolently turns her head to one side and spits.* VILLA *raises his hand to strike her, and she reaches quickly for her dagger. They are poised thus, deadlocked, when* LOPEZ *sticks his head through the front door.*)

LOPEZ. Eh, Chief, you ought to see Antonio in a hat . . . a new red hat!

 (*With loud laughter* VILLA *rushes out, with* ROSITA *close at his heels.* THE PROFESSOR, *his back to* FIERRO *who is playing a disinterested game of solitaire, looks down at his stiffly held right hand. For a moment he stares at it as though it were possessed by some other man, then he draws a handkerchief from his pocket and wipes it off with loathing. There are shouts of laughter from outside.* VILLA *re-enters, pushing in front of him a slender tall boy of twenty-two, dressed like the others in khaki, but instead of a straw or Texan hat he carries a bright red felt sombrero in his hands. This is* ANTONIO, *youngest of* VILLA's *personal staff. Honest, loyal, affectionate, and simplicity itself,* ANTONIO *has no place in the chaos of Revolution.*)

VILLA (*shouting jovially*). Behold, Professor! As fine a cock as ever crowed on a summer morning. (*Slapping* ANTONIO *on the back.*) Turn around, rooster, and flap your wings for us.

 (LOPEZ *and* ROSITA *have crowded into the room behind them.*)

LOPEZ. Put on your hat, bridegroom. Show us all your glory.

 (ANTONIO, *embarrassed but grinning good naturedly, puts on his hat at a gay angle and agreeably turns around so that they can look at him.* VILLA *is taking as much delight in the proceedings as though it were he, himself, who was showing off.*)

VILLA. By the five wounds, that is a magnificent hat!

ANTONIO (*proudly*). As magnificent a hat as a man was ever to be married in.

VILLA (*eagerly*). Let me put it on.

 (ANTONIO *passes it over to him, and* VILLA *puts it on.*)

LOPEZ. By God, Chief, it gives you a pretty look.

VILLA (*cocking his head as he tries to get a look at it on his own head*). As fine a hat as any in the Republic. Villa says it. (*He looks pleasingly at* ANTONIO.) Fine enough for a chief, eh, Antonio?

This Is Villa! | 199

ANTONIO (*embarrassed*). But I bought it for my wedding, Chief.

VILLA (*slowly taking it off and looking down at it in disappointment as he says childishly*). But I like the hat, Antonio.

ANTONIO (*nervously*). Even my horse Chato is yours, Chief. But my hat . . . three months I saved to buy that hat for my wedding. Please, Chief . . .

PROFESSOR (*dryly*). Weddings are for the giving of gifts. Not the receiving of them.

VILLA (*brightening a little*). True words, scholar. What a dropper of wisdom we have here. (*He puts the hat back on his head, sighs, takes it off, and reluctantly hands it back to* ANTONIO, *who grins shyly at him. Suddenly, with one of his inexplicable changes of mood,* VILLA *shouts with laughter and gives the boy a hearty slap on the back.*) St. Mary, St. Peter, and St. Paul, am I not Villa? Are there not a thousand red hats begging the honor of sitting on my head? Answer me that!

LOPEZ (*with a sigh of relief*). True words, Chief.

VILLA. Gifts for a wedding, is it? I'll give you a gift, little Antonio. Chew out your heart for me.

ANTONIO (*slowly*). There's only one thing I want, Chief but it's too grand a gift for this Antonio.

VILLA (*grandly*). Is it to be found in the three Americas?

ANTONIO. Ay, yes, Chief. It is only a little gift . . .

VILLA. Are you not Villa's friend? Does that not mean that if you want a mountain, St. Gabriel himself will carve one out of air for you?

ANTONIO. Nothing so grand as a mountain, Chief. I only want . . . (*He pauses and takes a deep breath.*)

VILLA. Speak up. Speak up!

ANTONIO (*hastily, before his courage deserts him*). Only your gun, Chief. (*Everybody except* VILLA *stares at the boy in consternation at his audacity.* VILLA, *however, lets out a roar of laughter and slaps his thigh.*)

VILLA. My gun, is it. There's a man talking here, and not a calf bawling for its mother's milk! (*He gives* ANTONIO *his gun, who takes it as though it were as fragile as a butterfly's wing.*) You know how to ask for a soldier's gift.

FIERRO (*with awe*). By the roar of God, Antonio! You're the only man who has ever unarmed Pancho Villa!

(*As though by magic,* VILLA *is transformed into a crouching tiger. He springs back under the window, his body bent forward, his hands low on his hips.*)

VILLA (*staccato sharp*). Give me a gun! (FIERRO *starts to draw his, but* VILLA's *snarl stops him.*) Your hands on your shoulders, Fierro!

ROSITA (*softly*). I'll bring you one.

VILLA. Throw Lopez's gun on the floor between us.

(*The tension is high in the room as she obeys the command. As* VILLA's *hand closes on the butt, not a person in the room knows whether he will live to draw one more breath. Then* VILLA *spins it in his fingers and drops it into his holster, and there is a gasping sigh of relief.*)

ANTONIO (*in an agony of horror*). The gift was too high. (*He extends the gun to* VILLA.) Take it back, Chief. Please.

VILLA (*once more easily in command, switches his mood back to gay camaraderie. Coming forward, he catches* ANTONIO's *shoulder.*). Villa never takes back a gift once given. And now, show me the bride.

ANTONIO (*his hands caressing the gun with delight*). It's beautiful, Chief, beautiful.

VILLA (*irritably*). Enough of the gun. Where is the bride?

ANTONIO. I told her to go around to the back. She's waiting in there. (*He nods toward the bedroom.*)

VILLA. Then we must steal a look at her. (*He turns to the door, then turns back, speaking almost humbly.*) Antonio, can I wear the hat, just until the wedding, eh?

ANTONIO (*hands it to him with a grin*). Until the wedding, Chief . . . it is yours.

VILLA (*laughing delightedly as a child, puts it on, thrusts his arm through* ANTONIO's *and starts toward the bedroom*). Come along all of you. Rosita, Lopez, Professor . . . even you, Fierro. We do honor to the bride, today.

(*They press forward into the back room. As* LOPEZ *passes him,* THE PROFESSOR *catches his arm and stops him.*)

PROFESSOR (*softly*). We saw history made just now, Lopez.

LOPEZ (*wiping his forehead with his handkerchief*). His eyes turned yellow.

Did you see them? I thought he was going to kill all of us . . . even the young Antonio.

PROFESSOR. He can't even trust his own men. A jungle cat he is, surrounded by jungle cats.

LOPEZ. I said three prayers. I didn't know I knew that many.

PROFESSOR. That boy unarmed him. We must remember that.

LOPEZ (*with a frightened look at the door*). Watch your tongue. Fierro has the ears of a nighthawk.

PROFESSOR (*softly*). Fierro is as fickle as a woman, and gold is a sweet lover.

LOPEZ. Eh, but me, I believe in safety. You lack caution.

PROFESSOR (*sternly*). The time for caution is past.

LOPEZ. I love my neck . . . and the man who kills Villa will not live long with these vultures tearing him to pieces.

PROFESSOR. Tearing Antonio to pieces. We are safe. Who would suspect us?

LOPEZ. You are a fool. Antonio loves Villa. He would rather kill himself.

PROFESSOR (*dryly*). Antonio has a bride, and Villa loves women. All women, especially the young ones. He won't be able to stay away from this delicate bird. And Antonio loves his bride better than Villa. If we have patience things will arrange themselves . . . (*Looking over* LOPEZ's *shoulder he says in a loud pleasant voice as he catches* LOPEZ's *arm significantly.*) Why should I lend you money? You would only lose it to Fierro in a card game. Better to give it to Fierro at once and be done with it.

(VILLA *comes into the room, the red hat on the back of his head, pushing* CARMEN *in front of him. Behind them come the others:* ANTONIO *smiling in bashful pride,* ROSITA *sulky at another woman's greater importance,* FIERRO *half amused as usual.* CARMEN, *her rebozo [the traditional Mexican shawl] draped over her head, is a shy sweet child who is very much afraid of this strange company, and only her deep love for* ANTONIO *gives her the courage to stay there.*)

VILLA (*jovially*). The Professor is too fine a gentleman to go and look at a woman, so we must bring the woman to look at him. What do you think of the bride, Professor?

PROFESSOR (*making a light bow*). This house is honored, señorita.

VILLA. Is that not a fine speech, Carmen? Burn with red jealousy, Rosita. He never called you by a title.

ROSITA *(snapping at him).* I never asked him to.

VILLA. Neither did Carmen, eh? Stand beside her, Antonio. Let me see you together. Here, put on your hat. *(Hands it to him, then playfully half jerks it back.)* Remember, it is mine until the wedding.

ANTONIO *(grinning shyly).* True words, Chief.

VILLA. Eh, I get a softness in my stomach when I look at you. What a grand thing marriage is. Me, I believe in it. It costs nothing, and it makes the women happier. All good Christians should marry and raise little soldiers for Villa, eh, Professor?

PROFESSOR *(coldly).* And raise little soldiers for the Republic.

VILLA *(striking out with anger).* Villa is the Republic! *(He laughs suddenly and loudly.)* To the first man-child I personally will stand godfather. Is that not a fine gift, Antonio?

ANTONIO *(almost with awe).* Do you hear that Carmen? The great Villa will be godfather to our son.

(CARMEN *draws her shawl across her face in sudden shyness.*)

ROSITA *(laughing tauntingly).* May I sleep in the devil's nose! She's a modest wench!

(ANTONIO *angrily steps between* ROSITA *and* CARMEN *who has drawn back. With a snarl* VILLA *turns on* ROSITA *and gives her a loud slap. Fingers curved, she springs on him, a low growl in her throat.* FIERRO *tears her off of him, half lifting her in the air, at which she starts to kick and bite. It is all he can do to hold her.*)

ROSITA *(screaming).* You eater of cow's meat . . . you pig with a fly in your snout . . . you son of three thousand black goats . . .

VILLA *(shouting above her curses).* Take her out of here.

(FIERRO *half carries, half drags her out, she fighting all the way.* LOPEZ, *unable to resist the excitement, follows them to the door. The noise of the struggle continues on the outside, as* VILLA *turns to* CARMEN.)

VILLA *(pleased).* She's jealous, that one. But her heart is as tender as a young calf's liver.

LOPEZ *(turning with delighted excitement).* She is sitting on Fierro's stomach and biting his ear for him. *(There are sudden shouts outside.)* Their fighting has frightened your Chato, Antonio. He has broken his halter. You'd better ride after him, quickly.

ANTONIO *(crying out).* Chato! *(He runs out of the room followed by* LOPEZ *and* THE PROFESSOR.*)*

> *(*CARMEN, *frightened, draws back closer to the wall.* VILLA *has passed her and nearly reached the door, when he pauses and turns to look at her. Very thoughtfully he examines her, then he rubs the back of his hand across his mouth and goes slowly up to her.)*

VILLA *(softly).* This Antonio of mine has a pretty taste in women.

> *(*CARMEN *turns as helplessly as a bird caught in a cage. Seeing the bedroom door she starts toward it when* VILLA, *with a quick movement, catches her wrist.)*

VILLA. Come, little bird. Tell your grandchildren Villa kissed you.

> *(He catches her in a bear's hug. She sinks her teeth, her only weapon, in his shoulder. With an exclamation of pain, he flings her from him. As she falls back her head hits the iron bar of the cot, and she falls in a crumpled heap to the floor.)*

VILLA *(nursing his shoulder).* I give your husband my gun, and his wife can't even give me a kiss. Is that gratitude, I ask you? *(When she does not move in answer he goes over to her and pokes her with his foot.)* Stand up, fledgling. I'm a rough, wild man, but I'd not harm a bird. *(She still does not move and he bends over her.)* See, I'm as harmless as a small black goat. We'll not tell Antonio I frightened you, eh, or he might take back his red hat.

> *(Something about the small limp figure makes him take a closer look at her. Fright shines for a moment in his face, as he realizes that the hand touching her head is covered with blood. He feels for the pulse in her wrist and, still not satisfied, puts his palm against her mouth. When no breath fans his fingers, he draws slowly back and up to his feet, gazing at her horrified.* FIERRO, *coming into the room, pauses before this strange spectacle, his sentence arrested in his mouth.)*

FIERRO. That Chato is a wild horse. Antonio has had to ride into the fields after . . . eh, do ghosts walk in this hut, Chief?

> *(*VILLA *looks at him wordlessly, then back to the still figure.* FIERRO *comes farther into the room and looks down at her. His eyes travel back to* VILLA.*)*

VILLA (*nervously*). I had no hand in it. She hit her head against the iron of the cot. She fell.

FIERRO (*thoughtfully*). She fell . . . from a little push, eh?

VILLA. I only poked at her.

FIERRO. You pushed another woman and I got scratched for it.

VILLA (*irritably*). This is no time for ass's ears. Put wisdom in your mouth!

FIERRO (*shrugs*). She was Antonio's woman, not mine. If he wants to kill you for it, that's his affair. (*He takes a cigarette from behind his ear and lights it.*)

VILLA (*startled at first, and then with certainty*). He will not try to kill me. The little rooster is my friend.

FIERRO (*with a curt gesture toward* CARMEN). So were you his friend.

VILLA (*turning away*). Take her out of here!

FIERRO. I've taken one woman out of here today. Call Lopez to do it, or the Professor . . . (*Adding as though it were a curse.*) . . . that fine gentleman.

VILLA (*knowing* FIERRO *too well to argue with him, shrugs, goes to the door, and calls*). Lopez! Bring the Professor in here with you. (*He turns back to* FIERRO.) Throw away that cigarette!

FIERRO. Why? Perhaps it's my candle for the dead.

VILLA (*not fully comprehending what has happened*). She's dead. And I never heard her speak. Silent she was, like a baby bird. I called her a bird. I didn't know she was dead.

FIERRO (*leaning forward and staring intently at her*). I wonder what she sees out there in the darkness. Every time I've killed a man I've wondered that. (*Like a shot of fire across his face, his cynical smile comes back to his mouth.*) Some day I'll know. I am a man of infinite patience.

(LOPEZ, *followed by* THE PROFESSOR, *enters.*)

LOPEZ. That Chato has been nervous all day. Antonio should have used a stronger rope on him.

PROFESSOR (*dryly*). Perhaps that horse knew he had lost his master's heart to a weaker rival.

FIERRO. The little bride has found a stronger lover.

(LOPEZ, *catching sight of the body, stops so abruptly that* THE PROFESSOR *nearly falls over him.*)

PROFESSOR. You clumsy . . . *(He, too, sees the body. For a moment there is silence, then, almost as though he had expected to find her so, he walks silently forward and arranges her rebozo across her face.)* She has a happy look.

FIERRO. She is more fortunate than Antonio. I was just wondering who was going to break the news to him.

VILLA *(in a strained voice).* Take her out of here.

FIERRO *(softly).* Are you going to tell him, Chief? *(The situation seems to provide him with diabolic laughter.)* How proud he'll be riding back as conqueror of the runaway Chato with his red hat on the back of his head. He'll be expecting a woman's praise, and a flash of pride in her eyes. He'll want her to smile at him. He'll want her silence to blossom into speech that will tell him what a great deed he has accomplished . . .

> (VILLA, *in voiceless rage, snatches his gun out of his holster and points it at* FIERRO, *who comes smoothly to his feet, his own hand on his gun.* THE PROFESSOR *catches* VILLA'S *arm, forcing the gun to point to the floor. Into this silence comes the shout of men's voices outside.)*

VOICES. Viva, Antonio! Viva! Was it a great chase, Antonio? The horse fears the bride, Antonio! Who would want a jealous horse? Ay-yay!

PROFESSOR *(quietly).* I'll tell him.

FIERRO. You have pretty phrases behind your teeth.

VILLA. Tell him I didn't mean to do it. I didn't know she was dead. She fell and . . . she'd never spoken to me. Not one word.

PROFESSOR. Take her out, Lopez.

> (LOPEZ, *with a nervous glace at the three men, picks her up as though she were a doll and carries her into the bedroom.)*

FIERRO. It is good luck to go out by the same door through which one enters. *(At the bedroom door he pauses.)* After you, Chief. You are the first mourner until Antonio comes.

VILLA *(slowly, to FIERRO).* Sometimes I think you want to die. *(He goes into the bedroom.)*

FIERRO *(lounging in the doorway, looks thoughtfully at THE PROFESSOR).* I've never killed a man with words. It must be an amusing sight.

> (*Just now* ANTONIO, *a bright eager look on his face, comes through the outer door. Seeing only* THE PROFESSOR *and* FIERRO, *his face lengthens in disappointment.)*

ANTONIO (*shyly*). Your pardon, Professor. I thought to find Carmen here.

FIERRO. She didn't like us, so she went away. Didn't she, Professor?

ANTONIO (*puzzled*). Went away? But she had no place to go. (*Relaxing with a grin at* FIERRO.) How you tease a man. (*Bending suddenly, he looks under the iron cot.*) Carmen! (*Not finding her, he rises, murmuring in shamefaced explanation.*) We play a little game. She likes to hide from me.

FIERRO. This time she has found an excellent hiding place.

PROFESSOR (*with revulsion*). Get out of here!

FIERRO (*in mock dismay*). I was only trying to help you, Professor.

PROFESSOR. I've heard the legend that you are Grandfather Devil reborn to taunt the souls of men. And it is a legend. The Devil is not so foul.

FIERRO (*slowly*). Live tongues wag easier than dead ones, friend Professor. (*He turns and goes into the bedroom.*)

ANTONIO. You shouldn't quarrel with Fierro, Professor. He has a hasty temper.

PROFESSOR. I doubt if he knows what it means to get angry. Sit down, Antonio.

ANTONIO. Thank you, sir. I have to go and find Carmen. She's very young and strange people frighten her.

PROFESSOR. She isn't frightened now, and she won't mind waiting. I want to talk to you.

ANTONIO. Yes, sir, but I can only stay one little moment. (*He sits nervously on the edge of a chair.*) What did you mean, Professor, that Fierro never gets angry?

PROFESSOR. Well, Antonio, some men want to die. Since they are too cowardly to kill themselves, they go about taunting other people into murder. It's a form of suicide. Do you have a match?

ANTONIO (*passing over a box of matches*). You know, Professor, you're wiser than I, and you've had learning out of books, but I think you're wrong about Fierro.

PROFESSOR. Eh, so?

ANTONIO. Yes, sir. You see, he loves Rosita and she hates him. Well, I know how I'd feel if Carmen hated me. But then you've never been in love, Professor. You wouldn't understand.

PROFESSOR. You're wrong, Antonio. I am in love.

ANTONIO *(interested but surprised)*. You are, Professor?

PROFESSOR. With the most beautiful, flamboyant of all creatures. Her eyes and her hair are as black as Popo in eruption. Her blood sings with the music of a peasant's heart. Her body is as graceful as banana fronds. And when I think of her I can see her face alive with the same wild freedom that it had before the Spaniards conquered her.

ANTONIO *(puzzled)*. Spaniards, Professor? But we are fighting Federals, not Spaniards.

PROFESSOR *(intently)*. Antonio, how would you feel if some man took your Carmen's throat in his hands and slowly choked the life out of her body?

ANTONIO *(who is beginning to think* THE PROFESSOR *is a little mad)*. Why, I would kill him, señor. Naturally.

PROFESSOR. And yet a man is strangling this woman who means more to you than Carmen ever could.

ANTONIO. No woman means more to me than Carmen, Professor.

PROFESSOR. No? And you call yourself a Mexican?

ANTONIO. I don't understand you.

PROFESSOR. I'm talking of our country, of our beautiful republic, who is having the life crushed out of her by men who are more ambitious for themselves than for her.

ANTONIO *(relieved to find that* THE PROFESSOR *isn't totally insane)*. Oh, yes, Professor. That's why we fight the Federals. And now if you'll excuse me, I'll go and find Carmen. *(He rises and starts toward the bedroom door.)*

PROFESSOR *(quietly)*. You won't find her, Antonio.

ANTONIO *(laughing easily)*. She can never hide so well that I can't find her.

PROFESSOR. You'll find her body, Antonio . . . that's easy enough to find.

ANTONIO *(puzzled)*. Her . . . body?

PROFESSOR. Saints in Heaven, perhaps the quick way is the best way . . .

ANTONIO *(striding to him and catching his arms)*. Spit out the words in your mouth. Where is Carmen?

PROFESSOR *(bluntly)*. She's dead.

> (ANTONIO *draws back from him, his face going blank with disbelief. His hand reaches blindly for a chair and he sinks down on it.)*

ANTONIO *(helplessly)*. Dead?

PROFESSOR *(gently).* Yes, Antonio. Dead.

ANTONIO. No. It's not true . . . when I left she was standing there smiling at me . . . we were going to be married this afternoon. *(He looks pleadingly up at* THE PROFESSOR, *who can not meet his eyes.)*

PROFESSOR. She died, Antonio. She . . . *(Desperately.)* Can't you understand why I'm trying to tell you?

ANTONIO. You mean . . . *(Horror flames in his eyes.)* You mean she was . . . *(He rises.)* Who did it? Who did it?

PROFESSOR *(his voice and outstretched hands trying to quiet the boy).* One moment, boy. One moment . . .

ANTONIO. Was it Fierro? Was it?

PROFESSOR. No, not Fierro.

ANTONIO. Lopez?

PROFESSOR. Do you think Lopez would touch your woman?

ANTONIO *(greater horror dominating him).* You mean . . .

PROFESSOR. Villa, Antonio. Villa did it.

ANTONIO *(half sobbing).* That's a lie. Villa is my friend.

PROFESSOR. He wanted your hat and he took it. He wanted your woman and he took her. He wants your country. Are you going to let him have her, too?

ANTONIO *(dazedly).* Villa . . . Carmen . . . Villa . . . *(With a sudden animal snarl.)* You lie in your mouth!

PROFESSOR. You needn't believe me. Look for yourself . . . she's in there. *(He points to the bedroom. There is silence, and then* ANTONIO, *half against his will, dreading what he knows he will see, drags himself slowly to the door and peers inside.)* And see Villa . . . your good friend . . . kneeling beside her, offering a prayer for her soul. *(As the boy sinks back against him, he leads him to the table and pours out a glass of mescal.)* Drink this mescal. It will pour fire into you.

    *(*ANTONIO *thrusts it violently away and buries his face in his arms.* THE PROFESSOR *looks thoughtfully down at him, then softly closes the bedroom door.)*

ANTONIO. She was so soft . . . so gentle. Why should Villa kill my Carmen?

PROFESSOR. Do you remember that girl in Chihuahua city? Walking along the street with no eyes for anyone, and Villa tried to kiss her. He pushed her under the stamping feet of his horse when she slapped his face for him.

ANTONIO. But Carmen . . .

PROFESSOR. And that pretty child in Saltillo. She fell backwards into a cauldron of scalding water . . . Remember?

ANTONIO. Ay, Blessed Jesus . . .

PROFESSOR. Your Carmen was fortunate. Her head struck the iron of the cot. Life left her gently . . .

ANTONIO. Holy Virgin . . .

PROFESSOR. I know, boy. I know how you feel. For three years now I've had the same pain in my own heart. You feel as though your bones were turning to water, and your skin rotting away from being near such filth.

ANTONIO. Blessed Mary . . .

PROFESSOR. But you're only one man. He's not doing this just to you. It's happening all over the country. Take your pain and multiply it by a thousand, and ten thousand, and a hundred thousand . . . that's the pain beating against Mexican earth this very morning.

ANTONIO. Carmen . . . Carmen . . .

PROFESSOR. Villa trusts you. He thinks you're too simple a fool to kill him for what he's done to you . . . you're the only man in the Republic who can walk up to him with a loaded gun in your hand.

(LOPEZ *enters from the bedroom.*)

LOPEZ (*in a low voice to* THE PROFESSOR). Villa is afraid to come in until he knows you've told Antonio about . . . about her.

PROFESSOR (*shaking* LOPEZ *away*). You're too close to the northern butcher. You haven't seen what is happening in the towns he's captured. He hasn't brought peace . . . he's brought nothing but terror and death and desolation.

(*After a startled, knowing glance at* THE PROFESSOR, LOPEZ *goes around on* ANTONIO's *other side so that the boy, gazing helplessly in front of him, is between two cross fires.*)

LOPEZ. You're the only one who can kill him. The Republic will make a hero of you. All the world will call you a hero. The hero who killed the northern butcher they'll call you.

PROFESSOR. If you could only see what is happening since Villa has become the northern general! Women are not safe in their own homes. Men dare not walk down the street alone at night. Human life doesn't mean anything anymore, and bullets are cheap.

LOPEZ. The Republic will even build a statue to you . . . to all of us, eh, Professor?

PROFESSOR. This afternoon Fierro shot a man because he sang a little song. God knows how many men he kills every day because he loves the feel of a gun in his hand. And Fierro isn't the only one. There are others who take what they want because Villa gives them the power to take it.

(None of them see VILLA *enter from the bedroom. Startled by what he hears, he stands perfectly still, watching them as a jungle animal watches its quarry.)*

LOPEZ. Villa killed your Carmen. Don't forget that. He killed her.

PROFESSOR. It isn't Carmen who matters any longer. It isn't you and Lopez and I who matter now! It's all the men and all the women who have been slaves for two hundred years, and who are having their new freedom ground into their faces by the heel of this butcher.

LOPEZ. He killed your Carmen. He killed your Carmen.

*(*ANTONIO *gives a wailing moan and half collapses.* THE PROFESSOR *pulls him to his feet, shaking him.)*

PROFESSOR. All the fine high dreams of the Revolution are in your hands, now. I'm putting a duty on you, Antonio. You must not fail!

LOPEZ. Do it with his own gun. That will be a fine death for this woman murderer.

PROFESSOR. He's in the bedroom with the body of your girl. You have only to walk in . . . to point the gun . . . to pull the trigger . . .

LOPEZ. Just into the next room, then out the back door to freedom.

PROFESSOR. Only the next room.

VILLA *(quietly)*. Not so far as that, little Antonio.

(At the sound of his voice the men swing around to face him. LOPEZ's *face twitches with terror. As though that particular voice were necessary to put life into his body,* ANTONIO *raises his hand, the gun pointed steadily at* VILLA.)

VILLA *(knowing that one false move will cause his death, speaks quietly as he takes a step forward)*. The northern butcher these squeaking mice have called me. Do you believe that, Antonio . . . about your friend?

LOPEZ *(screaming on a high thin note)*. Do it now, you fool!

VILLA. If you believe that . . . do it now, Antonio. *(Still looking at* VILLA, *but defeat in his body,* ANTONIO *slowly drops his gun hand.* VILLA *smiles faintly, then steps away from the bedroom door.)* I put a candle at her head. I left one for you to place at her feet.

> *(*ANTONIO *stumbles to the door. As he passes* VILLA, *he pauses, looking at him as though he'd never seen him before. Villa smiles again and places his hand on the boy's shoulder, but with sudden revulsion* AN-TONIO *shakes it off and walks slowly out.)*

VILLA *(with a shrug)*. The little one has only one fault . . . he is too loyal to his friends. *(Calling abruptly.)* Fierro! *(He smiles at* THE PROFESSOR.) Eh, you have nerves. I can smell them.

> *(*THE PROFESSOR *does not respond to this taunt.* FIERRO *strolls unconcernedly in.* LOPEZ *is held erect through the freezing power of pure fear.)*

VILLA *(gently)*. These baby heroes would save the Republic, Fierro. They would have men whisper with awe: "Here are the heroes who killed the northern butcher."

FIERRO *(without surprise)*. The soldier Gonzalez . . . You remember him, Chief . . . the one with the white patch over his eyes?

VILLA. I remember . . .

FIERRO. He has two gray rats in a cage. If we asked him with politeness, he might lend them to us.

VILLA *(nodding solemnly)*. He might. He has a generous heart, that one.

FIERRO. If we put these rats in a heated iron kettle . . . And if the kettle were tied to the bellies of these pretty heroes . . . I wonder what the rats would do, Chief?

VILLA *(laughing at the jest and slapping his own stomach)*. They'd eat their way out! *(*THE PROFESSOR'S *hand clenches convulsively, but his face does not change.* LOPEZ *topples to the floor in a dead faint. Slowly, as* VILLA *stares at* THE PROFESSOR *with admiration.)* By the tail of Judas . . . it's the soldier who faints! *(Just then there comes the sound of a shot from the next room.* FIERRO *half starts forward, but* VILLA *waves him back.)* Eh, good-bye, Antonio. And that takes courage, too. (*He takes off his hat and gravely crosses himself, then turns to* THE PROFESSOR.) I like courage. A Christian without courage is like a snake without poison . . .

FIERRO (*absently*). True words, Chief. What shall I do with the fragile one? (*He kicks at* LOPEZ.)

VILLA (*dismissing the subject, his eyes fastened on* THE PROFESSOR). Hang him.

FIERRO (*startled at last*). Hang! But I thought . . .

VILLA. Hanging is good enough for cowards.

FIERRO. Just as you say, Chief. (*He jerks his head toward* THE PROFESSOR.) And this one?

VILLA. I think the Professor and I would hold a conversation

FIERRO. Alone?

VILLA (*with simple dignity*). Am I not Villa?

    (FIERRO *shrugs and in a businesslike manner, totally lacking in emotion, drags out the senseless body of* LOPEZ. VILLA *gazes thoughtfully at* THE PROFESSOR, *who grows restive under the direct gaze.*)

PROFESSOR (*slowly*). What do you want to say to me?

VILLA (*scratching his head*). I don't know. Perhaps I wanted to tell you a little story about an Argentine man the Federals sent up here. He offered to kill me for two thousand pesos. Now I ask you, Professor. Is my death not worth more than two thousand pesos?

PROFESSOR (*in a low voice*). It is worth more than all the gold in the Republic.

VILLA. So. And you, my chicken . . . the Federals were going to pay you all the gold in the Republic for putting a bullet in my belly?

PROFESSOR (*sharply*). Lopez is the Federal, not I.

VILLA. Was the Federal, you mean. (*With a shout of laughter.*) Ha! Is it my good friend Carranza who sent you, then . . . or my pal Obregón who loves me more than his own mother? How they would both like to see me frying in the devil's fat?

PROFESSOR. Why must we have so much of speech? Get out your rats, or your ants and honey, or your hangman's rope, and be done with it.

VILLA (*watching him curiously*). So anxious for death, my bird?

PROFESSOR (*flaring into passion*). Better to die than to see you emperor of Mexico.

VILLA *(with a cry of delight)*. So you're one of those! An idealist by the thieves on the cross! *(He begins to pace up and down.)* Eh, you start the Revolution with your fine talk, but when a man who believes in action pushes the stone down the hill, you get frightened. You begin to weep and say you want your pretty overlords again. You're afraid of the brave fine soldiers who have come out of the mountains and valleys to make your dreams come true! When a man dies you tremble like a kitten and meow: "We want peace!"

PROFESSOR. We're not fools. Better an overlord who knows how to rule, than a blood-maddened butcher who turns loose a plague of black terror that crushes the heart out of a people.

VILLA *(delightedly)*. And now you're angry, by the seven kings of hell. *(He comes closer, his voice frankly curious.)* Tell me, man, why do you want to kill me? Have I murdered your brother, perhaps, or your father . . . or stolen your wife?

PROFESSOR. You've stolen my country.

VILLA *(impatiently)*. That's the difficulty. You idealists are always singing pretty words that don't mean anything. Me, I'm a man of action. I can't understand you. Isn't Mexico my country, too?

PROFESSOR. You should rule in hell, not in a country that is sick with war.

VILLA. Eh, and who told you she was sick of war? Every day hundreds of little men join my army because they want to fight. I don't go out and point a gun at them and force them to fight. They fight because they love fighting. Is that my fault?

PROFESSOR. You lead them. You stuff their ears with promises of gold and loot and women . . .

VILLA. I stuff their ears with nothing! Always you must have pretty words for what men do. Me, I want no words. I am living in the hills. Someone comes and says to me: "In the valley men are fighting. It is a beautiful battle." So what do I do? Am I not a man and human? Why should all the world have glory for a battle and Pancho Villa none? So I go down to the valley. I fight. After a while I am a captain. The battle moves out of the valley into the whole of the Republic. What use is a captain in such a big fight? So I am no longer a captain. I am a general. And that is the end of it.

PROFESSOR. That is not the end of it. Ambition blazes in you. What do you care for the reasons behind the Revolution. You only want to be a general . . . the greatest general in the north . . . in the south . . . in the whole of the Republic.

VILLA *(slowly)*. Better me than Carranza, or Obregón, or de la Huerta, or all those other little men. Do you think they fight because they love Mexico? *(Laughs curtly.)* And what a pretty joke that is! Each one wants to be the great general . . . not the great savior of his country.

PROFESSOR. They dream of peace. You think only of war . . . and more war until no man, nor woman either, will be anything more than bloody meat on the ground.

VILLA. And suppose I let them win. What will happen? Do you think they would cut a pack of cards to see which one would be the ruler of Mexico? If you think that, then you wear ass's ears.

PROFESSOR. Those generals know how to rule. They come of a ruling class . . . an educated class . . .

VILLA *(turning to him)*. And I from the people. I learned to read and write when I was a man grown. I learned it in prison . . . the prison your pretty generals put me in because they were afraid of me. As they're afraid of me now. No man in all the Republic knows what the people want so well as I. That's why they're afraid of me. Because they know that when I speak it is the voice of the people speaking in my mouth. Better for me to rule than a pretty uniform plastered with gold medals.

PROFESSOR. Much better. Better for you to turn loose a hoard of mad vultures with the right to murder and loot and rape . . .

VILLA *(with deadly quiet)*. And who has a better right? Do you know how my mother died? She was kicked to death by a drunken civil judge when I was five years old. I saw it happen. (THE PROFESSOR *jerks his head to one side and* VILLA *smiles grimly.*) And my sister was carried off by the son of a rich landowner when she was fourteen. My only brother was shot for desertion from the Federal army when he tried to go out and find me to keep me from starving to death. Eh, and my case is a simple one. Some of my men out there have uglier stories to tell. Would you like to hear them?

PROFESSOR *(half whispering)*. No.

This Is Villa! | 215

VILLA (*sneering*). You have thin chocolate in your veins. I know how it is with you men who've learned life out of books. I've met your kind before. You've fashioned the ideals of the Revolution into a pretty little song that you like to hear tinkling in the morning when you wake up. But your song has gotten lost in the thunder of my guns. You want your pretty tune back so that you cry in a corner and think that Villa will give it to you.

PROFESSOR. But you won't. I know that now.

VILLA. I can't give it back. And neither can anyone else. Suppose I am killed. Do you think the next man to stand in my shoes will be any better than I? Would you rather have me . . . or a man like Fierro?

PROFESSOR. Better you. Better you a thousand times. At least there is something human about you.

VILLA. You know, I like you, Professor. I don't execute you because I am angry with you. If it were left to myself, I'd say there is a horse tied to the bedroom door . . . Take it and ride down the river road to freedom. No one would stop you on the river road.

PROFESSOR. You wouldn't say that.

VILLA. No. because if I let you go, then some other fool would think this killing of Villa was an easy thing to do. I could not sleep peacefully in my bed because of heroes wanting to kill the northern butcher. You can understand my difficulty.

PROFESSOR. So I must die in order that Villa may have peace while he sleeps.

VILLA (*sullenly*). And now you make me sound like the king of fools! (*With a flare of temper, not at* THE PROFESSOR *but at himself.*) The trouble with me is that I'm a sentimental man . . . (*He goes to the bedroom door and suddenly closes it, then turns back into the room. Flaring up again.*) Take your eyes away from my face!

PROFESSOR. What are you going to do with me?

VILLA (*wearily*). I don't know. I ought to stand you up against a wall and shoot the brains out of your head. Antonio always admired your brains.

PROFESSOR (*with the dawning of a faint hope*). Antonio?

VILLA. He liked you, Antonio did. On the march he used to say, "Chief, when the Revolution is over I want to be a professor, too." Can you imagine a soldier saying a thing like that? And now . . . well, I'm a sentimental man.

PROFESSOR. I think I'm beginning to understand.

VILLA (*suddenly sitting down again*). Look, Professor, I'll make a bargain with you. If I let you escape will you swear by the sacred bones of your mother that you will never tell that you tried to kill Villa and he let you go free?

PROFESSOR. So you put your peaceful nights in my keeping?

VILLA. You know how it is. I like you, and Antonio liked you, and now . . . Will you do that, Professor?

PROFESSOR. Suppose I forget?

VILLA. I'll find you . . . and then the first hand to the gun, and the first bullet shot . . . (*He shrugs, then turns his back and faces the couch.*) There is a fork two kilometers down the river road. Take the turn to the right. If anyone stops you say you ride on business for Villa.

PROFESSOR. There is a horse tied at the bedroom door?

VILLA. I left it there. . . . Don't stop for questions, friend. I might remember to cut out your tongue for you.

> (THE PROFESSOR *starts to say something, then with an amused shrug goes quietly out the bedroom door.* VILLA *turns around, scratching his head. He is as sulky as a child, a little surprised at his gesture. Then he goes to the door and calls.*)

VILLA. Fierro! Are you done with hanging that flea-bitten mouse?

FIERRO (*outside*). I'm coming, Chief. (VILLA *walks to the table, picks up the pack of cards, shuffles them once, then flings them back down again. Next he walks to the bedroom door, but pauses at the entrance, rubbing his chin. With an impatient jerk of his head he slowly strolls back, resting his foot on a chair as* FIERRO *enters.*) We had to use all the water in the horse-trough to bring him to before we could hang him properly. What's the use, say I, of hanging a man if he doesn't know he's being hanged?

VILLA. Answer me with clear wisdom, Fierro. Suppose today were . . . were yesterday, and Carmen had never been here.

FIERRO. I do not like games.

VILLA (*harshly*). You will like this one.

FIERRO (*resignedly*). Very well, it is yesterday.

VILLA. And suppose a friend of Antonio's . . . a good friend, you understand . . . a man he respected and admired . . . tried to kill me. What would Antonio have done if he had been the judge at that man's trial?

FIERRO. Yesterday I would have said . . . Who knows? Today . . .

VILLA. Well?

FIERRO *(with a shrug)*. Antonio killed himself to keep from killing you.

VILLA *(snaps his fingers)*. I thought so. And here I have been sentimental for nothing.

FIERRO. Eh?

VILLA. You know the fork in the river road?

FIERRO. You let that four-eyed frog escape!

VILLA. Not yet. There's a tree at the fork. A tall tree with heavy branches. A man like you could hide in that tree. The leaves are so thick he could not see the gun in your hand.

(ROSITA *enters from the outside.*)

ROSITA *(petulantly)*. I want to get drunk. I always want to get drunk when I see a man hanged.

VILLA *(paying her no attention)*. Ride Antonio's horse. Go across the field. You can still reach that tree before the Professor gets there.

FIERRO *(delighted)*. I understand, Chief. *(He runs out the door.)*

VILLA *(runs to the door after him, shouting)*. Shoot him in the back. *(Turns and looks at* ROSITA.) A traitor's death, say I, for a traitor.

ROSITA *(flatly)*. I want to get drunk!

VILLA *(suddenly enthusiastic now that his problem is solved)*. We'll have music, Rosita. And you can dance. We'll get you a new pink dress and a red blouse . . . redder than Antonio's . . . *(He pauses, looks at the bedroom door, and suddenly goes out of the room.* ROSITA, *seeing the mescal bottle, goes over and takes a long drink from it. In a moment* VILLA *enters with* ANTONIO'S *red hat cocked on the back of his head. Staring at him in amazement, she slowly puts down the bottle.)* Eh, am I not a handsome man?

ROSITA *(accusingly, as to a child)*. But that's Antonio's hat.

VILLA *(sulkily)*. Well . . . he said I could wear it until his wedding.

(ROSITA *slowly walks up to him, studying the hat, then with a growing gurgle, she sweeps it off his head, tilting her head at him.)*

VILLA *(with a loud shout of laughter).* Eh, Rosita! Drunk did you say? *(Striding forward he pauses only long enough to fling her like a sack of flour over one shoulder. She laughs and beats him playfully on the back, and both are singing the "Adelita" as they disappear through the door.)*

> I'm a soldier and now I must leave you,
> For my country has called on me to fight.
> Adelita, Adelita, my loved one,
> You must not, dear, forget me tonight.

(The curtains close.)

The Ring of General Macías
A Drama of the Mexican Revolution

1943

The Federal troops were fighting for a way of living; the Revolutionists were
fighting for life itself. The outcome of such a struggle could never be in doubt.

Joaquín Peralta, *Essay on the Great Revolution.*

The Characters

MARICA, the sister of General Macías
RAQUEL, the wife of General Macías
ANDRÉS DE LA O, a captain in the Revolutionary Army
CLETO, a private in the Revolutionary Army
BASILIO FLORES, a captain in the Federal Army

PLACE: Just outside Mexico City
TIME: A night in April 1912

The Scene

*The living room of General Macías's home is luxuriously furnished in the gold
and ornate style of Louis XVI. In the right wall are French windows leading
into the patio. Flanking these windows are low bookcases. In the back wall is:
right, a closet door; and, center, a table holding a wine decanter and glasses.
The left wall has a door upstage, and downstage a writing desk with a straight
chair in front of it. Near the desk is an armchair. Down right is a small sofa*

with a table holding a lamp at the upstage end of it. There are pictures on the walls. The room looks rather stuffy and unlived in.

When the curtains part, the stage is in darkness save for the moonlight that comes through the French windows. Then the house door opens and a young girl in negligee enters stealthily. She is carrying a lighted candle. She stands at the door a moment listening for possible pursuit, then moves quickly across to the bookcase down right. She puts the candle on top of the bookcase and begins searching behind the books. She finally finds what she wants: a small bottle. While she is searching, the house door opens silently and a woman, also in negligee, enters. (These negligees are in the latest Parisian style.) She moves silently across the room to the table by the sofa, and as the girl turns with the bottle, the woman switches on the light. The girl gives a half-scream and draws back, frightened. The light reveals her to be quite young—no more than twenty—a timid, dovelike creature. The woman has a queenly air, and whether she is actually beautiful or not, people think she is. She is about thirty-two.

MARICA *(trying to hide the bottle behind her)*. Raquel! What are you doing here?

RAQUEL. What did you have hidden behind the books, Marica?

MARICA *(attempting a forced laugh)*. I? Nothing. Why do you think I have anything?

RAQUEL *(taking a step toward her)*. Give it to me.

MARICA *(backing away from her)*. No. No, I won't.

RAQUEL *(stretching out her hand)*. I demand that you give it to me.

MARICA. You have no right to order me about. I'm a married woman. I . . . I . . . *(She begins to sob and flings herself down on the sofa.)*

RAQUEL *(much gentler)*. You shouldn't be up. The doctor told you to stay in bed. *(She bends over MARICA and gently takes the bottle out of the girl's hand.)* It was poison. I thought so.

MARICA *(frightened)*. You won't tell the priest, will you?

RAQUEL. Suicide is a sin, Marica. A sin against God.

MARICA. I know. I . . . *(She catches RAQUEL's hand.)* Oh, Raquel, why do we have to have wars? Why do men have to go to war and be killed?

RAQUEL. Men must fight for what they believe is right. It is an honorable thing to die for your country as a soldier.

MARICA. How can you say that with Domingo out there fighting, too? And fighting what? Men who aren't even men. Peasants. Ranch slaves. Men who shouldn't be allowed to fight.

RAQUEL. Peasants are men, Marica. Not animals

MARICA. Men. It's always men. But how about the women? What becomes of us?

RAQUEL. We can pray.

MARICA *(bitterly)*. Yes, we can pray. And then comes the terrible news, and it's no use praying any more. All the reason for our praying is dead. Why should I go on living with Tomás dead?

RAQUEL. Living is a duty.

MARICA. How can you be so cold, so hard? You are a cold and hard woman, Raquel. My brother worships you. He has never even looked at another woman since the first day he saw you. Does he know how cold and hard you are?

RAQUEL. Domingo is my—honored husband.

MARICA. You've been married for ten years. And I've been married for three months. If Domingo is killed, it won't be the same for you. You've had ten years. *(She is crying wildly.)* I haven't anything . . . anything at all.

RAQUEL. You've had three months—three months of laughter. And now you have tears. How lucky you are. You have tears. Perhaps five months of tears. Not more. You're only twenty. And in five months Tomás will become just a lovely memory.

MARICA. I'll remember Tomás all my life.

RAQUEL. Of course. But he'll be distant and far away. But you're young . . . and the young need laughter. The young can't live on tears. And one day in Paris, or Rome, or even Mexico City, you'll meet another man. You'll marry again. There will be children in your house. How lucky you are.

MARICA. I'll never marry again.

RAQUEL. You're only twenty. You'll think differently when you're twenty-eight, or nine, or thirty.

MARICA. What will you do if Domingo is killed?

RAQUEL. I shall be very proud that he died in all his courage . . . in all the greatness of a hero.

MARICA. But you'd not weep, would you? Not you! I don't think there are any tears in you.

RAQUEL. No, I'd not weep. I'd sit here in this empty house and wait.

MARICA. Wait for what?

RAQUEL. For the jingle of his spurs as he walks across the tiled hall. For the sound of his laughter in the patio. For the echo of his voice as he shouts to the groom to put away his horse. For the feel of his hand . . .

MARICA *(screams)*. Stop it!

RAQUEL. I'm sorry.

MARICA. You do love him, don't you?

RAQUEL. I don't think even he knows how much.

MARICA. I thought that after ten years people slid away from love. But you and Domingo—why, you're all he thinks about. When he's away from you he talks about you all the time. I heard him say once that when you were out of his sight he was like a man without eyes or ears or hands.

RAQUEL. I know. I, too, know that feeling.

MARICA. Then how could you let him go to war? Perhaps to be killed? How could you?

RAQUEL *(sharply)*. Marica, you are of the family Macías. Your family is a family of great warriors. A Macías man was with Ferdinand when the Moors were driven out of Spain. A Macías man was with Cortés when the Aztecans surrendered. Your grandfather fought in the War of Independence. Your own father was executed not twenty miles from this house by the French. Shall his son be any less brave because he loves a woman?

MARICA. But Domingo loved you enough to forget that. If you had asked him, he wouldn't have gone to war. He would have stayed here with you.

RAQUEL. No, he would not have stayed. Your brother is a man of honor, not a whining, creeping coward.

MARICA *(beginning to cry again)*. I begged Tomás not to go. I begged him.

RAQUEL. Would you have loved him if he had stayed?

MARICA. I don't know. I don't know.

RAQUEL. There is your answer. You'd have despised him. Loved and despised him. Now come, Marica, it's time for you to go to bed.

MARICA. You won't tell the priest—about the poison, I mean?

RAQUEL. No. I won't tell him.

MARICA. Thank you, Raquel. How good you are. How kind and good.

RAQUEL. A moment ago I was hard and cruel. What a baby you are. Now, off to bed with you.

MARICA. Aren't you coming upstairs, too?

RAQUEL. No . . . I haven't been sleeping very well lately. I think I'll read for a little while.

MARICA. Good night, Raquel, and thank you.

RAQUEL. Good night, little one.

(MARICA *goes out through the house door at left, taking her candle with her.* RAQUEL *stares down at the bottle of poison in her hand, then puts it away in one of the small drawers of the desk. She next selects a book from the downstage case, and sits on the sofa to read it, but feeling chilly, she rises and goes to the closet at back right, and takes out an afghan. Coming back to the sofa, she makes herself comfortable, with the afghan across her knees. Suddenly she hears a noise in the patio. She listens, then convinced it is nothing, returns to her reading. But she hears the noise again. She goes to the patio door and peers out.)*

RAQUEL *(calling softly).* Who's there? Who's out there? Oh! *(She gasps and backs into the room. Two men—or rather a man and a young boy— dressed in the white pajama suits of the Mexican peasants, with their sombreros tipped low over their faces, come into the room.* RAQUEL *draws herself up regally. Her voice is cold and commanding.)* Who are you, and what do you want here?

ANDRÉS. We are hunting for the wife of General Macías.

RAQUEL. I am Raquel Rivera de Macías.

ANDRÉS. Cleto, stand guard in the patio. If you hear any suspicious noise, warn me at once.

CLETO. Yes, my captain. *(The boy returns to the patio.)*

(The man, hooking his thumbs in his belt, strolls around the room, looking it over. When he reaches the table at the back he sees the wine. With a small bow to RAQUEL *he pours himself a glass of wine and drains it. He wipes his mouth with the back of his hand.)*

RAQUEL. How very interesting.

ANDRÉS *(startled).* What?

RAQUEL. To be able to drink wine with that hat on.

ANDRÉS. The hat? Oh, forgive me, señora. *(He flicks the brim with his fingers so that it drops off his head and dangles down his back from the neck cord.)* In a military camp one forgets one's polite manners. Would you care to join me in another glass?

RAQUEL *(sitting on the sofa)*. Why not? It's my wine.

ANDRÉS. And a very excellent wine. *(He pours two glasses and gives her one while he is talking.)* I would say Amontillado of the vintage of '87.

RAQUEL. Did you learn that in a military camp?

ANDRÉS. I used to sell wines . . . among other things.

RAQUEL *(ostentatiously hiding a yawn)*. I am devastated.

ANDRÉS *(pulls over the armchair and makes himself comfortable in it)*. You don't mind, do you?

RAQUEL. Would it make any difference if I did?

ANDRÉS. No. The Federals are searching the streets for us and we have to stay somewhere. But women of your class seem to expect that senseless sort of question.

RAQUEL. Of course I suppose I could scream.

ANDRÉS. Naturally.

RAQUEL. My sister-in-law is upstairs asleep. And there are several servants in the back of the house. Mostly men servants. Very big men.

ANDRÉS. Very interesting. *(He is drinking the wine in small sips with much enjoyment.)*

RAQUEL. What would you do if I screamed?

ANDRÉS *(considering the request as though it were another glass of wine)*. Nothing.

RAQUEL. I am afraid you are lying to me.

ANDRÉS. Women of your class seem to expect polite little lies.

RAQUEL. Stop calling me "woman of your class."

ANDRÉS. Forgive me.

RAQUEL. You are one of the fighting peasants, aren't you?

ANDRÉS. I am a captain in the Revolutionary Army.

RAQUEL. This house is completely loyal to the Federal government.

ANDRÉS. I know. That's why I'm here.

RAQUEL. And now that you are here, just what do you expect me to do?

ANDRÉS. I expect you to offer sanctuary to myself and to Cleto.

RAQUEL. Cleto? *(She looks toward the patio and adds sarcastically.)* Oh, your army.

CLETO *(appearing in the doorway)*. I'm sorry, my captain. I just heard a noise. (RAQUEL *stands.* ANDRÉS *moves quickly to her and puts his hands on her arms from the back.* CLETO *has turned and is peering into the patio. Then the boy relaxes)*. We are still safe, my captain. It was only a rabbit. *(He goes back into the patio.* RAQUEL *pulls away from* ANDRÉS *and goes to the desk.)*

RAQUEL. What a magnificent army you have. So clever. I'm sure you must win many victories.

ANDRÉS. We do. And we will win the greatest victory, remember that.

RAQUEL. This farce has gone on long enough. Will you please take your army and climb over the patio wall with it?

ANDRÉS. I told you that we came here so that you could give us sanctuary.

RAQUEL. My dear captain—captain without a name . . .

ANDRÉS. Andrés de la O, your servant. *(He makes a bow.)*

RAQUEL *(startled)*. Andrés de la O!

ANDRÉS. I am flattered. You have heard of me.

RAQUEL. Naturally. Everyone in the city has heard of you. You have a reputation for politeness—especially to women.

ANDRÉS. I see that the tales about me have lost nothing in the telling.

RAQUEL. I can't say. I'm not interested in gossip about your type of soldier.

ANDRÉS. Then let me give you something to heighten your interest. *(He suddenly takes her in his arms and kisses her. She stiffens for a moment, then remains perfectly still. He steps away from her.)*

RAQUEL *(rage forcing her to whisper)*. Get out of here—at once.

ANDRÉS *(staring at her in admiration)*. I can understand why Macías loves you. I couldn't before, but now I understand it.

RAQUEL. Get out of my house.

ANDRÉS *(sits on the sofa and pulls a small leather pouch out of his shirt. He pours its contents into his hand.)*. So cruel, señora, and I with a present for you? Here is a holy medal. My mother gave me this medal. She died when I was ten. She was a street beggar. She died of starvation. But I wasn't there. I was in jail. I had been sentenced to five years in prison for stealing five oranges. The judge thought it a great joke. One year for each orange. He laughed. He had a very loud laugh. *(Pause.)* I killed

The Ring of General Macías | 227

him two months ago. I hanged him to the telephone pole in front of his house. And I laughed. *(Pause.)* I also have a very loud laugh. (RAQUEL *abruptly turns her back on him.*) I told that story to a girl the other night and she thought it very funny. But of course she was a peasant girl—a girl who could neither read nor write. She hadn't been born in a great house in Tabasco. She didn't have an English governess. She didn't go to school to the nuns in Paris. She didn't marry one of the richest young men in the Republic. But she thought my story very funny. Of course she could understand it. Her brother had been whipped to death because he had run away from the plantation that owned him. *(He pauses and looks at her. She does not move.)* Are you still angry with me? Even though I have brought you a present? *(He holds out his hand.)* A very nice present—from your husband.

RAQUEL *(turns and stares at him in amazement).* A present! From Domingo?

ANDRÉS. I don't know him that well. I call him the General Macías.

RAQUEL *(excitedly).* Is he well? How does he look? *(With horrified comprehension.)* He's a prisoner . . . your prisoner!

ANDRÉS. Naturally. That's why I know so much about you. He talks about you constantly.

RAQUEL. You know nothing about him. You're lying to me.

(CLETO *comes to the window.*)

ANDRÉS. I assure you, señora . . .

CLETO *(interrupting).* My captain . . .

ANDRÉS. What is it, Cleto? Another rabbit?

CLETO. No, my captain. There are soldiers at the end of the street. They are searching all the houses. They will be here soon.

ANDRÉS. Don't worry. We are quite safe here. Stay in the patio until I call you.

CLETO. Yes, my captain. *(He returns to the patio.)*

RAQUEL. You are not safe here. When those soldiers come I shall turn you over to them.

ANDRÉS. I think not.

RAQUEL. You can't escape from them. And they are not kind to you peasant prisoners. They have good reason not to be.

ANDRÉS. Look at this ring. *(He holds his hand out, with the ring on his palm.)*

RAQUEL. Why, it's—a wedding ring.

ANDRÉS. Read the inscription inside of it. *(As she hesitates, he adds sharply.)* Read it!

RAQUEL *(slowly takes the ring. While she is reading her voice fades to a whisper.).* "D. M.—R. R.—June 2, 1902." Where did you get this?

ANDRÉS. General Macías gave it to me.

RAQUEL *(firmly and clearly).* Not this ring. He'd never give you this ring. *(With dawning horror.)* He's dead. You stole it from his dead finger. He's dead.

ANDRÉS. Not yet. But he will be dead if I don't return to camp safely by sunset tomorrow.

RAQUEL. I don't believe you. I don't believe you. You're lying to me.

ANDRÉS. This house is famous for its loyalty to the Federal government. You will hide me until those soldiers get out of this district. When it is safe enough, Cleto and I will leave. But if you betray me to them, your husband will be shot tomorrow evening at sunset. Do you understand? *(He shakes her arm.* RAQUEL *looks dazedly at him.* CLETO *comes to the window.)*

CLETO. The soldiers are coming closer, my captain. They are at the next house.

ANDRÉS *(To* RAQUEL*).* Where shall we hide? (RAQUEL *is still dazed. He gives her another little shake.)* Think, woman! If you love your husband at all—think!

RAQUEL. I don't know. Marica upstairs—the servants in the rest of the house—I don't know.

ANDRÉS. The general has bragged to us about you. He says you are braver than most men. He says you are very clever. This is a time to be both brave and clever.

CLETO *(pointing to the closet).* What door is that?

RAQUEL. It's a closet . . . a storage closet.

ANDRÉS. We'll hide in there.

RAQUEL. It's very small. It's not big enough for both of you.

ANDRÉS. Cleto, hide yourself in there.

CLETO. But, my captain . . .

ANDRÉS. That's an order! Hide yourself.

CLETO. Yes, sir. *(He steps inside the closet.)*

The Ring of General Macías | 229

ANDRÉS. And now, señora, where are you going to hide me?

RAQUEL. How did you persuade my husband to give you his ring?

ANDRÉS. That's a very long story, señora, for which we have no time just now. *(He puts the ring and medal back in the pouch and thrusts it inside his shirt.)* Later I will be glad to give you all the details. But at present it is only necessary for you to remember that his life depends upon mine.

RAQUEL. Yes—yes, of course. *(She loses her dazed expression and seems to grow more queenly as she takes command of the situation.)* Give me your hat. (ANDRÉS *shrugs and passes it over to her. She takes it to the closet and hands it to* CLETO.) There is a smoking jacket hanging up in there. Hand it to me. (CLETO *hands her a man's velvet smoking jacket. She brings it to* ANDRÉS.) Put this on.

ANDRÉS *(puts it on and looks down at himself)*. Such a pity my shoes are not comfortable slippers.

RAQUEL. Sit in that chair. *(She points to the armchair.)*

ANDRÉS. My dear lady . . .

RAQUEL. If I must save your life, allow me to do it in my own way. Sit down. (ANDRÉS *sits. She picks up the afghan from the couch and throws it over his feet and legs, carefully tucking it in so that his body is covered to the waist.)* If anyone speaks to you, don't answer. Don't turn your head. As far as you are concerned, there is no one in this room—not even me. Just look straight ahead of you and . . .

ANDRÉS *(as she pauses)*. And what?

RAQUEL. I started to say "and pray," but since you're a member of the Revolutionary Army I don't suppose you believe in God and prayer.

ANDRÉS. My mother left me a holy medal.

RAQUEL. Oh, yes, I remember. A very amusing story. *(There is the sound of men's voices in the patio.)* The Federal soldiers are here. If you can pray, ask God to keep Marica upstairs. She is very young and very stupid. She'll betray you before I can shut her mouth.

ANDRÉS. I'll . . .

RAQUEL. Silence! Stare straight ahead of you and pray. *(She goes to the French window and speaks loudly to the soldiers.)* Really! What is the meaning of this uproar?

FLORES (off). Do not alarm yourself, señora. (He comes into the room. He wears the uniform of a Federal officer.) I am Captain Basilio Flores, at your service, señora.

RAQUEL. What do you mean, invading my house and making so much noise at this hour of the night?

FLORES. We are hunting for two spies. One of them is the notorious Andrés de la O. You may have heard of him, señora.

RAQUEL (looking at ANDRÉS). Considering what he did to my cousin—yes, I've heard of him.

FLORES. Your cousin, señora?

RAQUEL (comes to ANDRÉS and puts her hand on his shoulder. He stares woodenly in front of him.). Felipe was his prisoner before the poor boy managed to escape.

FLORES. Is it possible? (He crosses to ANDRÉS.) Captain Basilio Flores, at your service. (He salutes.)

RAQUEL. Felipe doesn't hear you. He doesn't even know you are in the room.

FLORES. Eh, it is a sad thing.

RAQUEL. Must your men make so much noise?

FLORES. The hunt must be thorough, señora, and now if some of my men can go through here to the rest of the house . . .

RAQUEL. Why?

FLORES. But I told you, señora. We are hunting for two spies . . .

RAQUEL (speaking quickly from controlled nervousness). And do you think I have them hidden someplace, and I the wife of General Macías?

FLORES. General Macías! But I didn't know . . .

RAQUEL. Now that you do know, I suggest you remove your men and their noise at once.

FLORES. But, señora, I regret—I still have to search this house.

RAQUEL. I can assure you, captain, that I have been sitting here all evening, and no peasant spy has passed me and gone into the rest of the house.

FLORES. Several rooms open off the patio, señora. They needn't have come through here.

RAQUEL. So . . . you do think I conceal spies in this house. Then search it by all means. Look under the sofa . . . under the table. In the drawers of the desk. And don't miss that closet, captain. Inside that closet is hidden a very fierce and wicked spy.

FLORES. Please, señora.

RAQUEL *(goes to the closet door)*. Or do you prefer me to open it for you?

FLORES. I am only doing my duty, señora. You are making it very difficult.

RAQUEL *(relaxing against the door)*. I'm sorry. My sister-in-law is upstairs. She has just received word that her husband has been killed. They were married three months ago. She's only twenty. I didn't want . . .

MARICA *(calling off)*. Raquel, what is all that noise downstairs?

RAQUEL *(goes to the house door and calls)*. It is nothing. Go back to bed.

MARICA. But I can hear men's voices in the patio.

RAQUEL. It is only some Federal soldiers hunting for two peasant spies. *(She turns and speaks rapidly to FLORES.)* If she comes down here, she must not see my cousin. Felipe escaped, but her husband was killed. The doctor thinks the sight of my poor cousin might affect her mind. You understand?

FLORES. Certainly, señora. What a sad thing.

MARICA *(still off)*. Raquel, I'm afraid! *(She tries to push past RAQUEL into the room. RAQUEL and FLORES stand between her and ANDRÉS.)* Spies! In this house. Oh, Raquel!

RAQUEL. The doctor will be very angry if you don't return to bed at once.

MARICA. But those terrible men will kill us. What is the matter with you two? Why are you standing there like that? *(She tries to see past them, but they both move so that she can't see ANDRÉS.)*

FLORES. It is better that you go back to your room, señora.

MARICA. But why? Upstairs I am alone. Those terrible men will kill me. I know they will.

FLORES. Don't be afraid. señora. There are no spies in this house.

MARICA. Are you sure?

RAQUEL. Captain Flores means that no spy would dare to take refuge in the house of General Macías. Isn't that right, captain?

FLORES *(laughing)*. Of course. All the world knows of the brave General Macías.

RAQUEL. Now go back to bed, Marica. Please, for my sake.

MARICA. You are both acting very strangely. I think you have something hidden in this room you don't want me to see.

RAQUEL (*sharply*). You are quite right. Captain Flores has captured one of the spies. He is sitting in the chair behind me. He is dead. Now will you please go upstairs!

MARICA (*gives a stifled sob*). Oh! That such a terrible thing could happen in this house. (*She runs out of the room, still sobbing.*)

FLORES (*worried*). Was it wise to tell her such a story, señora?

RAQUEL (*tense with repressed relief*). Better that than the truth. Good night, captain, and thank you.

FLORES. Good night, señora. And don't worry. Those spies won't bother you. If they were anywhere in this district, my men would have found them.

RAQUEL. I'm sure of it.

> (*The captain salutes her, looks toward* ANDRÉS *and salutes him, then goes into the patio. He can be heard calling his men. Neither* ANDRÉS *nor* RAQUEL *moves until the voices outside die away. Then* RAQUEL *staggers and nearly falls, but* ANDRÉS *catches her in time.*)

ANDRÉS (*calling softly*). They've gone, Cleto. (ANDRÉS *carries* RAQUEL *to the sofa as* CLETO *comes out of the closet.*) Bring a glass of wine. Quickly.

CLETO (*as he gets the wine*). What happened?

ANDRÉS. It's nothing. Just a faint. (*He holds the wine to her lips.*)

CLETO. She's a great lady, that one. When she wanted to open the closet door my knees were trembling, I can tell you.

ANDRÉS. My own bones were playing a pretty tune.

CLETO. Why do you think she married Macías?

ANDRÉS. Love is a peculiar thing, Cleto.

CLETO. I don't understand it.

RAQUEL (*moans and sits up*). Are they—are they gone?

ANDRÉS. Yes, they're gone. (*He kisses her hand.*) I've never known a braver lady.

RAQUEL (*pulling her hand away*). Will you go now, please?

ANDRÉS. We'll have to wait until the district is free of them—but if you'd like to write a letter to your husband while we're waiting . . .

RAQUEL (*surprised at his kindness*). You'd take it to him? You'd really give it to him?

ANDRÉS. Of course.

RAQUEL. Thank you. (*She goes to the writing desk and sits down.*)

The Ring of General Macías | 233

ANDRÉS (*to* CLETO, *who has been staring steadily at* RAQUEL *all the while*). You stay here with the señora. I'm going to find out how much of the district has been cleared.

CLETO (*still staring at* RAQUEL). Yes, my captain.

   (ANDRÉS *leaves by the French windows.* CLETO *keeps on staring at* RAQUEL *as she starts to write. After a moment she turns to him.*)

RAQUEL (*irritated*). Why do you keep staring at me?

CLETO. Why did you marry a man like that one, señora?

RAQUEL. You're very impertinent.

CLETO (*shyly*). I'm sorry, señora.

RAQUEL (*after a brief pause*). What do you mean: "a man like that one"?

CLETO. Well, you're very brave, señora.

RAQUEL (*lightly*). And don't you think the general is very brave?

CLETO. No, señora. Not very.

RAQUEL (*staring at him with bewilderment*). What are you trying to tell me?

CLETO. Nothing, señora. It is none of my affair.

RAQUEL. Come here. (*He comes slowly up to her.*) Tell me what is in your mind.

CLETO. I don't know, señora. I don't understand it. The captain says love is a peculiar thing, but I don't understand it.

RAQUEL. Cleto, did the general willingly give that ring to your captain?

CLETO. Yes, señora.

RAQUEL. Why?

CLETO. The general wanted to save his own life. He said he loved you and he wanted to save his life.

RAQUEL. How would giving that ring to your captain save the general's life?

CLETO. The general's supposed to be shot tomorrow afternoon. But he's talked about you a lot, and when my captain knew we had to come into the city, he thought perhaps we might take refuge here if the Federals got on our trail. So he went to the general and said that if he fixed it so we'd be safe here, my captain would save him from the firing squad.

RAQUEL. Was your trip here to the city very important—to your cause, I mean?

CLETO. Indeed yes, señora. The captain got a lot of fine information. It means we'll win the next big battle. My captain is a very clever man, señora.

RAQUEL. Did the general know about this information when he gave his ring to your captain?

CLETO. I don't see how he could help knowing it, señora. He heard us talking about it enough.

RAQUEL. Who knows about that bargain to save the general's life beside you and your captain?

CLETO. No one, señora. The captain isn't one to talk, and I didn't have time to.

RAQUEL *(while the boy has been talking, the life seems to have drained completely out of her)*. How old are you, Cleto?

CLETO. I don't know, señora. I think I'm twenty, but I don't know.

RAQUEL *(speaking more to herself than to him)*. Tomás was twenty.

CLETO. Who is Tomás?

RAQUEL. He was married to my sister-in-law. Cleto, you think my husband is a coward, don't you?

CLETO *(with embarrassment)*. Yes, señora.

RAQUEL. You don't think any woman is worth it, do you? Worth the price of a great battle, I mean?

CLETO. No, señora. But as the captain says, love is a very peculiar thing.

RAQUEL. If your captain loved a woman as much as the general loves me, would he have given an enemy his ring?

CLETO. Ah, but the captain is a great man, señora.

RAQUEL. And so is my husband a great man. He is of the family Macías. All of that family have been great men. All of them—brave and honorable men. They have always held their honor to be greater than their lives. That is a tradition of their family.

CLETO. Perhaps none of them loved a woman like you, señora.

RAQUEL. How strange you are. I saved you from the Federals because I want to save my husband's life. You call me brave and yet you call him a coward. There is no difference in what we have done.

CLETO. But you are a woman, señora.

RAQUEL. Has a woman less honor than a man, then?

CLETO. No, señora. Please, I don't know how to say it. The general is a soldier. He has a duty to his own cause. You are a woman. You have a duty to your husband. It is right that you should try to save him. It is not right that he should try to save himself.

RAQUEL *(dully)*. Yes, of course. It is right that I should save him. *(Becoming practical again.)* Your captain has been gone some time, Cleto. You'd better find out if he is still safe.

CLETO. Yes, señora. *(As he reaches the French windows, she stops him.)*

RAQUEL. Wait, Cleto. Have you a mother—or a wife, perhaps?

CLETO. Oh, no, señora. I haven't anyone but the captain.

RAQUEL. But the captain is a soldier. What would you do if he should be killed?

CLETO. It is very simple, señora. I should be killed, too.

RAQUEL. You speak about death so calmly. Aren't you afraid of it, Cleto?

CLETO. No, señora. It's like the captain says . . . dying for what you believe in—that's the finest death of all.

RAQUEL. And you believe in the Revolutionary cause?

CLETO. Yes, señora. I am a poor peasant, that's true. But still I have a right to live like a man, with my own ground, and my own family, and my own future. *(He stops speaking abruptly.)* I'm sorry, señora. You are a fine lady. You don't understand these things. I must go and find my captain. *(He goes out.)*

RAQUEL *(rests her face against her hand)*. He's so young. But Tomás was no older. And he's not afraid. He said so. Oh, Domingo—Domingo! *(She straightens abruptly, takes the bottle of poison from the desk drawer, and stares at it. Then she crosses to the decanter and laces the wine with the poison. She hurries back to the desk and is busy writing when* ANDRÉS *and* CLETO *return.)*

ANDRÉS. You'll have to hurry that letter. The district is clear now.

RAQUEL. I'll be through in just a moment. You might as well finish the wine while you're waiting.

ANDRÉS. Thank you. A most excellent idea. *(He pours himself a glass of wine. As he lifts it to his lips, she speaks.)*

RAQUEL. Why don't you give some to—Cleto?

ANDRÉS. This is too fine a wine to waste on that boy.

RAQUEL. He'll probably never have another chance to taste such wine.

ANDRÉS. Very well. Pour yourself a glass, Cleto.

CLETO. Thank you. *(He pours it.)* Your health, my captain.

RAQUEL *(quickly)*. Drink it outside, Cleto. I want to speak to your captain.

(The boy looks at ANDRÉS, *who jerks his head toward the patio.* CLETO *nods and goes out.)* I want you to give my husband a message for me. I can't write it. You'll have to remember it. But first, give me a glass of wine, too.

ANDRÉS *(pouring the wine).* It might be easier for him if you wrote it.

RAQUEL. I think not. *(She takes the glass.)* I want you to tell him that I never knew how much I loved him until tonight.

ANDRÉS. Is that all?

RAQUEL. Yes. Tell me, captain, do you think it possible to love a person too much?

ANDRÉS. Yes, señora. I do.

RAQUEL. So do I. Let us drink a toast, captain—to honor. To bright and shining honor.

ANDRÉS *(raises his glass).* To honor. *(He drains his glass. She lifts hers almost to her lips and then puts it down. From the patio comes a faint cry.)*

CLETO *(calling faintly in a cry that fades into silence).* Captain. Captain.

> (ANDRÉS *sways, his hand trying to brush across his face as though trying to brush sense into his head. When he hears* CLETO, *he tries to stagger toward the window but stumbles and can't quite make it. Hanging on to the table by the sofa he looks accusingly at her. She shrinks back against her chair.)*

ANDRÉS *(his voice weak from the poison).* Why?

RAQUEL. Because I love him. Can you understand that?

ANDRÉS. We'll win. The Revolution will win. You can't stop that.

RAQUEL. Yes, you'll win. I know that now.

ANDRÉS. That girl—she thought my story was funny—about the hanging. But you didn't . . .

RAQUEL. I'm glad you hanged him. I'm glad.

> (ANDRÉS *looks at her and tries to smile. He manages to pull the pouch from his shirt and extend it to her. But it drops from his hand.)*

RAQUEL *(runs to French window and calls).* Cleto. Cleto! *(She buries her face in her hands for a moment, then comes back to* ANDRÉS. *She kneels beside him and picks up the leather pouch. She opens it and, taking the ring, puts it on her finger. Then she sees the medal. She rises and, pulling out the chain from her own throat, she slides the medal onto the chain. Then she walks to the sofa and sinks down on it.)*

MARICA *(calling off)*. Raquel! Raquel! (RAQUEL *snaps off the lamp, leaving the room in darkness.* MARICA *opens the house door. She is carrying a candle, which she shades with her hand. The light is too dim to reveal the dead* ANDRÉS.) What are you doing down here in the dark? Why don't you come to bed?

RAQUEL *(making an effort to speak)*. I'll come in just a moment.

MARICA. But what are you doing, Raquel?

RAQUEL. Nothing. Just listening . . . listening to an empty house.

    (Quick curtain.)

Backgrounds
Reviews and Letters

Mexican Grass Roots
Carleton Beals, Saturday Review, *13 October 1945*

Miss Niggli, utilizing her intimate knowledge of Mexican village life, spins a series of highly bizarre and romantic fictional tales, in which such tourist delights as cockfights, bullfights, witchcraft, generals, and violence, play important roles.

⁓

[Miss Niggli's]community—Hidalgo—is more than a village; it is a town on the crossroads big enough to have two plazas and many stores, one of those frowsy Northern desert towns, largely mestizo, but shading off to Indian or to white hidalgo. It is a place where trains stop and even some traveling theatre troupe plays for a night. It is near Mexico's largest industrial city—Monterrey—and on the dry austere mesa, where the dust of Texas plus Texans blow in, where the heat sears vegetation and folk, and the revolution still rules memories, causes feuds, and shakes family loyalties like dice in a cup . . . In her book feuds and hates are charmingly healed: good people are happily rewarded, and unconventional folk, even if noble, come to a tragic end. . . .

⁓

Miss Niggli writes with fine feeling for form and color, and her story of the reconciliation of two clashing villages is warm with humor, although the plot is little more than Romeo and Juliet, divorced of shoes, and provided with a cockfight and a happy ending. Several of her bullfight scenes are breathtaking, and her story of the horse race is magnificent, even the artificial clever turn at the end which will provide a hearty laugh. Her sense of pathos is much better than her theatre, for her high-keyed emotional passages tend to break down into raucous banality; and as a result her story of the courtship of the village old maid by the timid schoolteacher is a sweet little yarn that glows in one long after the book is laid aside. When she strains for a vivid denouement, the relations of her people and the social groups are distorted and thrown out of focus, but when she forgets the bizarre and her infatuation with native witchcraft, she tells about daily life with an authentic touch.

Review of *Mexican Village*
Orville Prescott, New York Times, *16 October 1945*

In the State of Nuevo León not far from Monterrey between two ranges of purple mountains there lies upon the desert floor the sun drenched village of Hidalgo. It is a small village of not more than one thousand souls. Some twenty years ago all of its citizens were poor, except Don Saturnino Castillo, the richest man in the Sabinas Valley, whose family had been great in Mexico for three hundred years. They were poor, but they hadn't time to worry about such a trifle. Life in Hidalgo was too intense, too crowded with excitement, comedy and tragedy. Everyone knew all there was to know about everyone else, at least they thought they did. A new love affair, a practical joke, a matter of village honor, or some dark deed of Latin melodrama was always there to provide fresh material for the gossiping tongues of Hidalgo. No wonder that Bob Webster, who came to Hidalgo to manage the cement quarry for a year only, could never tear himself away. No wonder that it is almost equally hard to divert your attention from the utterly absorbing pages of *Mexican Village* by Josephina Niggli.

This remarkable book by a greatly gifted Mexican writer is one of the notable works of fiction of the year, one of the finest books about Mexico I have ever read. Miss Niggli was born in Monterrey, taken to Texas at the age of two, and brought back to live in Hidalgo at ten. She knows the people of Hidalgo intimately. More important, she has the creative ability to make her readers feel as if they, too, know them as well. Although Miss Niggli has described Hidalgo as accurately as possible and although her characters are not imaginary, *Mexican Village* is fiction. Miss Niggli is a natural and expert storyteller. She likes drama and suspense and surprise endings and so, in order to make use of them most effectively, she has rearranged reality and invented colorful details.

Easy and Delightful Reading

It is well that she has. Too many writers become so absorbed in the social significance and the economic background of their characters that they forget to tell a story. But Miss Niggli is so steeped in the life of Hidalgo she does not have to examine it like a researcher; instead she can tell her stories with zest and narrative skill and occasional outbursts of unashamed romanticism. So *Mexican Village* is easy and delightful reading. It is only when you set it down at last that you realize how much of Mexico itself is here, not only concrete facts but the very spirit of the people.

Josephina Niggli writes a warm, supple, simple English that never once shows evidence that it is not her native tongue. Her book is richly and wonderfully Mexican in its scene and atmosphere, but there is nothing local, either Mexican or American, about the manner of its writing or its underlying point of view, which is just compassionately human. Miss Niggli is a true citizen of the international kingdom of creative literature. She has cast her book in an unusual form. It is not a novel at all, but a collection of ten completely independent novelettes. Each has a separate existence of its own, but they are all linked loosely together by their common scene and the reappearance of the same people. Each story has a different group of principal characters, who usually appear to play only minor roles in the other stories. This complex pattern Miss Niggli has worked out with precise dexterity.

Exotic and Colorful Goings On

Hidalgo may be a typical Mexican village of no great importance. But to Northern readers it will seem an astonishing place, filled with exotic and colorful goings on. There religious faith is deep and unquestioning, but pagan cults are also reverenced. Old Tía Magdalena, Bob Webster's housekeeper, was an eagle witch and the daughter and granddaughter of eagle witches. Tía Magdalena prayed to the saints and sacrificed goats and cocks to the old gods with equal fervor. Everybody in Hidalgo feared her. But they feared goatherds, too, for it was well known that goatherds were well-beloved sons of the devil.

The good people of Hidalgo were poor and ignorant, but they were courteous, honorable, and respectfully reverent of learning. It was this reverence that explained their feud with the village of San Juan Iglesias. The feud was over the possession of the bones of a distinguished historian, a native of Hidalgo who had unfortunately died in San Juan Iglesias. How could such a matter be settled except by a cockfight? Honor was a ritual in Hidalgo. It caused women to fight each other even on Sundays when they would be fined, although no fine for feminine squabbles was imposed on weekdays. And, naturally, love was a great power in Hidalgo. It made Porfirio, the wood carver, and Andrea Trevina, an owner but not a herder of goats, put up with surprising indignities from their women.

Love also inspired even greater follies and tragedies in the cases of Anita O'Malley, the dancer, and Maria, the beautiful outcast. Both their stories are love stories of a traditional and sentimental sort, and both are touching and dramatic. Love has a way of being sentimental and traditional and Miss Niggli is willing to admit it. Bullfighting stories also have a way of conforming to established rules. Miss Niggli's does, and at the same time manages to be an excellent bullfighting story. In fact, it might not be excessive to say that *Mexican Village* is excellent and let it go at that.

Review of *The Peacock Sheds His Tail,* by Alice Tisdale
Hobart, and *Mexican Village,* by Josephina Niggli
Norah Piper, Commonweal, *14 December 1945*

The criterion of the many is the altitude a book achieves on the best-seller
list, so I am going out on a limb in expressing a preference for one of two
recorded books on Mexico. *The Peacock Sheds His Tail* is by an established
writer of sugarcoated contemporary history in fictional form; *Mexican Village* is a first novel. Mrs. Hobart's book smells of research and ties its plot
to several of the quaint customs about which she has heard. Her villain is
privilege, with a discreet, oh, very discreet sideswipe at the Church as its
handmaiden. She goes all out on the subject of the Sinarquistas as a perfectly safe scapegoat, linking them to Germany and Spain, and portraying
them as a sort of Mexican Ku Klux Klan. Superimposed on this background is a marriage between a young American diplomat and a Mexican
girl from an old, conservative family, shaken well and spiced with social
significance. Miss Niggli's book is based on a much deeper knowledge of
the country. Laid in the Sabinas Valley in the northern part of the country
instead of in the capital, its flaws spring from too much sentimentality. She
writes in a golden haze of days remembered and a slight confusion arises
from her dividing the book into ten separate tales, more or less overlapping
in time, although the device plus Miss Niggli's own feeling for Mexico give
the book a folk quality and authenticity that Mrs. Hobart lacks. Except in
its final pages, *The Peacock Sheds His Tail* has the deftly woven plot of the
professional storyteller but it is a United States idea of Mexico and what
ought to be done about it. The "plots" of the ten tales in *Mexican Village*
arise so inevitably from the characters portrayed that we have a sense of
classic drama or comedy in spite of the tendency to be over-idyllic. But
here are two books about that country of complexities, where one civilization was forcibly imposed on another, where the old religion is not completely dead, a country struggling with inertia, illiteracy, and the attempts
of each succeeding party to perpetuate itself once it has achieved power.

Review of *Mexican Village*
Mildred Adams, New York Times, *16 December 1945*

Nuevo León, say the experts, is the least Mexican of all Mexican states. Up near the northern border, having only a small Indian population, feeling the magnetic pull of the United States, its characteristics are its own, and few people have noted them in books. Its beautiful women have golden hair and green eyes, and its men are tall. Even speech is different here.

These tales of a Nuevo León village have pace and charm. Josephina Niggli, born in Mexico, is a storyteller in the fine tradition. In her pages people come alive. She wastes little time pulling strings or presenting stereotypes. These slender lads, the girls that court and flout and serve them, the elders that watch over them, are individuals. The sum of all that they think and do is the village itself, the collective life which also is an actor in the dramas here set forth.

Many things make this volume memorable in the modern spate of tales about Mexico. Not the least is the fact that it has no axe to grind, it demands no ideological bias on the part of the reader. It is not upholding the cause of the Indian as against the Spaniard, of the peasant as against the landlord, of Mexico as against the United States—or vice versa. Also, the curse of the cute, which prevails in too many books about Mexico, is only faintly present.

The revolution is there. It happened; it left memories and legends. It is part of Nuevo León's background, but not the whole of it. North American influence is there. Bob Webster, hero and mystery man, is a "yanqui," and his quarry is owned by North American capital. But North American influence, male or female, capitalist or proletarian, is only one thread in the complex tapestry of village living.

The title of the volume is unfortunate. It sounds like a sociological study and may prejudice readers fed on too many sociological studies of our neighbors to the south. And that would be a pity, for these are tales that are fun to read and rich in that rarest of modern fictional commodities, the true flavor of human life. Their Mexican microcosm is adult, knowing its own values, asking no favors from a bigger neighbor.

Review of *Mexican Village*
John Gillin, Social Forces, May 1946

I do not see how anyone can fail to enjoy this book, whether or not he is interested in community studies or in Latin American life. Although the book is a valuable document, it is not a scientific report, but rather a work of art of high merit. It consists of ten long short stories, most of which involve the same cast of characters, who are the inhabitants of a small Mexican town named Hidalgo in the State of Nuevo León. The fact that this is a real town and that most of the characters are real people whom the author knew in her childhood there may render the book more "authentic" for social scientists, but I think that is beside the point. I have never been in Hidalgo, but I have been in and lived in a number of small Latin American communities from Mexico to southern Peru. I cannot, therefore, say from personal observation whether Miss Niggli gives a factually accurate report of the setting, social organization, personality type, and culture of Hidalgo, but it does seem to me that she has captured with remarkable skill many of the main facets of Ibero-American rural community life— and produced a work of fascinating literature as well. So, if *Mexican Village* were really an artistic synthesis of a whole series of communities, it would still satisfy me. For the author's lively style, skilled narrative technique, and sound knowledge of values have brought to life the people of a small Mexican town and their design for living more vividly than any sociological or ethnological report of the conventional type. Most social scientists—and their readers as well—might wish they had Miss Niggli's gift of expression.

The structure of the book is not that of a mere collection of sketches. Rather, each story is plotted in itself and in turn fits into an overall plot which, on the whole, sustains reader interest from beginning to end. For my taste, the larger plot seems to be unnecessarily melodramatic in its denouement. But this is not a journal of literary criticism, and we shall not dwell further upon the technical features of the author's literary craftsmanship, which has already received high praise in the appropriate places.

One asks himself, however, after reading a book like this whether it would not be better if all community and cultural studies were presented in this form. Does not art, based on sound observation, far outstrip science in presenting the life of a people? What do the ponderous monographs, dull in their very form, which we social scientists persist in turning out, offer which a book such as this does not present much better?

This is not the place for an extended philosophical discussion of science and art, but I believe that it would be desirable if both media could be used for the exposition and elucidation of community life. If the artistic reconstruction of Hidalgo makes that community and its people "live" on the printed page, it also necessarily leaves much unsaid. There are many "facts" of cultural importance which are not clearly set forth in Miss Niggli's account of Hidalgo, and this is some measure of her ability as a creative artist. For the literary writer, in the interest of dramatic values and compositional symmetry, must select certain aspects of the scene upon which to throw his spotlight, leaving many corners of the stage in shadow or barely suggested by subdued lighting. One of the tasks of the scientific reporter, on the other hand, is to set forth in painstaking detail all aspects of the cultural configuration he is studying. Many of these details are undramatic and many a pattern of culture in real life is "lopsided" rather than displaying that balance which is so essential to the artistic effect. In Hidalgo, for example, one would need to know some details about land tenure, about the relationship system and the scheme of godparenthood, about markets and exchange, about division of labor, and so on, which are not fully described in this book, if one were to have the requisite data for a competent scientific interpretation of the culture. What Miss Niggli gives us in the form of "data" is undoubtedly "true," but it is not the whole story.

Thus the artistic presentation of a culture has many advantages, especially if a writer has the narrative skill of Miss Niggli and her ability to create human character in a given cultural setting. Such a presentation is most valuable, either as an introduction to the culture for those who know nothing about it otherwise, or as a synthesis and highlighting for those who are familiar with the detailed and sometimes dull "facts" of the scientific fieldworker. If all cultures could be presented by literary artists and scientific investigators, I feel that much of the indifference and muddled thinking regarding foreigners and strangers which often characterizes even our "educated" classes would tend to disappear.

Review of *Mexican Village*

Agapito Rey, Journal of American Folklore, *July–September 1947*

At the age of ten, Miss Niggli went to Hidalgo, where her father was manager of a cement plant. Her childhood impressions of Hidalgo form the basis for the present work. Hidalgo is located in the Sabinas Valley near Monterrey, birthplace of the author. Because of this isolation, this Mexican Village still preserves many of its simple characteristics, traditions, and superstitions.

This book is not a novel, but a series of pictures drawn from everyday happenings in the village. The story opens in 1920 when Bob Webster, born in San Antonio, arrives in Hidalgo to manage a quarry that furnishes stone to the cement mills at Monterrey. The author's father has held this position years before.

Many of the characters are drawn from life. That is true particularly of the ruler of the Sabinas Valley. The "big four": the doctor, the priest, the mayor, and the judge. The doctor was still living at the time this book was published. It was at his invitation that the author returned to Hidalgo in 1920. They had met at El Paso, Texas, in one of the doctor's frequent trips from his home in Chihuahua. The other three died between 1931 and 1941.

Adjusting himself to his new environment, Bob Webster establishes a home and engages a housekeeper, one recommended to him by the village priest. She is a small withered old woman, an eagle witch; and through her we are introduced to various forms of witchcraft, interesting, if not new. Tía Magdalena is more than a housekeeper. She watches over the needs and comforts of her young master with the affection and firmness of a grandmother. Bob's plans in coming to the Sabinas Valley were to stay one year, save a couple of thousand dollars in that time and return to the States to enter into business in partnership with an aviator. Tía Magdalena in all her years has never seen or heard of a man flying. Only witches and drunks take to the air. To save her young charge from ruin she must devise some means of keeping him in the Valley. He will never leave once he becomes identified with its people and life. The story ends ten years later, and by then Bob is as much a part of the Sabinas Valley as the rocks of the Sierra Madre that enclose it.

In the presentation of many village characters and their usual activities, the author introduces us to a great deal of folklore. There are descriptions of courting and marriage customs. One of the local women is a gypsy, sister of a famous bullfighter. In order to narrate her life the author takes us to arenas in Spain and Mexico, filling in quite a few details from the technique of the ring.

Hidalgo is a typical Mexican village. There are no Indian communities in the Sabinas Valley. The people are a mixture of native and foreign elements well assimilated after hundreds of years. They are very religious, although in their worship there is a great deal of paganism. In their domestic troubles, and in love difficulties, the people light candles to their favorite images in the churches. A saloonkeeper promises to light one to his patron saint after a good drinker and a generous customer patronize his place. The most intense period of devotion is before a cockfight sponsored by rival villages as a means of settling a long-standing feud. Each one seeks heavenly favor for his rooster. Even the priest helps to get the birds in trim. But the cocks coming from the same flock would not fight—an example people should emulate.

A retiring widow in the village is a former dancer. Her triumphs on the stage at the capital, the tragic deaths of her sweetheart, her husband, and her drunkard father are vividly told. Several dances are described throughout the work, as are also horse races and other games and amusements typical of a small town. Once a troupe of strolling players came to the Village to entertain and edify the public. They staged a Spanish version of *Uncle Tom's Cabin.* The performance ended in a fight. A drunken rancher in the audience insisted on bidding for Eliza when she was auctioned as a slave on the stage.

All through the book there are bits of songs and poems, which the people recite on various occasions. There are also many riddles and proverbs, to which peasants everywhere are much inclined. All of this folkloric material is given in English, but the titles are given in Spanish, so it is not hard to identify them. The title of *La Verbena de la Paloma* is badly garbled.

It is an interesting and well-written book with live pictures of a typical Mexican Village. In a few more years these quaint little towns will give way to modern life and standardization.

Review of *Step Down, Elder Brother*

Bonaventure Schwinn, Commonweal, *19 December 1947*

Monterrey with its three hundred years of history in the shadow of Saddle Mountain is the setting of Josephina Niggli's novel of contemporary Mexican life, and more than in most stories the place is a part of the plot. Miss Niggli knows the old city like her own back yard. Her love for its local color and her sympathetic understanding of the Mexican mind shine on every page, and she has a sufficient knowledge of Mexican history to give depth to her background.

The story is about the aristocratic Vázquez de Anda family, who have done so much to make Monterrey what it is and who, in turn, have been molded into a pattern by the Creole culture of their environment. But the city is changing under the influence of the strong young force of the mestizo, half Spanish and half Indian, who is beginning to assert himself. And besides being affected by the new social order, the Vázquez de Anda family is changing internally, as its children arrive at maturity, declare their independence, fall in love, and throw off the tyranny of the rich banker uncle who has dictated all the important decisions for a generation. There are romances, conflicts, crises, and surprises galore. The characters are widely diversified and well-drawn. The center of interest is always Domingo, the eldest son, who has everything except happiness. Bound by invisible cords, he is dominated by influences he is not strong enough to overcome, and his story is a study in frustration. The novel is happily free from the lush lubricity of such books as *Forever Amber* and *The Hucksters,* but it is infected with the naturalism characteristic of most contemporary fiction. Fornication is planned and committed without any sense of sin and it is not followed by remorse.

Miss Niggli's *Mexican Village,* a collection of sketches published in 1945, created something of a sensation. This is her first novel. She has not as yet mastered the art of the longer narrative form. She is not so overwhelmingly convinced of the reality of her story that she lets it tell itself. Even making allowances for the fact that Márgara is like the Xtabay of the Mayan legend, Domingo's love for her, especially at first, seems inadequately motivated, and his giving her up at the end is equally hard to understand. The narrative lags a little at times in the wrong places. Miss Niggli's reach exceeds her grasp, but she has a whacking good story to tell.

Review of *Step Down, Elder Brother*

Betty de Sherbinin, Saturday Review of Literature, *24 January 1948*

An American tourist could go many times to Monterrey and gain less insight into its ways and manners than the reader will gather from this novel. Its pages are of that Mexican city, pictures of streets, plazas, modern homes, old houses that echo with traditions and stories of the past. The features, the voices, the daily routine, the vices, the habits, the characteristics of Monterrey's quarter of a million inhabitants come to life and give the book humor, vitality, and interest.

This is primarily the story of Domingo Vázquez de Anda, native of Monterrey and heir to its oldest and finest heritage. He loved and gave up an American girl because she would never have fitted into the life of the city in which he had been born. He is, years later, faced with an arranged marriage to a more suitable girl whom his family has chosen. While he accepts these ties that hold him and direct him, he is resentful of them and anxious sometimes to break with them. But the old habit of family and family authority, as well as a deep sentimental love for his own people keeps him from severing these bonds.

In his restlessness he finds Márgara, the daughter of a local photographer, and his hungry need for life makes him see her as a woman of mystery. To him she becomes the enchantress, the Xtabay of Maya Legend; when he thinks of her it is in terms of Mexican poetry he has read through the years. The Xtabay never materializes for the reader and these moments are further over-laden when the author asks her readers questions: "Was he in love with her?," "And even if it were not too late what could he say?," "Would she be destroyed and he left to mourn her in the closed room of his memory?"

The stories woven around this central theme are less high-flown and more realistic. Domingo's family, as they move about in the limiting confines of their environment, as they succeed in achieving their ends, holds the makings of a livelier, more full-blooded story than the one the author has chosen to tell. Uncle Agapito, the striving banker who governs the family and whose say is final; Serafina, the servant girl who accepts the child as docilely as she accepts the love that brought it to her; Mateo, the chauffeur with the yen to sell real estate—all are convincing creatures who are out of step with the novel's central theme.

Time and again this book suggests that this is a novel that might have been written in Spanish for a Spanish-speaking audience. Josephina (and why is it not Josefina?) Niggli's prose has the same sweep as Spanish prose; her sentences have an echo of Spanish construction. When she takes her readers to Don Primitivo's to drink beer and to talk and sing, she does not treat them as foreigners entering the closed circle. She translates for them the conversations of habitués, prepares special dishes for them, teaches them the words of songs that are being sung. Skillfully, she opens door after door for them without assuming the role of the overanxious writer who is explaining the ways of an alien people.

It is only when the reader must follow Domingo's vagaries, when Márgara, the lady of the shadows, moves across a room to disappear behind a curtain, that one regrets that a writer who commands the gift of painting a picture as vivid and as real as her descriptions of Monterrey should build her novel on this kind of romanticism.

Review of *Step Down, Elder Brother*
Mildred Adams, New York Times, *8 February 1948*

A year ago a new writer joined those whose pleasant and difficult occupation it is to write well about Mexico for readers in the United States. She bore the curiously bilingual name of Josephina Niggli, and in a book called *Mexican Village* she revealed a close knowledge of rural Mexico, a quick skill in presenting it. Her method, to tell the tales of a town and through them to present the place and the people, delighted readers tired of too much sociological documentation on the one hand and too many rosy travelogues on the other. She was greeted as a perceptive observer and a born storyteller whose contribution to the zest of reading was as great as to a knowledge of the land she wrote about.

Now Miss Niggli presents her first novel, and it should be reported that she shows in it the same keen eye and acute understanding which distinguished her earlier book. This is the story of a proud Mexican family of Monterrey. Monterrey is to Mexico City what Pittsburgh is to New Orleans, and what happens to money and industry in Monterrey is more important than what happens to blood. Ideals must yield to practicality, romanticism be disciplined by realism.

The older generation sinned, but with a bow to noblesse oblige, the youngsters merely sin. Thus the breakup of class lines, with which Miss Niggli, like most Mexican novelists, is concerned, is here presented in terms that are simple and human instead of revolutionary and grandiloquent. It is one of the book's distinctions that in it the revolution, which has been expressed in so many hundreds of thousands of purple words, becomes a thing seen through the pages of a photograph collection and the memories of old men.

As a novel the book cannot be said to be completely successful. Where the short tales in Miss Niggli's *Mexican Village* were breathlessly compact and dramatic, this one in the longer form moves too slowly, is too long drawn out, its love story tasting at times of the saccharin and pink tinting its hero so deplores. Nor is the conflict between love of woman and love of younger brother clearly resolved. Yet for all that, the skill with people, the sense of place and dialogue, the ability to make the reader smell and taste and feel, which mark a born writer, are here.

On *Mexican Village* and *Step Down, Elder Brother*

William C. Parker, Raleigh News and Observer, *29 February 1948*

Plays by Miss Niggli have found their way into anthologies all over the world. Many awards have gone to the author: two Rockefeller fellowships in playwriting, one of the Theatre Guild's new play fellowships, a scholarship of the Bread Loaf Writers' Conference and the 1946 Mayflower Cup awarded by the North Carolina Literary and Historical Society.

Her road to fame has not been at all easy, and encouragement was not always fast to come. Once, after she had written *Mexican Folk Plays,* which was published by the University of North Carolina Press in 1938, she was asked by W. T. Couch, the Press's onetime director, to write a book of nonfiction on Mexico.

For many months she worked on it until she felt "bogged down" and realized that fiction would come to her much more easily. So she wrote a couple of stories and sent them to the Press. After not hearing something from them for a considerable length of time she had given up all hope of arousing interest in her Mexican fiction by the Press.

She took a job as secretary and assistant to Playwright Paul Green and bided her time until one day she encountered Mrs. G. L. Paine, one of the Press's editorial readers, who raved over the stories and asked when they would all be finished. Still not sufficiently encouraged, Josephina retrieved the stories from the vault of the Press and took them to Betty Smith, author of *A Tree Grows in Brooklyn,* for an opinion. Betty said anyone would be a fool not to finish a book like that, so *Mexican Village* grew into being. Its success was slow at first, but finally it rose to full stature with immense popularity. Later it was made into a movie.

Rinehart and Company commissioned Miss Niggli to write the stirring new novel laid in the city of Monterrey. Its story of the turning tide of the new generation, the revolt of the children of tradition, is one that you will soon come to know and never forget.

Strong characterization, which is certainly the major trait of any successful novel, is surely to be found in the emotions and behavior of those people she writes about as if they were her own flesh and blood.

An elder brother who is attracted to the beautiful Márgara; a daughter who finds her feeling is for the family's chauffeur, a mestizo; and the artistry of her self-expression, its poetic-prose qualities—all among the many reasons supporting the Book-of-the-Month Club's excellent choice.

Tar Heel Back Home: Realism in Adaptation of Her Book to Films Seen by Josephina Niggli

Carol Leh, Greensboro Daily News, *13 January 1952*

Chapel Hill, January 12—Back in North Carolina after her first adventure as a Hollywood screenwriter, Josephina Niggli, author of *Mexican Village* predicts that the film version of her best-selling book will be treated with realism as well as Technicolor.

"We chose three stories from the original ten—'The Cockfight Story,' 'The Bullfight Story,' and 'The Alejandro María Story'—to build our plot around," Miss Niggli explained from the antique-filled living room of her small white home near the University of North Carolina. ("We" means *Mexican Village* producer Jack Cummings and director–co-writer Norman Foster.) "From these three yarns interwoven, we believe that the movie, like the book, will dissect a Mexican village and show different economic levels, from a beggar on a dirt street to a wealthy scion who summers in Europe.

"But," she added with frank warning, "I'm a storyteller, not a sociologist."

Cast Chosen

The screen version, to be made in Mexico with an all-Mexican cast, except the principals, will be shot this Spring. Hollywood scouts are hunting locations now, probably in April. ("We are waiting for clouds because Mexican rain runs on a time schedule, and much of the script calls for exteriors.") It will star some of the brightest names at Metro-Goldwyn-Mayer, the producing studio.

Ricardo Montalban will play Pepe Gonzales, most famous character from the book, in "The Cockfight Story," with Cyd Charisse taking the feminine lead. Ava Gardner and Fernando Lamas will be co-starred in "The Alejandro María Story," with Lamas in the title role. Sally Forrest also may appear in this part of the picture. Although "The Bullfight Story" is as yet uncast, Metro officials are looking toward Elizabeth Taylor and Mexican actor Victor Mendoza.

Screen rights to the fourteen-language book, which is required reading in Spanish and Latin American history courses in every United States university, were purchased last summer in the dramatic fashion by which Hollywood operates. At least the action came with swiftness and financial impact for the rosy-cheeked, brown-eyed writer, who dwells here quietly with her mother, Mrs. G. M. Niggli, retired concert pianist.

M-G-M Buys Book

"I had been making a speech in Corpus Christi, Texas, at the Southwestern Writers Conference last June—went off innocent as a child—and when I stepped from the plane at the Raleigh–Durham airport I sighed with relief: 'I'm so glad to be home I don't know what to do.' 'Don't settle yourself, you're leaving for California tomorrow,' mother said. 'Your agent just long-distanced to say that M-G-M has bought your book and wants you to do the screenplay.'"

That announcement was the first indication Miss Niggli had that screen rights were even in negotiation. But two days later she arrived in Los Angeles, with the same three unpacked suitcases she'd brought home from Texas.

"I went for ten weeks—and stayed six months," Miss Niggli reported, confirming the modus operandi of Hollywood. All this time she was on full salary (besides the original purchase price of the book)—and it is not uncommon for top screenwriters to receive several thousand dollars a week. Yet an astronomical income hasn't affected her in the least, and she continues to be known around Chapel Hill as "a regular girl," plump and jolly, with a rich voice and ready laugh, and a fondness for dark clothes with a dash of color.

"It was most disconcerting—they knew a lot more about the book at Metro than I did." she confessed. "I wrote it ten years ago [it was published in 1945 by the University of North Carolina Press], and hadn't read it since—once I've finished a job, I'm through with it—but the producer and director quoted whole passages by heart. And when they threw some lines at me in an unsuspecting moment I said, 'That's pretty. Where's it from?' '*Mexican Village,*' they answered."

Los Angeles wasn't new to Miss Niggli—she had visited with Mr. and Mrs. Paul Green of Chapel Hill, when he was on assignment for Metro— but being there as a unit in motion-picture production was a new experience. "I never worked so hard in my life—every day from 10 to 5 except weekends," she declared. "But it was good and we accomplished a lot, and I learned a lot."

From Metro-Goldwyn-Mayer, writer Niggli received the cherished treatment. The studio arranged a plush apartment for her in the Sunset Strip section. She was always accompanied to the commissary and never ate a meal alone—somebody from the Front Office was always there to furnish companionship, introduce her to Clark Gable or Joan Crawford or whoever happened to be passing, and to pick up the check. If she needed to use a phone at the studio—perhaps she was out of paper for her typewriter— there was always someone to make the call.

Born In Mexico

A graduate of the University of North Carolina with the class of 1937, the author was born in Monterrey, Mexico, where her father, Frederick Ferdinand Niggli, was general manager of a cement company. Her paternal ancestors were Mexican and Catholic; her maternal line stems from the Episcopal Morgans of Alexandria, Virgina. ("Great-Great Grandfather John William Morgan ran guns for the confederacy.")

Hollywood's Version of Niggli Story
Carol Leh, Durham Morning Herald, 15 February 1953

Hollywood, California—Fidelity to her native Mexican people and countryside is promised by Chapel Hill, North Carolina, authoress Josefina Niggli for the forthcoming Technicolor film *Sombrero*, produced by Metro-Goldwyn-Mayer from her book *Mexican Village*.

Co-scripted by Miss Niggli and the movie's director, Norman Foster, *Sombrero* was lensed during six weeks of shooting in Mexico last year, with a full Hollywood company including Tar Heel writer Niggli. It will be released in March.

A few changes have been made from the original plans. At first the studio retained the book title for the cinema version, then decided *Sombrero* would have more box-office appeal than *Mexican Village*. Early announcements mentioned Ava Gardner for a lead feminine role, but this casting was abandoned. The author's name underwent a slight revision. She phoneticized it from "Josephina," printed on the jacket of her novels, to "Josefina," used in Hollywood.

Final talent roundup for the picture includes five of M-G-M's top stars and an array of bright new names. Ricardo Montalban plays Pepe Gonzales "who lives for love and laughter." Cyd Charisse is the strangely sad Lola, sister of a famous matador. Vittorio Gassman, Italian star of *Bitter Rice*, takes the part of Alejandro, scion of the valley's proudest family. Pier Angeli is the young and merry Eufemia Calderón. Yvonne De Carlo becomes the beautiful outcast María.

Besides the five co-stars, the film introduces José Greco, Spanish dancing star and former partner of the late Argentina.[*] Greco portrays the gypsy matador and performs a spectacular solo. Another newcomer to the screen is handsome Rick Jason, Broadway actor who plays a gentle candy vendor in *Sombrero*. Although Gassman is well-known in European cinema, the M-G-M picture will be his initial performance for an American studio.

---

[*]Editor's note: Greco's partner was the legendary Spanish dancer La Argentinita.

Consisting of three interwoven love stories in unusual treatment, *Sombrero* is built on a bitter feud which rends a peaceful valley. The feud is waged between two villages and involves the six lovers. One romance is tragic, with Gassman and Miss De Carlo; one tempestuous, with Miss Charisse and Jason; one gay, with Montalban and Miss Angeli.

Miss Niggli has declared that her goal in writing the screenplay like the book was to reveal the real Mexicans of various social strata, as she came to know them during the years she lived in Monterrey. She wanted, she says, "neither to idealize the poor downtrodden Indian nor to make a political issue of him." She admits she wrote the book originally because of resentment over previous works that had done just these things.

Highlights of the movie version include a wild, mountainside dance by Cyd Charisse to the accompaniment of a crashing storm; a bullfight; a cockfight during which armies of villagers charge toward the boundary line with banners and bands; a cemetery scene during which Montalban and Jason try to dig up the bones of a dead poet.

Shot on location in Mexico City and in the quaint villages of Tetacala and Tepotlan,* *Sombrero* became much more than a Technicolor motion-picture production. It developed nuances of internationalism, honeymoonism, and something of the appearance of a mobile zoo.

Romance off-camera started when Shelly Winters, Gassman's bride, arrived by Pan-American plane. About the same time, Kurt Kasznar, who depicts the good Padre Zacaya in *Sombrero,* took himself a Broadway-actress bride, Leora Dana, and together they flew from New York to Mexico for his part in the picture.

Miss Charisse's husband, Tony Martin, was with the troupe during a large part of location.

Along with the glamour girls and boys who joined *Sombrero* in curricular or extracurricular capacities were a number of lesser creatures. Script called for so many cows, pigs, chickens, and burros that a full-time veterinarian was employed.

The international complications were both expected and unexpected. A certain amount of clearance and red tape is essential whenever a

---

*Editor's note: The correct name of the town is Tepoztlán.

motion-picture company works on foreign soil. These matters were arranged by the studio with fair ease. But slicker gloves were needed to convince the Mexicans, still smarting from previous treatment by American studios, that *Sombrero* would be different.

Four persons connected with the movie contributed to reassurance of the Mexicans: Miss Niggli; Montalban, who was born in Mexico and first won stardom there; Foster, hailed in the local press as "un gran amigo de Mexico" since his directorial stint at Mexico City's Churubusco Studios from 1940–47; and producer Jack Cummings, who made *Fiesta* in Puebla six years ago.

Once the Mexicans were satisfied that Hollywood would do right by them this time, they tumbled head over heels to cooperate. Cooperation also was accelerated by the American dollars that poured in during production.

The villages of Tepotlan (population 1,400) and Tetacala (2,600) added another note: a competitive spirit, to see which could contribute the most to, and benefit the most by, this Hollywood location. With many residents carrying folding pesos in their pockets for the first time, the two towns suddenly realized that the location prosperity might be the beginning of a bigger tourist boom if they looked attractive on the screen.

With gratitude the Latins accepted two stone angels M-G-M erected outside the huge Tetacalan cathedral—for photographic purposes. The natives welcomed a new modern sanitation system in the schools. But when Tepotlan citizens discovered that their green benches from the plaza had been "borrowed" a few days for a colorful scene in Tetacala, the rightful owners prepared to descend in the middle of the night to retrieve the property.

It took a lot of fast Hollywood talk to convince the Mexicans that "Manyana" is still a sound philosophy.

Review of *Sombrero*
Bosley Crowther, New York Times, 23 April 1953

M.G.M.'s colorful *Sombrero*, which was skimmed into Loew's State yesterday, is a big, broad-brimmed, squashy sort of picture, as massive as the garment for which it is named. It is also as ostentatious and full of torpid hot air. Although it is labored under by a distinguished and resolute cast, it engulfs and obliterates its people in a huge, mottled, shape-obscuring shade.

The reason for this is easily obvious. It was made to cover a lot of area, and the people who put it together didn't have the large-scale skill for the job. Based on a book called *Mexican Village,* a volume of lively folktales by the talented author, Josefina Niggli, it is aimed to blend three or four of these into a flowing and dramatic panorama of life in rural Mexico. But the stories themselves are told so poorly and the jointing is so curious and confused, in a clumsy, staggered fashion, that the sum is a jumbled, tedious blob.

Though it starts off in gay and gaudy humor, with that playboy Ricardo Montalban making himself a charming nuisance in his village by painting mustaches on the portraits of the local girls, it is soon slanting off in the direction of a moody young grandee, played by Vittorio Gassman, who pines for a slightly sullied belle. And from this situation it moves abruptly to the problem of another local lad, played by Rick Jason, who is captured by the sad eyes of a hapless city girl.

Thus launched, with incidental by-plays, it goes back and forth among the three, picking up episodes and people with odd and bewildering unconcern. There's the quaint little girl whom the playboy encounters most cheerfully in—of all spots—a neighboring village graveyard. She is played by Pier Angeli. There's the business of the moody young grandee being persuaded by his smoky "river girl"—no one but Yvonne De Carlo—to marry aristocratic Nina Foch, not knowing, we gather, that her lover is doomed by some morbid brain disease. And there's the arrogant bullfighting brother of the sad city girl, Cyd Charisse, who so dominates his dismal sister that he very nearly drives them both mad. (As a matter of fact, he soon ends up on the damaging horns of a bull.)

In the uneven switching of attention from one to another little group, the mood of the picture is altered and garbled unmercifully. One minute you'll be watching and listening to the ebullient Mr. Montalban singing a spicy Latin number and the next you'll be hearing Mr. Gassman wheeze, furiously clutching at Miss De Carlo and making tedium with many stuffy words. Or now you'll be watching José Greco doing a hot, electric Mexican dance in his role of the jealous bullfighter and, a minute later, you'll be sampling village farce, knocked out by a gang of pseudo-Mexicans, of whom Kurt Kasznar is one as a village priest.

It is all very odd and disconcerting, and—except for three or four things, such as that dance by the graceful, snake-hipped Greco or a wild dance that Miss Charisse does—it is utterly lacking in excitement and dramatic character. Miss Niggli and her associate, Norman Foster, who also directed, are to blame.

But this must be said for *Sombrero*—it is beautifully photographed in very fine Technicolor and the actual countryside of Mexico, in which it is set, is lovely. There, at least, it is not in the shade.

Focus on *Sombrero* Below the Border
John Rothwell, New York Times, 1953

Cuernavaca, Mexico—The nearby villages of Tetecala and Tepoztlán, two quaint little settlements steeped in ancient legend and, until recently, drowsing contentedly in an almost unbroken siesta, have been playing hosts for some time now to the first Hollywood motion-picture troupe either has seen. The results have been a sudden awakening, with their customary "mañana" outlook on life giving way to a surprisingly competitive spirit that seems most Norte-Americano in flavor.

Their energetic eagerness to cooperate with the moviemakers, here to film Metro-Goldwyn-Mayer's *Sombrero,* apparently can be traced to two causes. First, they feel the visitors spell a lucrative boom ahead. Second, they are confident that Hollywood is about to "do right" by its neighbor to the south.

Enthusiasm

Whether or not future free-spending tourists will make Tetecala and Tepoztlán regular points of call after seeing their charms on the screen, as is the hope of the two villages, only time will tell. Nevertheless, they've been outdoing each other in showing their enthusiasm for the project. And it takes a lot of doing to ready a community for an invasion of its main streets, markets and plazas by Technicolor cameras and some 150 guests.

That there has been no hint of the antagonism displayed at the treatment of Mexico and its nationals in some previous Hollywood productions can be attributed, however, to the recent arrival on the scene of Josefina Niggli, the author, and a producer-director team recognized as being sympathetically understanding of the Mexicans. Miss Niggli came from her home in Chapel Hill, North Carolina, to view the filming based on her book *Mexican Village.*

Authentic

She immediately confirmed the belief that the movie, like her book, would be as faithful to the Mexican people as to the scenic countryside. She said her writing had been aimed to show the real Mexican people of various social strata, as she came to know them during the years in which she was raised in Monterrey. She wanted neither to idealize "the poor, downtrodden Indian," nor make a political issue of it. She resented previous works that had done so.

She confided that she was surprised when producer Jack Cummings became interested in her novel last year and induced M-G-M to purchase it. She was amazed when he wanted no changes in it for pictures. Unlike the first publishers to whom she submitted her writings, he didn't even request that a North American hero be added. During six months in Hollywood as collaborator with director Norman Foster on the screenplay, she found herself in the unique position, according to the usual Hollywood conception, of being an author who wanted to make some changes in her creation while the studio folk were insisting upon sticking to her original story.

Cummings and Foster also seem to have instilled a confidence in Mexicans that they possibly are in better hands than in previous undertakings south of the border. Cummings has been a regular visitor since filming *Fiesta* in Puebla six years ago and is highly regarded. Foster was a top-flight director in Mexico City while living there for seven years prior to returning to Hollywood in 1947. During ten days of filming in Mexico City, before the movie troupe moved to Cuernavaca for the Tetecala and Tepoztlán sequences, he consistently was referred to in the local press as "un gran amigo de Mexico."

A similar "homecoming" atmosphere surrounded the return of Ricardo Montalban as a star of the new film. Born in Mexico City, he first became a star there under Foster's direction before being beckoned by Hollywood. All but three of the Mexican crew members, working alongside the Hollywood crew in accordance with local union regulations, had been associated with either Foster or Montalban on earlier pictures.

Although Miss Niggli's book comprised ten separate but interwoven stories, only three of these have been employed for *Sombrero*. Each is a love story, one tragic, another tempestuous, and the third, gayly comic. The same characters run throughout, but Vittorio Gassman and Yvonne De Carlo are featured as the lovers in the first, Cyd Charisse and handsome newcomer, Rick Jason, in the second, and Pier Angeli and Montalban in the third. Nina Foch, Walter Hampden, Kurt Kasznar and José Greco, who divides two solo dance numbers with Miss Charisse, augment the unusually large cast.

With so many familiar personalities on hand, Mexico City took on the air of a movie-struck metropolis during the filming there, starting with the troupe's arrival by plane to a rousing serenade by five mariachi groups. It is in the villages of Tetecala and Tepoztlán, however, that the impact of Hollywood has been felt most—economically and physically as well as mentally.

Windfall

Many natives of both, with never more than a few coins in their pockets before, now have folding pesos to spare. The 400-seat theatre in Tetecala, closed for over a year because repairs for its ancient sound system couldn't be afforded, soon will be open now that its owner has been working for the Hollywooders. Tepoztlán, with a population little more than half of Tetecala's 2,600, doesn't have a theatre. But two of the local benefactors from the picture promise there'll be one in time to bid against Tetecala for the film's world premiere.

On at least one occasion, however, the inter-village rivalry threatened to develop into a full-fledged feud. This happened when Cummings and Foster, after giving Tetecala its first coat of paint in several decades and a new, modern sanitation system in its school, decided the old stone seats in the plaza weren't sufficiently photogenic in Technicolor. Their solution was to borrow the colorful green metal benches from Tepoztlán's plaza.

Gift

Upon discovering their seats were to enhance Tetecala's beauty on the screen, a loyal band of Tepoztláns gathered quickly. They announced they would march upon the other village and retrieve their property by whatever means necessary.

A quick meeting of the Hollywood masterminds followed. Then came the announcement—two stone angels, replicas of those which Tepoztláns had admired so long and so enviously in another nearby town, were being built and would be placed in niches at the entrance to Tepoztlán's church. They would be used in the picture, but they would remain there permanently as a token of Hollywood's appreciation to the people of the village.

Now, under the benevolent gaze of the angels from Hollywood, Tepoztláns once more are looking forward to the prospects of a prosperous future.

Letter from Bernadette Hoyle to Richard Gaither Walser, 20 June 1955

Your book of Mrs. Harris is splendid. I finally got a copy of it last week—Mrs. Hopkins at the Extension Library. I went by to see her when I went to interview Josephina Niggli. And by the way, Josephina is leaving N.C. to go to England to teach—selling the house, etc. I didn't learn that until I was halfway through the interview. Now, how does that place her in my series—a Tar Heel writer who is not a Tar Heel writer and who is leaving Tar Heellia! Won't your friend Nell B. L. have a good one there. I don't know just exactly what to do about including her in the series. What do you think? I have interviewed her—yet she wouldn't let me photograph her—gave me a glossy made ten years ago, I know, doesn't look a bit like her—long black braids wound round her head and a wistful expression—Yet, I hate to leave her out of the series—what should I do about it?

Letter from Josephina Niggli to Maren Elwood, 11 May 1957

. . . When I was a young kid, starting out as a writer, I had a shining goal. I was going to present Mexico and the Mexicans as they had never before been presented. Well, I did. I made [it] big time. I even made M-G-M and Book-of-the-Month. You see, I reached my goal and passed it.

Then I decided I would try the American fiction market, and I ran head on into a very interesting obstacle. I couldn't write about Americans. Their psychology completely baffled me.

As though this were not enough, another obstacle faced me. I don't like magazines. Except for a stray Ellery Queen, I haven't read a magazine since the 25¢ pocket book went on the stands. (I'm excluding the two technical photography magazines published in Germany to which I subscribe). What do I read? Well, since last April 1, I've read: A new translation of seven Ibsen plays, re-read Highet's *The Classical Tradition,* Laver's *Victorian Vista* (a study in the social customs of the Victorians), *1848, the Story of a Year, A Study in Elizabethan Cosmology,* besides my regular reading in Shakespeare and the Bible. None of these were required for my schoolwork. This happens to be the kind of reading I like. I also read about thirty-four pocket books . . . the 25¢ variety of mystery and detection.

I love detective stories. Indeed the one course you offer that I particularly want to take is the one in the Mystery and Detective Story. You see, Miss Elwood, I don't have to write for a living. M-G-M took care of my income, and I make a very good salary in my job . . . and I'll be making even more at the University of Texas. I write because I can't help writing. And since yesterday I've come to the conclusion that it's just plain foolish tieing myself down to something I'm simply not interested in: the average short story.

Now, keeping in mind the point that creating an American character is a real problem to me, do you think I'd be better off in Advanced Fiction — or could I exchange it for the Detective and Mystery Story? You've dealt with all sorts of writers. I've only dealt with me. And you know your own courses. Twenty years of college has taught me that in the long run the expert always knows best.

Letter from Josephina Niggli to Paul Green, 18 December 1964

Thanks so much for your nice letter about *Miracle*. I do hope you get to read the ending as I'm right proud of it. I know that it was a lot of fun to read. As for the history, that was a dictionary of dates, a map of Mexico in 1536, the documents on the miracle, and all the rest was memory. After all, I've been specializing in Mexico for a lot of years.

Right now I'm hard at work on *Lightning from the East,* the play for the Texas State Historical Theatre at the San Jose Mission in San Antonio. It will run for bout four weeks, beginning the middle of June. If you're in Canyon City then, I hope you get a chance to go down to see it. I know that I'm anxious to see your Canyon City job. I'll be in S.A. during rehearsals the early part of June, and even if your play hasn't opened, perhaps they'd let me see some rehearsals. I hear you're going to use a lot of the light and sound techniques you saw in Spain. I've got quite a gimmick on *Lightning* that I'm real proud of . . . through a modern narrator (visible) the mission itself . . . or rather herself . . . that Queen of Missions . . . tells the story. The main pay-off . . . no need to worry about language: Spanish, English, Indian, as the Mission remembers in English!

Josephina Niggli, Autobiographical Article, no date

I have reached the age which my grandma always said was the stopping point for birthdays. At any rate, I was born in Monterrey, N.L., Mexico, in a very small hospital directly across the street from the biggest nightclub in the Republic. (The last time I was in Monterrey, the hospital had been torn down, and the nightclub had been turned into a private garden, rented only for banquets and weddings.)

At that time my father was general manager of a cement plant in a small town thirty-five kilometers west of Monterrey called Hidalgo. It so happens that seventy-five kilometers north of Monterrey is another town called Sabinas Hidalgo, and that poor town has had to suffer for a book I wrote when I grew up. Which proves that authors should be careful—very careful indeed.

Hidalgo was a nice little town with one automobile and lots of horses. I didn't have a horse. I had a donkey named Senacharib (for the only poem I was ever able to recite all the way through). Here I learned Spanish, and how to crochet. Also, my mind was molded into a Spanish pattern which even today dominates all my thinking processes.

My mother was sick, and we wandered around a bit during my growing-up years, so I never had any formal schooling until I was sent to San Antonio, Texas, to high school. I told everybody I was a junior—I didn't know what it meant, but it was a pretty word—and apparently everyone believed it. At any rate, I graduated when I was fourteen and went to college. (My cousins have never forgiven me for this duplicity. They had to go their full three and a half years.)

My college was the Incarnate Word, the largest Catholic womans' college in the South. I had lots of fun, although I never learned to spell. My English teacher said, "Just learn to punctuate. Publishers hire editors to correct bad spelling." This was wonderful advice because it was perfectly true. During this time I decided to be a poet. The Texas Poetry Society is very kind to young writers, and I won several contests. I also wrote a short story for the *Ladies' Home Journal* which won second place. This ended my other two major ambitions: to be a bank clerk or a train conductor (they handle little strips of paper, and I love little strips of paper).

The year I graduated from college, the director of a local theatrical group asked me to write a play. It was the worst play ever written, but I kept on. All my plays at that time were strictly *tres lousee* as I had not yet encountered my Mexican treasure house. Everyone said, "Write about what you know," so I wrote about the people who surrounded me, and they happened to be Americans about whom I knew absolutely nothing.

Then my mamma sent me to the University of North Carolina. Her name was Goldie, and the first play I ever saw on the Playmaker stage was Wilbur Dorset's *Goldie*. I felt as though the whole theatre was welcoming me. And Proff Koch said, "Write a play about Mexico." So I wrote *The Red Velvet Goat*. That was in September of 1935. In September of 1940 this little play was being produced every night in England—in bomb shelters, and subways, and wherever people gathered to forget the war.

I wrote quite a number of plays that year—enough to make a book of them. Bill Couch of the University Press telephoned me and asked if I'd like to write a nonfiction book for the Press. He'd read the plays, thought I had talent, and it was time for me to do a book. We signed a contract, and I went to work. But I couldn't get anywhere. I wrote enough to paper a house, and none of it was worth even that.

In the meantime I'd won a couple of fellowships—one at Bread Loaf Writers' Camp where I met Herschel Brickell; and one sponsored by the Theatre Guild in New York. Herschel, who edits the O'Henry Prize Collection of short stories, told me not to be silly. If I couldn't write the book as nonfiction, write it as fiction. So I did. I called it *Farewell to My Valley* as a working title, but as the book shaped up, that title was no good. Nobody could find a title until Noel Houston said, "Call it *Mexican Village*."

It's had a strange and long career. It's still selling. It's been translated into six languages, including Korean. Latin American departments of universities use it as supplementary reading. It won the North Carolina Mayflower Cup, and now M-G-M is producing it as a movie. They're hunting a new title, too, but the publicity releases still call it *Mexican Village*.

Bill Couch released me to Rinehart's, so I wrote a book for them called

Step Down, Elder Brother. This was a Book-of-the-Month choice, which was nice, too.

My father and grandmother died during the war, so my mother and I moved to Chapel Hill. We bought a house on Gimghoul, right next to the castle, and I was delighted to be living at last in my enchanted town. This was in 1945. Since then—my mother figured it up the other night—I've been home over a scattered period of eighteen months.

And now I'm going away again. That's why I'm never seen downtown. I have to stay in the backyard studio pounding out my new book: *Beat the Drum Slowly.*